the Complete Book of
ELECTRIC VEHICLES

by Sheldon R. Shacket

DOMUS BOOKS

Chicago • New York

BOOK DESIGN AND PRODUCTION: **MacDonald-Ball Studio**
EDITORIAL DIRECTOR: **Betty Ritter**
SPECIAL ILLUSTRATIONS: **Robert Tanaka**

Cover photo courtesy of
General Motors Corporation.

Copyright © 1981 Quality Books, Inc.
Published by
Domus Books
400 Anthony Trail
Northbrook, Illinois 60062

Manufactured in the United States of America

1   2   3   4   5   6   7   8   9   10

Library of Congress Cataloging in Publication Data

Shacket, Sheldon R., 1941–
   The complete book of electric vehicles.

   Bibliography p. 224 **Revised 2nd Edition**
   Includes index
   1. Electric vehicles. I. Title. II. Title:
Electric vehicles.
TL220.S53   1981   629.2'293   81-2453
ISBN 0-89196-085-6   AACR2
ISBN 0-89196-086-4 (pbk.)

Contents

Introduction

The *Electric Vehicle is coming!* It is an integral part of man's future and survival on this planet. Today we are observing the stepping stones that will bring technology and imagination together to create truly efficient vehicles and energy systems worthy of the 21st Century.

Out of the nation's energy crisis and air pollution problems has come a mandate for electric vehicle development. Because petroleum is an irreplaceable commodity, we will look at how we can save this natural resource for better and more strategic uses such as air defense, the production of plastics, and the manufacture of fertilizers. We will show how the electric vehicle fits into an electric society where the accumulated alternate energy sources will, if intelligently promoted and developed, bring us energy independence.

The need for electric vehicles becomes clear when we realize the following facts:

1. About 54% of the petroleum used in the U.S. is used in the internal combustion engine.
2. The U.S. imports 45% of all oil it consumes, spending over $100 billion a year for imported petroleum.
3. Less than 17% of all U.S. electricity is generated from oil.
4. Of the 100 million cars in this country, about 40% are "second cars" (usually gas guzzlers), 90% of which are replaced every five years.
5. About 87% of automobile trips are 15 miles or less and 95% are less than 30 miles. Electric vehicles can easily replace the "second car".

We see before us a new and potent industry that will offer overwhelming opportunities. Public need is the handmaiden of all successful business—companies that satisfy the need for electric vehicles will surpass those firms that continue to feed the appetite of the internal combustion engine.

Some day our cities will be powered by the energy of the universe, nuclear fusion. Handfuls of sea water will yield more energy than an oil supertanker. A new electric society will control its environment to benefit nature, not destroy it. With a little patience, we will see new technological advances emerge like mushrooms in a field. The threshold of a new age is upon us. It is ours to behold.

This book is dedicated to Evelyn and Jan Shacket
with many thanks to:
Joseph Seliber, P.E.
William E. Siegfriedt, M.E.
Robert Myers (Know-It-All)
Denise Reig, Arlene Pabian, Nancy Hoffmann,
Phyllis Betenia, John Newell,
Sarah Sample, Barbara Blumenthal,
Lydia Conca, Linda Grossman and
Jeanne Hoffman.
And special thanks to Dr. Yao from
Argonne National Laboratories for
his assistance with the battery chapter.

chapter 1

Electric Vehicle History

The last decade of the 19th century provided an atmosphere that was particularly suited to the development of new modes of transportation.

The emerging cities required alternatives to the noisy and dirty steam- powered locomotives and horse-drawn city carriages. This was a period when Americans owned over 25 million horses and the principal form of personal transportation was that mechanical marvel, the safety bicycle. Ten million bicycles gave Americans a new freedom—the freedom from feeding and maintaining a horse. The bicycle also encouraged the construction of paved streets and brought about improvements in metallurgy, bearings, wheels, and power transmissions. These technical advances opened the door to a host of mechanized forms of transportation. Suddenly, curious new self-powered vehicles began appearing on city streets. Steam, internal combustion and electric carriages could perform the functions of the horse or bicycle.

The electric vehicle quickly became popular with city dwellers. People had grown familiar with electric trolleys and railways, and technology had produced motors and batteries in a wide variety of sizes. The Edison cell, a nickel-

The horse-drawn tramcars of 1894 were converted to electric power after 1898 by the Glasgow, Scotland Department of Transportation. The cars seated 18 passengers inside and 26 outside.

Photo courtesy of
The Museum of Transport, Glasgow

THE CHICAGO INTERMURAL
The world's first electrically operated elevated railroad cars were on display at the World's Columbian Exposition in 1893.

Photo courtesy of
The Chicago Historical Society

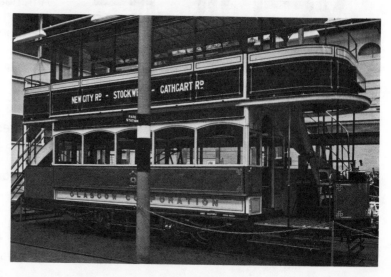

The Standard electric Tram No. 779 of 1900 seated 24 people on the lower level, 42 on top. Scotland Department of Transportation.

Photo courtesy of
The Museum of Transport, Glasgow

iron battery, developed by Thomas Edison in 1910, became the leader in electric vehicle use.

For a short period of time in the early days of automotive development the electric vehicle reigned supreme, and became a dominant factor in the personal transportation scene prior to the turn of the century.

A SIMPLIFIED HISTORY OF EARLY POWERED TRANSPORTATION

This chart depicts the development of various modes of transportation and their relationship to the electric vehicle prior to the turn of the century.

1600	*Simon Steven* of Holland: a wind powered sailing chariot.
1769	*Nicolas Cugnot* of France: a three-wheeled, 3-mph (4.8 km/hr) steam-powered, cannon wagon.
1801	*Richard Trevithick*, England: steam-powered carriage.
1804	*Oliver Evans*, America: steam amphibian.
1822	*Sir Goldworthy Gurney*, England: 30-mph (48 km/hr) steam carriage.
1834	*Thomas Davenport*, America: battery-powered electric car used on a short track (non-rechargeable).
1838	*Robert Davidson*, Scotland: 5-ton electric locomotive (non-rechargeable).
1847	*Moses Farmer*, America: electric car, 2-passenger, non-rechargeable (experimental).
1851	*Charles B. Page*, America: 19-mph (31 km/hr) electric car (non-rechargeable).
1859	*Gaston Plante,*: development of lead storage battery.
1874	*Sir David Salomons*, England: battery-powered carriage.
1879	First non-battery locomotive exhibited in Berlin, Germany.
1881	*Camille Favre,*: storage battery improvement.
1881	First use of a third rail for rail locomotives. (Electricity produced by dynamo generation early in 1870's.)
1885	*Karl Benz*, Germany: gasoline-powered tricycle car.
1886	*Frank J. Sprague:* first successful electric trolley system. (Prior method was horse-drawn rail carriages.)
1886	*Gottlieb Daimler*, Germany: gasoline-powered automobile.
1888	*Fred Kimball*, America: electric car operated in Boston.
1891	*William Morrison*, America: electric car operated in Chicago.
1893	Electric carriages used at Chicago World's Fair to carry visitors.
1893	*Duryea Bros.*, America: gasoline-powered buggy.
1895	First electric rapid transit, Chicago.

1899 RIKER

Photo courtesy of Smithsonian Institute

The turn of the century marked the beginning of electric vehicle dominance in the pleasure car field. In the year 1900, 4,200 automobiles were sold. Of these, 38% were electric, 22% gasoline-powered, and 40% steam.

In the early 1900's, the electric Brougham and Victoria carriages were the preferred method of transportation among New York's wealthy elite. Closed-body electrics followed regal carriage lines many years before gasoline automobiles offered enclosed bodies. Equipped with chauffeur and footmen, the elegant "electrics" carried wealthy families to plays, operas, and fashionable gatherings. Their cost was in the $5,000 to $6,000 range, easily equivalent to a Rolls Royce of today.

Sales of the automobile had risen sharply. Only fifteen years had passed since the development and introduction of the 1885 Karl Benz gasoline-powered tricycle, which used a 110-pound (50 kg), 1/2-horsepower engine. The vehicle could maintain speeds of only a few miles per hour and was unable to negotiate even the mildest grade.

The first primitive American gasoline-powered buggy was the 1893 Duryea. In the same year, electric carriages were already "for hire" at the Chicago World's Fair. Early development and expert marketing gave electrics a clear edge over gasoline-powered vehicles.

In this period, the bicycle industry in America was very strong. The largest bicycle maker in America was the Pope Manufacturing Company. Pope "Columbia" bicycles were respected throughout the world. But Colonel Albert A. Pope, the company's founder, believed that, although the bicycle was the simplest form of transportation imaginable, requiring little care, producing no pollution, and providing healthful exercise for the owner, there was a clear cut destiny for the electric car and truck. By the end of 1898, Pope had produced about 500 electric automobiles under the name "Columbia Electric."

In 1899, the Pope firm was purchased by the Electric Vehicle Company. The EVC was a huge conglomerate by the standards of that day and pursued the acquisition of all electric car and taxi companies in the United States. Its net worth was over 18 million dollars in 1899, yet by 1907, having staked everything on the continuing dominance of electrics over gasoline-powered vehicles, it was totally bankrupt.

Another early electric car manufacturer was the Electric Carriage and Wagon Company owned by Henry G. Morris and Pedro G. Salom. The Morris and Salom "Electrobat" cab of 1895-1897 operated in New York City in January 1897 in a fleet of twelve public taxis. Like Pope, the company was absorbed by The Electric Vehicle Company.

The Riker Electric Motor Company of America was founded by A. L. Riker in 1896 and produced a variety of electric cars and trucks until

1904 COLUMBIA
Photo courtesy of
the Smithsonian Institute

1914 RAUCH & LANG

Photo courtesy of the Smithsonian Institute

1902. After Riker sold out to the Electric Vehicle Company, he began producing gasoline vehicles.

The Kriéger Company of Paris, France, was an important contributor to electric vehicle technology and was awarded a prize at the 1897 Paris Motor Cab Trials. This amazing vehicle had four-wheel brakes and power steering utilizing a motor on each of the front wheels. The speed of 15 mph (24 km/hr) and range of 50 miles (80 km) per charge was respectable for the 2,530-pound (1147 kg) carriage. M. Kriéger was an ingenious man who experimented with an alcohol-electric hybrid in 1902. In 1904, he marketed, without much success, a car powered by both gasoline and electricity. Before his company went into bankruptcy, he patented a turbine-electric hybrid. Fairly advanced for 1909!

The French B.G.S. Electric Car of 1900 held the world's electric distance record of almost 180 miles per charge (290 km). The B.G.S. company made cars, trucks, buses, and limousines from 1899 to 1906. They designed and produced batteries specifically for their own vehicles.

The Woods Motor Vehicle Company of Chicago, Illinois, was founded in 1899 and sold vehicles until 1919. One model in 1903 was made to look like a gasoline automobile by utilizing a false hood or "bonnet." With prices ranging up to $4,500, Woods did not achieve a large sales volume but the firm's longevity proved that it had a respectable following. The Woods 1915 model featured solid rubber tires and claimed a 40-mph (64 km/hr) top speed with maximum range (at cruising speeds) of up to 100 miles (160 km) per charge. One of their last vehicles was a 1917 gasoline-electric hybrid featuring a 4-cylinder engine and electric motor. A 20-mph (32 km/hr) cruising speed on electric power alone could be augmented by the gasoline power plant to produce speeds of 25 mph (40 km/hr) in combination.

The Buffalo Electric Carriage Company of Buffalo, New York, built automobiles in various

Photo courtesy of the Museum of Transport, Glasgow

1899 MADELVIC ELECTRIC BROUGHAM
The Madelvic Motor Carriage Co. of Edinburgh, Scotland, produced this unusual model which featured exceptional coachwork. A small fifth wheel located behind the front carriage wheels supplied power to the ground. The entire 3-wheel front half of the vehicle could be attached to conventional horsedrawn vehicles. The company produced vehicles only until 1900.

1906 KRIEGER-BRASIER ELECTRIC LAUNDAULET

The Crawford Auto Museum of Cleveland, Ohio has on display the world's finest example of a 1906 Krieger electric carriage.

The front-wheel drive Krieger was manufactured and sold for $4,000 in 1906 by Campagnie Parisienne des Voitures Electriques Krieger in France. This magnificent example of coachbuilder's art has a bright yellow and deep green exterior with black patent leather fenders and a dark green broadcloth interior.

A total of 56 Edison nickel-iron battery cells, comprising 60% of the vehicle's total weight, power a pair of 4-hp traction motors located in the front wheel hubs. A mechanical controller—an advanced design for its time—incorporated eight forward speeds and one reverse with a position for "dynamic" or electrical braking. Top speed was 25 mph (40 km/hr) with a maximum range of 50 miles (80 km) per charge.

The Frederick C. Crawford Auto-Aviation Museum is located at 10825 East Boulevard, Cleveland, Ohio, 44106 and has one of the world's outstanding collections of electric vehicles.

Photo courtesy of the Frederick C. Crawford Auto-Aviation Museum

THE 1904 KRIEGER

The 1904 Krieger electric brougham of France featured power steering, four-wheel brakes and front-wheel drive. Kriegers were produced from 1897 to 1909; some later models used gasoline-powered generators to supplement battery energy.

In 1909, Krieger patented a gas turbine-electric with rear wheel drive, but was forced into bankruptcy before the vehicle could be produced.

Photo courtest of Photo Hutin Compiegne, Paris

Photo courtesy of The National Motor Museum, England

1897 HEADLAND ELECTRIC DOGCART
The Headland Electric Storage Battery Company of London, England, produced batteries and vehicles from 1897 to 1900.

1917 WOODS DUAL POWER 12-HP COUPE
This vehicle had an electric motor and a 12-hp, 4-cylinder Continental gasoline engine. Maximum speed for electric power was 20 mph (32 km/hr) and 35 mph (56 km/hr) using both engine and motor.

The Woods Motor Vehicle Company of Chicago, Illinois, produced a variety of electrics from 1899 to 1919.

Photo courtesy of The Henry Ford Museum, Dearborn, Michigan

1907 ELECTROMOBILE
The British Electromobile Company of London produced vehicles from 1901 to 1920.

Photo courtesy of the National Motor Museum, England

Photo courtesy of the National Motor Museum, England
QUEEN ALEXANDRIA AND HER 1901 COLUMBIA ELECTRIC.

km/hr). The road conditions of the day did not allow for high speeds. Cities were congested, therefore the top speed of electrics was perfectly acceptable.

The phenomena of overcrowding, congestion, and traffic jams are not indigenous to our times. Studies from the early part of this century indicate there may have been more traffic jams and congestion in the center of large cities then, than there are today. The combination of gasoline, horsedrawn, steam, and electric vehicles, inadequate streets, and the absence of proper traffic controls caused unbelievable tie-ups. (But then, for that matter, there were traffic jams in ancient Rome during the reign of Julius Caesar.)

Women were the champions of the electric automobile of the past. Comfortably positioned at the tiller of her dependable, quiet, and stately electric carriage, the lady driver could entertain an entire parlorful of her friends while traveling to her destination. Her vehicle was replete with plush interior, and exhibited only the most discreet road manners. The absence of the brutal and dangerous hand-cranked starter made the electric appealing to the genteel trade.

Electric vehicles flourished in cities where the streets were paved and the trips short, and in areas devoid of mud-tracked, hilly terrain and uncivilized driving conditions. The cities were the domain of the early electrics because the cities had electricity and in addition, many wealthy patrons who were the primary users of electric vehicles.

THE DEPARTURE OF THE ELECTRIC CAR

The causes of the disappearance of the early electric automobile were complex and totally devastating. Many factors led to its downfall, the most important of which was the perfection of a device that was composed of all the elements of the electric car itself. The inventor was Charles F. Kettering; the year, 1911; the invention, the automobile starter motor.

Kettering's early experience as an engineer for National Cash Register Company allowed him to produce an electric motor system to open cash register drawers. When asked by Henry M. Leland of the Cadillac Motor Company to develop an easier method of starting cars, Kettering applied the technology of the cash register motor to the automobile.

price categories from 1901 to 1906. Their light two-seater had a range of 75 miles (120 km) per charge. Prices ranged from $1,650 to $5,000 for six-seater models. Buffalo cars were later manufactured by Babcock from 1906 to 1912.

The Milburn Company of Toledo, Ohio, was one of the most successful manufacturers. Over 7,000 Milburns were sold from 1914 to as late as 1927. They included conventional models such as the five-passenger brougham. The 1919 Milburn limousine, and several other models, were designed to appear as gasoline automobiles to the extent that they not only had a hood but also incorporated a simulated radiator.

The year of 1912 was most prolific for electrics. Nearly 34,000 electric cars were registered, with scores of trucks and commercial vehicles to boot.

Early electric "town automobiles" had speeds of about 20 to 30 miles per hour (32-48

The automotive starter is a simple device, yet in 1911 there was not one successful, practical solution. Engineers had been working on the problem since the invention of the automobile. More than 25 years of hand cranking cars had passed. Many engineers argued that if an electric motor could be developed that would spin an internal combustion engine, it would weigh about 135 pounds and require several hundred pounds of batteries, (the payload of the vehicle itself).

But Kettering didn't look at it that way. He merely considered the problem and reasoned that a very small motor, over-loaded several times its capacity, could put out enough power to crank an engine for a brief period if it were allowed to cool between uses. The technique worked, much to the astonishment of the scientific community.

The new gasoline-powered automobiles with electric starters attracted the female driver who, until then, had relied on the "easy-to-drive" electric. This eliminated a major part of the market for the electric car.

Another man with an idea finished the electric car off for good. The man was Henry Ford. His mass-produced Model T's, originally priced at $850 in 1909, were selling for $260 in 1925. The Model T comprised over 40% of American motor car sales and records show that half of the cars on the road were "tin lizzies." The low price of the "T" enabled many people to purchase an automobile for the first time. The irony of this story is that of the 15 million Model T's sold during its reign, virtually every one had a hand-crank starter.

The lure of the countryside provided a market that was ripe for the gasoline vehicle which could extend its range indefinitely by merely storing or carrying more fuel. The gasoline automobile encroached upon the domain of the electrics because its range was double or triple that of an electric at a fraction of the cost.

The early electric car continued to plod along and eventually faded out because it became an anachronism. And, while talented designers used their imagination to build electric vehicles of the highest caliber, they had to stand by and watch the world go by while patiently awaiting new technology. To an extent, we are still waiting for that technology to catch up with the gasoline automobile.

In 1899, general scientific opinion was that batteries would become more efficient. Study was ongoing and scientists considered it a mat-

ter of time before a lightweight energy system would be invented. The electric vehicle industry waited with great optimism in the same way we are waiting today, 81 years later, for the arrival of a "superbattery".

The final blow to the electric car was that it could not appeal to the rural dwellers because they had no electricity. Although Thomas Edison's inventions electrified cities in the 1870's, rural electricity was sparse until well into the 1920's, 30's and 40's.

How primitive was the early electric automobile? In a recent road test conducted by *Machine Design Magazine,* a 1915 Detroit Electric was tested. Compared with modern electric cars, it did quite well. It was, in fact, recommended "Best Buy."

The interior, replete with overstuffed seats and tieback curtains, was reminiscent of grandma's parlor. Powered by twelve 6-volt batteries and a 5.5 horsepower motor, it produced an 80-mile (129 km) range, using large diameter, high-pressure tires designed for the electric automobiles of the day. A top speed of 25 mph (40 km/hr) could quietly be achieved. The car carried five passengers, two of whom sat in chairs facing rearward and three in a main seat facing forward. Although the seating position design was more of a concession to pleasant parlor conversation, the visibility for the driver was excellent. The high, flat-pane windows were designed for full visibility in all directions even

Photo courtesy of Gilbert Heinrich

1915 DETROIT ELECTRIC
This elegantly-restored 1915 Detroit Electric belongs to Mr. Gilbert Heinrich of Electric Vehicle Associates, Cleveland, Ohio. A top speed of 25 mph (40 km/hr) and range of 80 miles (129 km) per charge were noted.

ELECTRIC SURREY IN OPERATION.

ELECTRIC SURREY CONSTRUCTED ON "THE RIKER SYSTEM," SHOWING DETAILS OF WORKING PARTS

when carrying a full complement of passengers. The Detroit Electrics displayed the excellent quality of a finely made machine. Although fitted with modern batteries, it is basically as it was originally, in an era when designers knew how to build electric cars. Let us hope that we will see some of our 1981 models "street-working" in sixty years or so.

Today, as large corporations and positive governmental forces begin to work, we will begin acquiring the technology our forefathers so desperately desired. The electric car today has an opportunity to succeed as never before.

The following companies have produced electric vehicles:

D = Germany   F = France   US = U.S.A.   B = Belgium   CH = Switzerland
A = Austria   GB = Great Britain   J = Japan   NL = Holland

1893-1900

Jeantaud (F)—1893-1906

Morris & Salom (US)—1895-1897

Riker (US)—1896-1902

Columbia (US)—1897-1913

Headland (GB)—1897-1900

Krieger (F)—1897-1909

General Electric (US)—1898-1899

Jenatzy (B)—1898-1903

Lohner (Lohner-Porsche Electric Cars) (A)—1898-1906

Madelvic (GB)—1898-1900

Waverly (US)—1898-1903

American Electric (US)—1899-1902

Baker (US)—1899-1916

B.G.S. (F)—1899-1906

Cleveland (US)—1899-1901

Eastman (US)—1899-1902

Henschel (D)—1899-1906

Scheele (D)—1899-1910

Woods (US)—1899-1919

1900-1915

Cardinet (F)—1900-1906

National (US)—1900-1904

Electromotion (F)—1900-1909

Bachelle (US)—1901-1902

Buffalo (US)—1901-1906

City & Suburban (GB)—1901-1905

Electromobile (GB)—1901-1920

Studebaker (US)—1902-1912

Tribelhorn (CH)—1902-1920

Borland (US)—1903-1916

Pope-Waverly (US)—1903-1907

Regina (F)—1903-1908

Fritchle (US)—1904-1917

Rauch & Lang (US)—1905-1928

Silvertown (GB)—1905-1910

Babcock (US)—1906-1912

Siemens-Schuckert (D)—1906-1910

Bailey (US)—1907-1915

B.E.F. (D)—1907-1913

Detroit Electric (US)—1907-1938

Waverly (US)—1908-1914

Broc (US)—1909-1916

Grinnell (US)—1910-1913

Kimball (US)—1910-1912

Ohio (US)—1910-1918

Hupp-Yeats (US)—1911-1919

Argo (US)—1912-1914

Church-Field (US)—1912-1913

Flanders (US)—1912-1913

Tiffany (US)—1913-1914

Flanders (US)—1914-1915

Milburn (US)—1914-1922

Chicago (US)—1915-1916

World War I 1914-1918

S.B. (D)—1920-1924

Post-World War I

Automatic (US)—1921

Chelsea (GB)—1922

Elektric (D)—1922-1924

World War II 1939-1945

Chapeaux (F)—1940-1941

During World War II

Le Dauphin (F)—1941-1942

Faure (F)—1941-1947

Stela (F)—1941-1944

After World War II

Tama (J)—1947-1951

B.M.A. Hazelcar (GB)—1952-1957

NOTE: Some manufacturers produced many models for a number of years. The 1913 Waverley, for example, offered 11 models of trucks and cars. The Studebaker Company of South Bend, Indiana, produced over 1,800 electrics from 1902 to 1912, one of which was specially designed for the personal use of Thomas A. Edison.

More Luxury—New Conveniences—Greater Comfort
in the Magnificent New Baker Coupé

The mere announcement of the magnificent New Baker Coupe resulted in the sale of hundreds of cars throughout the country, even before the first lot had received the final touches in their careful course through the big Baker plant.

There could be no more emphatic proof that this handsome model—the latest creation by the oldest, foremost and largest electric car builders in the country—fully meets the demand for a thoroughly stylish, yet conservative, coupe. It is a big, roomy motor car, with full limousine back, longer wheel base, graceful, low-hung body lines and new hoods of French design.

REVOLVING FRONT SEATS are one of the innovations introduced in this Baker Model. These permit the occupants to face forward or turn about. Easy view of the road is possible from the rear seat because of the exceptionally low front and front quarter windows.

Either Lever or Wheel Steer

The former from rear seat, the latter from left front seat (with controlling lever attached to steering mast). In every detail this new Baker is a car of supreme convenience and luxury.

Baker luxury endures, because the car itself was built *first;* the luxury was added afterward. With Baker beauty is unquestioned mechanical excellence—the kind that gives the car its long life; its remarkable ability to climb hills and to stand up under the hardest service, always at a *lower cost of upkeep* than any other electric.

THE BAKER MOTOR VEHICLE COMPANY, CLEVELAND, OHIO

Builders also of Baker Electric Trucks   CANADA: The Baker Motor Vehicle Company of Canada, Ltd., Walkerville, Ont.

Photo courtesy of the National Motor Museum, England

1922 CHELSEA ELECTRIC COUPE
This model had the distinction of having a simulated radiator in a front grill assembly. The Wandsworth Engineering Works of London was the manufacturer.

THE ELECTRIC BICYCLE

Conceived as early as 1895, electric bicycles were well ahead of their time. The design of the battery and the use of motor as an integrated propulsion system were in many respects similar to today's electric bicycle. However, despite the advanced nature of their design, the weight of the motors, batteries, and bicycle frames limited their use.

Among the numerous patents issued for electric bicycles prior to the turn of the century, one incorporated a motor within the hub of the front wheel. This innovative design configuration did not reappear until almost eighty years later.

The present popularity of the electric bicycle can be attributed to advances in technology resulting in improved efficiency using compact, lightweight motor and battery designs.

BAKER ELECTRICS
(facing page)

The Baker Electric Company (1899-1916), later Baker, Rauch & Lang, Cleveland, Ohio, was one of the most important electric vehicle producers in the U.S.

The firm was formed by Walter C. Baker, a pioneer in electric vehicle development. As early as 1893, Baker had assisted in the building of the "Electrobat" for the World's Columbian Exposition in Chicago. He was also associated with the development of ball bearings for automotive use, and engineered the lightweight alloy axles for the Model T Ford.

The accomplishments of Walter Baker are manifest, from his experimental Baker "Torpedo" racer of 1902 to the myriad of dependable production electrics he provided Americans. His death at 87 in 1955 did not erase the name of Baker from the roster of electric vehicle manufacturers— electric forklifts are produced today by the Baker Industrial Truck Division of Otis Elevator Corporation, Cleveland, Ohio.

The Rauch & Lang Company was active from 1905 to 1928. In 1916 they merged with Baker to form Baker, Rauch & Lang. After 1922 the vehicles were called Raulangs.

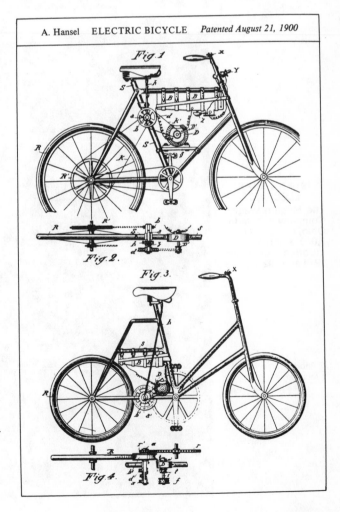

A. Hansel ELECTRIC BICYCLE *Patented August 21, 1900*

1913 BAILEY MODEL F PHAETON

This model had the distinction of resembling a gasoline-powered automobile more than an electric. The top speed was 20 mph (32 km/hr); range was from 80 to 100 miles (129 to 161 km) per charge. The S. R. Bailey Co. of Amesbury, Mass., produced electric cars from 1907 to 1915. Today, the Bailey Company produces precision rolled products.

Photo courtesy of the Henry Ford Museum, Dearborn, Michigan

1919 MILBURN ELECTRIC

The Milburn Wagon Company of Toledo, Ohio, produced over 7,000 electric automobiles between 1914 and 1922.

Photo courtesy of the Museum of Science & Industry, Chicago

1913 COMMERCIAL TRUCK

Photo courtesy of the Smithsonian Institute

EARLY COMMERCIAL VEHICLES

Imagine that you are a truck fleet owner faced with the proposition of changing your vehicles to either electric or gasoline. The trucks in your metropolitan area are about 50% electric and 50% gasoline-powered. Some friends suggest that gasoline would be the more economically feasible route, yet others proclaim electrics as the wave of the future. The question is difficult and you weigh your decision carefully. This is not the year 2000, but 1905. It actually happened.

From 1900 to 1920, thousands of electric trucks and delivery vehicles were in use because of the unique nature of the driving public of the day. Delivery men, usually accustomed to horse and carriage, found the gasoline vehicles difficult to operate. Complicated gear reductions and elaborate transmissions proved confusing to men whose only mechanical experience was that of holding the reins and speaking to the engine. Electric trucks had simple controls and lacked the smoke, noise, and vibrations of the gasoline

versions. When speeds of 8 or 10 mph (13 or 16 km/hr) were commonplace, roads were half-paved and deliveries were largely local (leaving cross-country freight to the railroading industry), the electrics thrived. When all of these advantages disappeared, the electric truck was soon to follow.

The assortment of electric commercial vehicles in the 1898 to 1918 period was a formidable group indeed. Some were fire engines, taxicabs, garbage collectors, tractors, lightpole repairers, heavy haulers, train switchers, crane carriers, freight handlers—but the largest group was light multistop delivery vans.

The "van," an English term for a lightweight truck, was and *is* an ideal use of electric power. To cite an example: a 1915 Lansden van could run 93 miles (150 km) a day, making 100 stops or deliveries on a single charge. It weighed 2,460 pounds (1116 kg) and could carry a 2,000-pound (907 kg) payload. It was equipped with an Edison, nickel-iron battery system that weighed

THE STEERING SHAFT AND ELECTRIC CONTROLLER OF AN EARLY COMMERCIAL TRUCK.

A COMMERCIAL ELECTRIC "TRIMMER'S WAGON."

Photo courtesy of the Smithsonian Institute

1,200 pounds (544 kg). This type of vehicle was used by department stores and express delivery companies in New York, Chicago, and other large cities. Some vans were used 14 to 18 hours a day and charged at night with large 40- amp battery chargers.

In 1915, one New York firm alone used 350 delivery vans. No fewer than 2,300 electric vehicles with over 100 garages for recharging existed in New York in that year. Over 45 firms had "fleets" of 10 units or more. Berlin had almost 1,000 electrics, mostly post office trucks and taxicabs.

Although Paris used electrics for garbage and refuse service, and England utilized both British and German electric postal service trucks, it was New York City with seven million dollars worth of electrics and equipment that led the field.

Reliability was the keynote. Greater reliability than the gasoline truck, especially for 80% of city deliveries, made the electric attractive. Low maintenance, combined with a minimum amount of "down time" enabled many electrics to show an average of 297 days in service out of a 300-day work year.

FIFTY TWO-TON BAKER ELECTRIC DELIVERY VANS
These vans were used by the American Express Company, one of two hundred companies using fleets of Bakers in 1912. They were never equalled for economy or dependabililty.

A GERMAN ELECTRIC TAXICAB, WITH ROOF BAGGAGE RACK.

The names of some of the truck manufacturers during the prolific 1898-1915 period were Waverly, Baker, Milburn, Riker, Orwell, Detroit, G.M.C., G.V., Commercial, Landsen, Buffalo, Clayton Couple-Gear, Walker, Urban, Ward, Voltacar, Guy, Eldrige, and Field, to name a few.

Early electric trucks, it must be understood, traveled at extremely slow speeds. A five-ton truck would travel at only seven miles per hour—slightly faster than walking speed—and carried 10,000 pounds (4,530 kg) for 35 miles (56 km) on one battery charge. The lightest trucks, the 1/2 ton variety, traveled at 12 mph (19 km/hr), with a load capacity of 1,000 pounds (453 kg) and a 45 mile (72 km) range per charge. Although a 45 mile (72 km) range for a lightweight van would be acceptable by today's standards, the 12 mph (19 km) top speed would be absurd. The vehicles of that day did not require high speeds in heavy city traffic situations. However, when the speed and distance requirements became higher, the electric truck disappeared.

Solid rubber tires were preferred for the electric trucks of that day. Manufacturers dis-

AN EARLY GENERAL VEHICLE
ELECTRIC DELIVERY VAN.

AN EARLY WARD
TWO-TON ELECTRIC TRUCK.

AN EARLY WAVERLY ELECTRIC TRUCK.

couraged the use of pneumatic tires because of their unreliability.

The earliest electric trucks were understandably primitive; although the Riker of 1898 had the appearance of a large "horseless" covered wagon, it nevertheless incorporated dual-geared rear wheels and a rear gate for loading, much like the modern trucks of today.

The Commercial electric truck of America was a very rugged, diversified carrier. One truck was reported to be used daily for over fifty years. The Couple-Gear truck was used for heavy hauling, fire engines, garbage trucks and a variety of uses, including a four-wheel drive truck fitted for passenger use. One model of

AN EARLY WARD ELECTRIC
DELIVERY VAN.

THE INTERNAL VIEW OF A COUPLE-GEAR TRUCK WHEEL SHOWING THE
BUILT-IN MOTOR.

The unusual strap-steel drive shaft assembly
of an early G.M.C. electric van.

this type had four-wheel drive, four-wheel steering and "power steering." To turn left, power was applied to the right front wheel, thus pushing the vehicle to the left. This was made possible by the use of a sophisticated geared motor built into the hub of the wheels. Another model had a four-cylinder gasoline engine powering a generator, eliminating the batteries and the transmission, while not complicating the ease of operation. This was one of America's most effective electrics built between 1910 and 1918.

The G.M.C. Electric Wagon's unique drive train used a long strap of spring steel to connect the motor to the differential, thus elimin-

THE DUAL MOTOR REAR
AXLE DRIVE OF A COMMER-
CIAL TWO TON ELECTRIC
TRUCK. Note double hard rub-
ber tires.

ating the drive shaft and universal joints normally used with this type of drive. The steel strap created a buffer effect that eliminated jerky start-ups when power was applied.

The early electric truck simply could not meet the needs of the trucking industry, especially when cross country hauling became necessary.

But even so, locally-used electric commercial vehicles do exist today. There are over 100,000 electric fork lifts in use in the United States alone. Britain delivers milk, eggs and other perishables in small electric vans called "milk floats," which number upwards of 50,000. And the electric golf cart is so uniquely suited for its job that it is predominant in its field.

RECENT HISTORY

In America, during 1966 and 1967, General Motors, Ford, and American Motors were developing modern electric passenger car prototypes. More than a dozen of these vehicles have been produced and demonstrated. This resurgence of electric vehicles interest followed in the wake of statements made by several influential public officials condemning the combustion- engined vehicle as a menace to public health.

General Motors brought out two prototype demonstration vehicles, namely a Chevrolet Corvair called the ElectroVair and a GMC electric fuel cell van called the ElectroVan. The batteries GM selected were silver-zinc with extremely short cycle life and extraordinary high cost. The fuel cell for the ElectroVan had to be replenished every 125 miles (201 km) and was complicated as well as bulky. The fuel cell required a fluid electrolyte which was pumped through the cells. The ElectroVair's range was only 80 miles (129 km) per charge coupled with an extremely low number of potential recharge cycles. The batteries for the ElectroVair II were priced at $15,000 in 1967, which is equivalent to about $30,000 today.

The ElectroVair I was built on a 1964 Corvair body and chassis; the ElectroVair II was built on a 1966 Corvair body and chassis. The 680-pound (308 kg) battery pack powered a 115-horsepower alternating current, induction motor which required oil for cooling because of a 13,000 rpm motor speed. Problems with the vehicle, as described by GM, were short range, short battery life, long recharge time, heavy weight and bulky size of the battery and drive systems, costly components and materials, difficult cooling requirements, safety problems with lack of engine braking as a possible hazard, and radio and TV interference.

The General Motors ElectroVairs are an example of an effort to produce high technology with no regard to practicality. The silver-zinc batteries were unrealistic, to say the least, as an inclusion into an electric vehicle. The 13,000 rpm motor, which was of an alternating current design, did not provide engine braking of any kind. This posed a safety hazard. Cooling of the motor, components and unusual complexity of design marred this valiant attempt to produce a usable vehicle.

The 1966 GMC HandiVan which was converted to produce the ElectroVan utilized a fuel cell system. The hydrogen-oxygen fuel cells used were extremely bulky and required that a hydrogen and oxygen tank be fitted into the back of the van. Basically, motor and controls were the same as the ElectroVair II.

The illustration shows the complexity of the first fuel-cell-powered van ever to be built. The 7,100-pound (3219 kg) ElectroVan powered by a 125 hp AC motor, had a top speed of 70 mph (112 km/hr) and a range of 100 to 150 miles (161 to 241 km).

Among the problems encountered by GM with the ElectroVan were heavy weight and large volume, short lifetime, costly components and materials, complicated and lengthy start-up and shut-down procedures, gas bleeds and gas leaks, complexity of the three separate fluid systems (electrolyte, hydrogen, and oxygen), a long list of safety problems, possible collision hazards, hydrogen leaks, electrolyte leaks, high voltages, and so on. Perhaps this is why we see very little fuel cell research activity for electric vehicles. The system is too expensive and complicated.

Besides the ElectroVair and ElectroVan, General Motors produced some special-purpose urban electric cars in 1969. These cars are generally acknowledged as excellent small-vehicle designs. The GM512 Series car uses one basic body with three separate experimental power plants. One is a battery-electric, another is a hybrid gasoline-electric, and a third is a gasoline-engine vehicle. The two- passenger vehicle has an overall length of 86.3 inches (220 cm) and a width of 56 inches (145 cm). Access to the vehicle is from the front, much like the BMW Isetta, which was a small German car popular in the 50's.

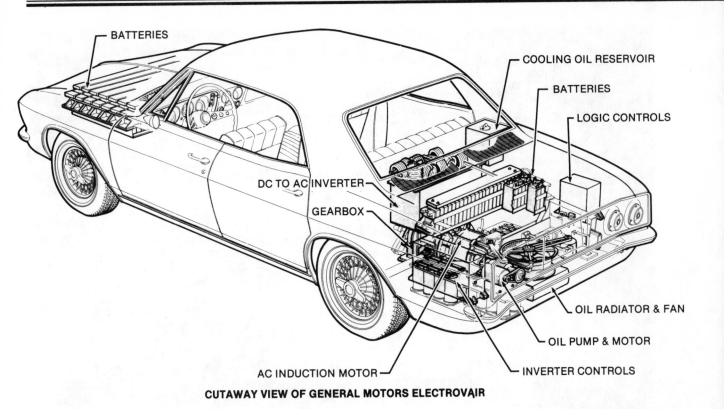

BATTERIES

COOLING OIL RESERVOIR

BATTERIES

LOGIC CONTROLS

DC TO AC INVERTER

GEARBOX

OIL RADIATOR & FAN

OIL PUMP & MOTOR

INVERTER CONTROLS

AC INDUCTION MOTOR

CUTAWAY VIEW OF GENERAL MOTORS ELECTROVAIR

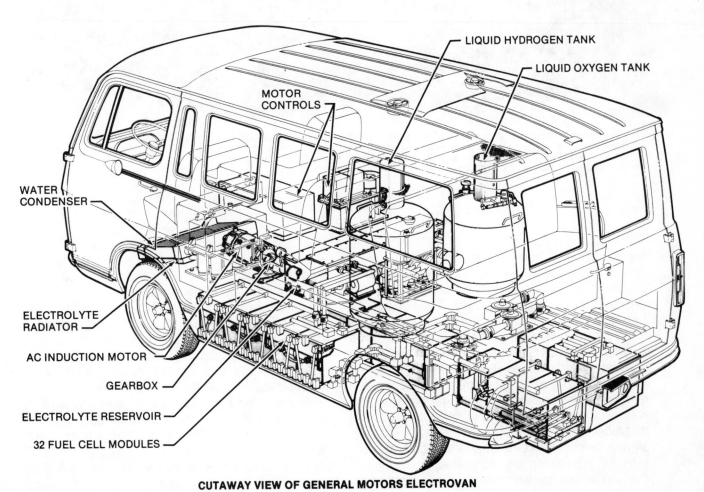

LIQUID HYDROGEN TANK

LIQUID OXYGEN TANK

MOTOR CONTROLS

WATER CONDENSER

ELECTROLYTE RADIATOR

AC INDUCTION MOTOR

GEARBOX

ELECTROLYTE RESERVOIR

32 FUEL CELL MODULES

CUTAWAY VIEW OF GENERAL MOTORS ELECTROVAN

This gasoline-electric hybrid is one of three experimental 512 series of special-purpose cars developed by General Motors Engineering Staff in the late 60's. Its power system consists of a 12-cubic-inch gasoline engine coupled with a series DC electric motor through an electro-magnetic clutch. It runs either in electric or hybrid mode.

Photo courtesy of General Motors Corp.

The battery pack consisted of seven lightweight 85 amp-hour, 47-pound (21 kg) units. This vehicle used an SCR controller and a Delco-Remy DC series-wound motor, capable of producing 8-1/2 horsepower. The hybrid 512 Series vehicle used a gasoline engine and electric motor combination. Electric drive was used zero to 10 mph (16 km): At speeds of 10-13 mph both power plants operated together. At speeds greater than 13 mph, (21 km) the gasoline engine was used exclusively. The gasoline engine was a 2-cylinder, 11.7 cubic inch (195 cc) displacement variety of a rather inefficient design. Attempts had been made to modify the engine by increasing the compression ratio, but the unit would not withstand the excess power.

The 90-volt, 20-ampere alternator was belt-driven at engine speed to recharge the battery, or conventional 115-volt AC outlets could be used. The constant-speed fuel economy was 45 to 50 miles per gallon (19.5 to 21.2 km/l). In the electric mode, the range and speed varied from 5.2 miles (8.3 km) at 30 mph, to 9 miles (14 km) at 10 mph (16 km). Unfortunately, more than one acceleration run every 2.5 miles (4 km) would result in battery depletion.

In fact, the top speed of the electric was 45 mph (72 km/hr) and the top speed of the hybrid was only 40 mph (64 km/hr). The electric was also faster in acceleration.

This vehicle was experimental and cannot be considered the culmination of high technology.

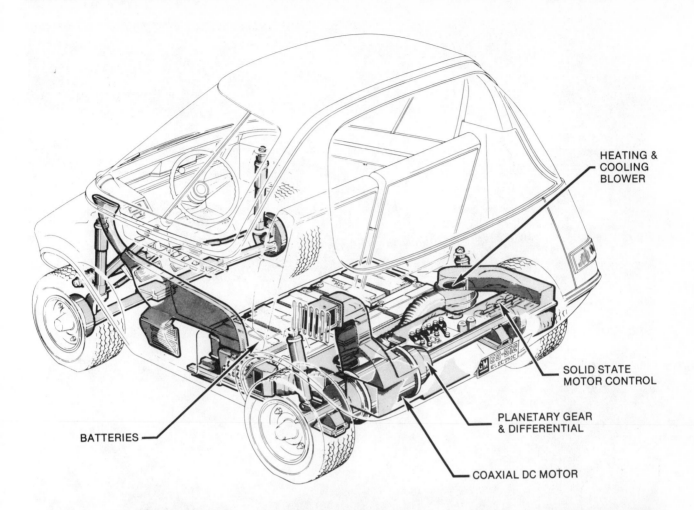

HEATING &
COOLING
BLOWER

SOLID STATE
MOTOR CONTROL

PLANETARY GEAR
& DIFFERENTIAL

BATTERIES

COAXIAL DC MOTOR

Photo courtesy of General Motors Corporation

THE G.M. SERIES 512 CARS

The XP512E electric car is powered by 12 maintenance-free lead acid traction batteries. Features include a DC motor, solid-state motor control and a canopy which could be removed.

FORD COMUTA

Photo courtesy of Ford Motor Company

The Ford Motor Company contribution to the "volt-rush" of the late 60's was the Comuta which was developed by the Ford of Britain Research Staff. The vehicle was only 80" (203 cm) long.

A modern Honda Civic or Toyota could approach the mileage of this hybrid and maintain complete road-worthiness and meet all safety requirements to boot.

Ford

The Ford Motor Company announced the development of an experimental electric car in June, 1967. The Ford Comuta was designed by Ford of Britain's Research Staff. The vehicle is 80 inches in overall length, which is less than half the length of its contemporary, the 1967 Ford Mustang. The photo shows the chassis with batteries in position.

American Motors Amitron

While General Motors and Ford were building prototypes in the 1960's, American Motors introduced a very sophisticated prototype called the Amitron. This sleek, efficient, teardrop-

FORD COMUTA

shaped coupe had a 50-mph (80 km/hr) cruising speed. A maximum range of 150 miles (241 km) per charge was based on moderate cruising speed.

The battery systems used in the Amitron were developed by Gulton Industries, a major battery manufacturer. Two different types of batteries were used: lithium-nickel fluoride and nickel-cadmium bipolar units. The two lithium batteries had a storage capacity of up to ten times as much energy as conventional lead-acid batteries of the same size.

The two nickel-cadmium bipolar batteries provided the energy reserve to allow acceleration of up to 50 mph (80 km/hr) in 20 seconds. Also the bipolar batteries could be recharged from the lithium batteries while the car was in a cruising mode. The advantage of the nickel-cadmium units was 1,000 recharge cycles over a three year period. A 4-hour recharge capability helped make this comparatively lightweight, 200-pound (91 kg) battery supply very attractive.

The vehicle also incorporated a regenerative

THE AMITRON

The American Motors' entry to the electric car development program of the late 60's, designated the "Amitron."

This three-passenger prototype had a Gulton lithium battery system, regenerative braking and solid-state controls.

A range of 150 miles (241 km) per charge, and speeds of up to 50 mph (80 km/hr) were claimed. Acceleration was 0 to 50 mph (0 to 80 km/hr) in 20 seconds.

Two lithium-nickel fluoride batteries* rated at 150 watt-hours per lb (331 watt hours per kg) used with two nickel-cadmium batteries in combination. Battery weight was only 200 lbs (91 kg).

braking system that could recapture part of the lost energy of braking into electric storage.

Another interesting aspect of the vehicle was weight-saving, air-filled seats which could be lowered to increase cargo carrying capacity. Also featured were helicopter-style instrumentation behind the steering wheel, a clam-shell-type door which when open exposed the entire roof via a counterbalanced pivot system, and bumpers made of vinyl-rubber that could absorb impact and return to their original shape.

The Amitron project was not further developed, in spite of the fact that it was very well received publicly when it was introduced in 1968. The expensive batteries and other factors contributed to the decision of AMC to suspend testing of this vehicle.

*Batteries will be discussed in detail in Chapter 4.

"THE GREAT ELECTRIC CAR RACE"

One recent "historical event" in electric vehicle development occurred in August, 1968. The event was "The Great Electric Car Race," conducted by students from the California Institute of Technology (CalTech) in Pasadena and students from the Massachusetts Institute of Technology (MIT) in Cambridge. The object of the race was for the MIT electrically-converted Chevrolet 1968 Corvair (borrowed from General Motors), to reach the CalTech campus before the CalTech converted 1958 Volkswagen Microbus, called the "Voltswagen," could reach the MIT campus.

The CalTech vehicle was owned by Wally Rippel, a graduate student in physics. It was supplied with twenty lead-cobalt batteries worth about $600, weighing 95 pounds each, and pro-

CAL TECH ELECTRIC VAN

duced by the Electric Fuel Propulsion Company of Ann Arbor, Michigan. E.F.P. Company's president, Mr. Robert Aronson, had also made arrangements for some mid-trip recharging stations. The CalTech car was accompanied by another ten- year-old vehicle, a 1958 Chevrolet, which towed a portable generator trailer for emergency recharging. There were five other vehicles which assisted the CalTech entry besides the 220-volt generator vehicle.

The MIT vehicle was a bit more sophisticated, besides being ten years newer. It carried 2,000 lbs. (907 kg) of nickel-cadmium batteries worth about $20,000 and supplied by Gulton Industries. The MIT Corvair was a laboratory model which had not been driven until shortly before the race. In fact, a pre-race trial run almost burned up their batteries. The MIT vehicle had an advanced, experimental, motor weighing 80 pounds (36 kg) and developing 30 horsepower. The permanent magnet motor was equipped with a high power, solid state control system much more advanced than the CalTech

vehicle. The CalTech vehicle used a 20 horsepower traction motor such as the type used in forklifts. Both vehicles had the same range per charge, but the Corvair traveled five to ten miles (8 to 16 km) per hour faster and a recharge took 15 minutes versus 45 minutes for the Voltswagen. Both vehicles consumed about $25.00 worth of electricity on the entire trip. But the trip was fraught with obstacles:

1. MIT proceeded without much difficulty across the Midwest after starting the race August 26, 1968. The only real problem the first few days was the overheating which occurred in the nickel-cadmium battery pack. This problem was solved by packing ice around the batteries and resorting to a four hour charge.

2. The second day for CalTech brought crew problems when one member contracted the mumps and had to be replaced. Also, the armature of the motor disintegrated about 400 miles (644 km) out, which resulted in a 23-hour wait for a new motor shipped by air to Phoenix,

Arizona, from the Electric Fuel Propulsion Company.

3. The CalTech vehicle was experiencing overheating as well, while recharging the lead-cobalt battery. The recharging rate had to be slowed down, which lost precious time that could have been used for driving.

4. One member of the CalTech crew lost a contact lens which cost forty minutes of driving time. The lens was not found.

5. The MIT car caught fire when being recharged at Elkhart, Indiana. The fire was put out quickly, but damage caused a ten-hour delay.

6. The MIT car had problems with overheating in Springfield, Illinois. The method for cooling motor overheating problems was to pour water on the motor.

7. The CalTech car blew out three diodes in its recharging circuit. More ice had to be continuously applied to batteries, using a siphon-hose purchased in McLean, Texas, to remove water from the battery enclosure.

8. The MIT car reached California first, but crew members did not like the charging setup at Newbury, so they decided to tow their vehicle to the next point, Victorville. One member of the crew, however, forgot to take the vehicle out of low gear, and the electric motor burned up by being towed at 65 mph (105 km/hr). The MIT car had to be towed directly to CalTech, bypassing the last two charge points, in order to reach the finish line.

9. The CalTech car reached Cambridge on September 4, without having to be towed at all.

10. The winning time was 210 hours and 3 minutes for the 3,300 mile (5309 km) cross-country race. Although the MIT car arrived in Pasadena 7-1/2 days after the start, with the CalTech entry coming into Cambridge 37 hours and 20 minutes later, the CalTech entry was voted the winner after certain penalties were deducted. These penalties involved deductions for towing time, recharging with a portable generator between official charging stations and time lost replacing parts. In effect, the tortoise had beaten the hare, and the tortoise made it on its own power. The entire trip was judged on both sides by representatives from Machine Design magazine. A good deal of press coverage and public participation made this event the circus that one would expect it to be.

At this point, we must review a few details. The electric vehicle was never intended for cross-country use. The pollution in the middle of Arizona is not high enough to warrant much concern for emission control. However, the test that was made showed public interest in electric vehicles, and pointed out the improvements necessary to produce an efficient product. The batteries, produced by Electric Fuel Propulsion Company, have been revised and improved in the last ten years, as have solid state speed controls and motor systems. The electric vehicle as a commuter car and commercial truck for urban use is still a very attractive vehicle. While we may not see thousands of them running on the highways, we will definitely see millions of them on our city streets in the 21st century.

During the 1970's programs were initiated to develop electrics in Europe, Japan and the United States. The motivating force which caused the return of the electric was due in part to the Arab Oil Embargo of late 1973. Since then, a concerted effort on the part of manufacturers in all countries has developed many prototypes and a number of limited-production vehicles.

ELECTRIC VEHICLE SPEED RECORD HISTORY

The dominance of early electric vehicles was evidenced by the fact that in 1899, the world's fastest vehicles were electric. Two pioneers in electric vehicle development, both Frenchmen, Charles Jeantaud and Camille Jenatzy, fought to achieve the world's speed record. Jeantaud set the record of 39.24 mph (63.1 km/hr) in December of 1898. Jenatzy a month later returned with a speed of 41 mph (66 km/hr), only to be beaten by Jeantaud with 43.69 mph (70 km/hr). The final speed record of 68.8 mph (110 km/hr) was attained by Jenatzy in the "La-Jamais Contente" ("The Never Satisfied") in 1899. After each high speed run, the vehicle batteries were so heavily discharged that they were worthless. The battle that raged between these two Frenchmen made them popular heroes and further galvanized the stronghold of electric automobiles.

The great speed race was not the first en-

Photo courtesy of the
Musée National du
Chateau de Compeigne

JENATZY'S "LA JAMAIS CONTENTE"
The world's speed record holder in 1899, a bullet-shaped
electric race car. A speed of 68.8 mph (110 km/hr) captured
the record, yet the racer had a top speed, unofficially, of 75
mph (121 km/hr). "La Jamais Contente" means "The Never
Satisfied."

counter Jeantaud and Jenatzy had with each other. They had previously competed in the 1898 "Paris Motor Cab Trials," which was a test designed to determine the best manufacturer of Paris taxis. Jeantaud had won this demonstration with his taxi design. Both Jeantaud and Jenatzy produced electric vehicles commercially during the period of 1893 to 1906. Eventually, both turned their interest away from electric vehicles and began producing gasoline-powered automobiles in 1902.

In 1902, a Baker electric, racer, called the "Torpedo," recorded an unofficial speed on Staten Island Boulevard in New York of 78 mph (126 km/hr), after which it crashed. In 1904 a rebuilt version of the Torpedo, called "The Torpedo Kid," achieved 104 mph (167 km/hr) at Daytona, in the U.S.A.

A non-stop distance record in France was established by a 1901 Krieger which traveled 192 miles (310 km) on a single charge.

Formerly, the French B.G.S. Electric Car held the world's distance record for electrics of almost 180 miles per charge (262 km) in 1900.

The next speed record specifically designed for electric vehicles was set in 1968 by Jerry Kugel with a "flying mile" record of 138 mph (223 km/hr) in the Autolite Lead Wedge at Bonneville, Utah, U.S.A. The vehicle weighed about

one ton (1,015 kg) and was powered by a 120 horsepower AC motor. Lead-acid batteries supplied the power.

In August 1972, the Eagle-Picher "Silver Eagle" produced a flying mile record of 146.437 mph (237 km/hr), at Bonneville. The silver-zinc batteries were the same variety that were used in the "Lunar Rover." A 102 horsepower DC motor was used.

The world's land speed record for an electric-powered motorcycle was set by Mike Corbin on August 19, 1974, with a speed of 165.367 mph (266 km/hr). The silver-zinc batteries, developing 1,000 amps at 120 volts, pushed the "Quicksilver" to 171.102 mph (275.3 km/hr) during qualification. The vehicle measured nine feet in length and weighed over 700 pounds (408 kg). Power was supplied by two jet aircraft engine starter motors developing 100 horsepower each.

On August 23, 1974, the "Battery Box" of Roger Hedlund captured the flying mile and kilometer speed record at 175 mph (281.5 km/hr). The efficiency of the vehicle which used lead-acid batteries was very high. At 175 mph (281.5 km/hr) the vehicle consumed electricity at a rate equivalent to 55 miles per gallon (23.3 km/l) of gasoline.

THE BATTERY BOX

Photo courtesy of John B. Newell

Roger Hedlund's record holding electric car at the Bonneville Salt Flats, Utah, August 23, 1974.

Photo courtesy of Corbin-Gentry, Inc.

CORBIN-GENTRY "QUICK SILVER"

On August 19, 1974, the world's fastest electric motorcycle was driven by Mike Corbin at the Bonneville Salt Flats, Utah, U.S.A. The "Quicksilver" established a new record speed of 165.367 mph (266 km/hr) with a trap speed during time trials of 171.1 mph (275 km/hr). The vehicle was powered by Yardney; silver-zinc batteries supplied by the Yardney Electric Company, Pawcatuck, Conn.

Photo courtesy of Ford Motor Company

THE LEAD WEDGE

The Lead Wedge was built jointly by the Autolite Corporation and the Ford Motor Company for the 1968 Bonneville Salt Flats speed record. The chassis housing motor and batteries is shown in foreground. Fiberglass body shell is in background.

EAGLE PICHER "SILVER EAGLE"

Photo courtesy of Eagle-Picher Company

The Silver Eagle established 21 records for electrics—14 national and 7 international—at the Bonneville Salt Flats, Utah, U.S.A., in August, 1972.

The vehicle had an unofficial top speed of 152.59 mph (245.5 km/hr).

Photo courtesy of The Boeing Aerospace Company

THE LUNAR ROVERS

(An electric vehicle that was really out of this world.)

Three "LRV," Lunar Roving Vehicles, were produced by the Boeing Aerospace Company under the direction of NASA, the U.S. National Aeronautic and Space Administration. The "Moon Buggies" accompanied the Apollo 15, 16 and 17 flights during 1971 and 1972.

The 462-lb (209-kg) Rovers carried up to four times their weight, or 1,606 lbs (728 kg) and performed in temperatures from − 200 to + 220 F (93 to 104C).

Features included: four-wheel steering with a 1/4-hp, series-wound motor at each wheel, lightweight aluminum chassis construction, woven wire wheels to reduce weight, and two unrechargeable 59-lb (27-kg) silver-zinc 36-V primary batteries, manufactured by the Eagle Picher Industries, Joplin, Missouri, rated at total of 242 amps. The Rovers carried television, communication equipment and navigational equipment.

A maximum range of 57 miles (92 km) and a top speed of 10 mph (16 km/hr) was possible, although range never exceeded 22 miles (35 km) and speed of 8 mph (13 km/hr).

The Lunar Rovers were carried on three Apollo missions and performed every function flawlessly. The program record ended with three successful missions in three attempts.

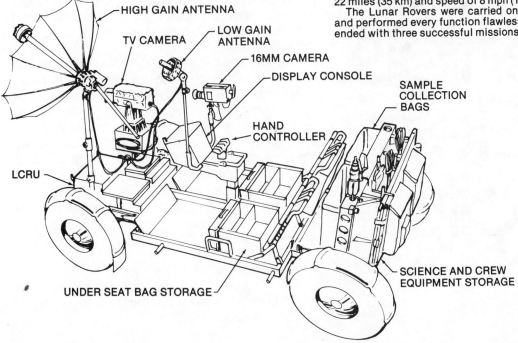

HIGH GAIN ANTENNA
TV CAMERA
LOW GAIN ANTENNA
16MM CAMERA
DISPLAY CONSOLE
SAMPLE COLLECTION BAGS
HAND CONTROLLER
LCRU
SCIENCE AND CREW EQUIPMENT STORAGE
UNDER SEAT BAG STORAGE

Funda-mentals of Elec-tricity

In the spirit of making this book an easy-to-read guide to electric vehicles, we will discuss electricity as simply as possible.

The word "electric" comes from a Greek word meaning "amber." Amber is a translucent mineral composed of fossilized resin. The ancient Greeks used the words "electric force" to refer to the mysterious forces of attraction and repulsion exhibited by amber when it was rubbed with a cloth.

For the sake of simplicity, we will use the following theory to describe electricity. When electricity flows through a wire, it is very much like water flowing through a garden hose. If a 50-foot garden hose is attached to a faucet and the faucet is turned on, water begins to flow. As the faucet is turned on and off, the water responds by flowing or stopping at the end of the 50-foot hose.

Water, flowing in a current, is affected by three factors:

1. Pressure
2. Rate of flow
3. Resistance to flow

Electric current running through a conductor exhibits similar characteristics:

1. Voltage

2. Current
3. Resistance

There are two types of electrical charges: positive and negative. A basic law of electricity is that like charges repel each other, and unlike charges attract each other. In other words, positive charges repel each other and negative charges repel each other, but negative and positive charges attract each other. Figure E-1.

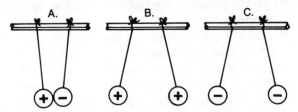

Figure E-1. **REACTION BETWEEN CHARGED BODIES**

In a battery, chemical action causes positive charges to collect on the positive terminal and negative charges to collect on the negative terminal. Because unlike charges attract, there is

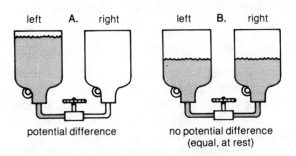

potential difference | no potential difference (equal, at rest)

Figure E-2. **WATER ANALOGY OF DIFFERENCE IN ELECTRIC POTENTIAL**

A few seconds after you open the valve, the level of the water in the two bottles will be equal.

Before you opened the valve, you had a "potential difference" between the two bottles. Now you have no potential difference. A piece of plain copper wire has no potential difference; connect it to a battery and you have a potential difference.

a force-attraction between the electrified particles concentrated at the positive and negative terminals. There is an electromotive force which exists between the two terminals. We call that force *potential difference* or, more commonly, *voltage*. Figure E-2

If we connect a wire to the two battery terminals, an electrical current will flow in the wire. We measure that flow in *amperes*. The number of amperes, or "amps," refers to the quantity of electrons passing a given point in one second. Figure E-3

In an electrical system, the conductor of electricity is usually a wire. When the electrical current runs through a wire, the wire creates a

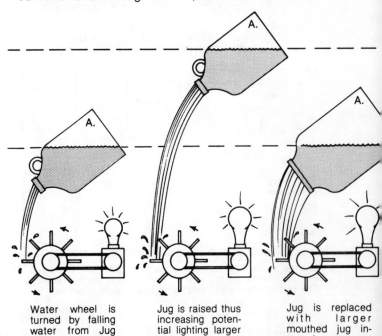

Water wheel is turned by falling water from Jug "A", lighting small bulb.

Jug is raised thus increasing potential lighting larger bulb.

Jug is replaced with larger mouthed jug increasing current and lighting larger bulb.

Figure E-3. **FALLING WATER ANALOGY DESCRIBING INCREASED POTENTIAL**

Figure E-4. WATER PIPE SIZE ANALOGY OF ELECTRICAL RESISTANCE

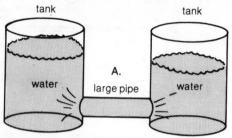

The water from the left tank in **A.** can reach the right tank through a large pipe. There is little resistance to the flow of water because the pipe is large.

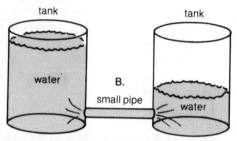

The pipe in **B.** is much thinner and smaller inside. It takes longer for the water to flow from one tank to another because the thin pipe offers more resistance to the flow of water.

Figure E-5. WATER HOSE CONSTRICTION ANALOGY OF ELECTRICAL RESISTANCE

water pipes

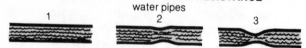

By squeezing the pipe resistance is increased.

Figure E-6. WATER HOSE LENGTH ANALOGY OF ELECTRICAL RESISTANCE

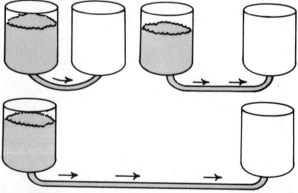

In the three sets of tanks above, the length of the hose connecting the tanks is another way to judge the resistance. The further the water must travel, the more resistance.

resistance to the current flow. To illustrate this, we can again use the analogy of water flow, as shown in Figures E-4, E-5, and E-6.

The *ohm* is the unit we use as a measure of electrical resistance. All substances resist, to a greater or lesser degree, the flow of electricity. Most metals are good conductors offering little resistance. On the other hand, rubber, wood, and glass are poor conductors offering high resistance, so we use these materials as insulators.

We can determine the amount of resistance in a conductor, or circuit, by dividing the voltage by the amps:

$$\frac{volts}{amps} = ohms$$

Let's say we have a circuit with a 200-volt potential and which has a 100 amp current. Using our formula, we find that the circuit is offering 2 ohms of resistance:

$$\frac{200 \text{ volts}}{100 \text{ amps}} = 2 \text{ ohms}$$

The higher the ohm rating, the more voltage is required to have a circuit with, in this case, a 100-amp flow.

The resistance to the flow of electricity in a light bulb filament is what causes the wire to burn brightly.

When we connected our two battery terminals with a wire to create a flow of electricity, we produced a source of power that we can harness to do work. We measure that power in *watts*. The combination of force, or voltage, and quantity of flow, or amps, creates watts, the unit of power. We express this in a simple formula:

$$volts \times amps = watts$$

If our positive and negative battery terminals have a potential difference of 5 volts between them, and we connect them into a circuit carrying 2 amps of current flow, we produce 10 watts of power:

$$5 \text{ volts} \times 2 \text{ amps} = 10 \text{ watts}$$

Some other units we use to describe electrical power are *horsepower* and *kilowatts*. These are related to watts, the basic power unit. One horsepower equals 746 watts. One kilowatt equals one thousand watts.

We use watts to do work for us—to light a bulb, turn a motor, or lift a weight. In households, electrical current is produced by utility generators. The more work you require electricity to do, the more wattage is consumed. Electric bills are usually stated in "kilowatt hours" of electricity used. A kilowatt hour is 1,000 watts (which is one kilowatt) used for one hour. If a light bulb uses 100 watts per hour, in ten hours it will have consumed one kilowatt hour of electricity. Or ten 100-watt bulbs burning for one hour each will also have consumed one kilowatt hour of electricity.

There are two types of electric current: alternating and direct. Direct current (DC) is the type of current produced by a battery. Direct current flows in one direction from its source. Alternating current (AC) fluctuates from positive to negative in a specific number of cycles per second. In the U.S. household current, which is AC, fluctuates at 60 hertz (or cycles per second), thereby producing 120 alternating pulses per second. Figure E-7

Figure E-7. **AC CURRENT**

AC current can be represented by a wave motion. We will discuss AC current later in the chapter on "motors."

THE MAGIC OF MAGNETISM

In ancient Greece, Socrates noted that a series of iron rings could support themselves, forming a chain, if held by a lodestone or "magnet." A natural magnet is a magnetic oxide of iron which attracts normal iron. The word meaning "magnet" was the name the Greeks gave the lodestone because of its discovery near Magnesia, in Thesaly.

A magnet has a north and south pole. When a magnet floats on a cork in water, it aligns itself with the north and south poles of the earth, because the earth is actually a large magnet.

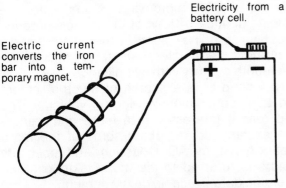

Figure E-8. **ELECTROMAGNETISM**

When an electric current flows through wire wrapped around a bar of iron, an electromagnet is created. When the flow of electricity ceases, the magnetism ceases.

As early as 1000 A.D., the Chinese used magnets to create compasses, making use of the magnet's ability to point a needle north.

In 1820, Hans Christian Oersted discovered a relationship between magnetism and electric current. In an experiment, he noticed a compass needle move when placed next to a wire through which passed an electric current produced by a battery. Figure E-8. This observation was amplified by other scientists. From their experiments came electromagnetism, electric induction, electric generators and motors, plus a host of important milestones in science.

ELECTRIC INDUCTION

If the experiment shown in Figure E-9 had not worked, the world would be a vastly different place in which to live.

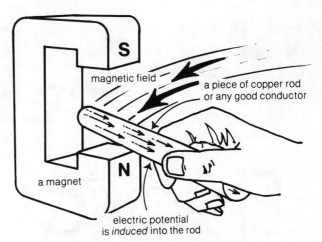

Figure E-9. **ELECTRIC INDUCTION**

When the metal rod is passed through the magnetic field, electricity is created by *induction*. The phenomenon above is the principle of the electric generator. That is, spinning a large conductor (rotor) within a magnetic field. Every time the rod passes through the magnetic field, electricity is "induced" into the rod.

Electric induction is, to my mind, one of the most important discoveries of science. Induction allowed the electrification of cities, and the use of motors in industry, transportation, farm mechanization, and much more.

We have looked briefly and simply at electricity and magnetism. Hopefully, this foundation of basic information will entice the more aggressive reader to research these subjects in greater depth. In any case, we now have enough information to proceed into the following chapters on motors, batteries, controls, and vehicles.

Electric Motors

Electric motors affect the life of virtually every person in the world. If an individual does not come into contact with electric clocks, trains, air conditioners, automobiles or any of the thousands of electric motor applications in his daily life, then he would have to be considered a primitive.

The similarity between a generator and a motor is that a generator converts mechanical energy into electrical energy, while an electric motor is a device that converts electrical energy into mechanical energy. The components of a DC motor and DC generator are almost identical. They both use or produce direct current. The discovery that a motor and a generator were interchangeable shook the nineteenth century with its brilliance.

This chapter is a sketch of electric motors and their application to electric vehicles. The avid reader interested in a more comprehensive explanation regarding some of the more exotic types of AC induction and specialty motors is referred to the many textbooks and scientific data available on the subject.

The basis of all electric motors is a relationship between an electric current and magnetism. An electric current sets up a magnetic field at right angles to a wire carrying the current, as shown in Figure M-1.

Figure M-1. MAGNETIC FIELD PRODUCED BY ELECTRIC CURRENT
A current sets up a magnetic field at right angles to a wire carrying the current.

If a compass is placed over a wire through which an electric current passes, the compass needle will be deflected. This discovery by Hans Christian Oersted in the early 19th century led to the application of electric induction, and the development of generators and electric motors.

The idea that like magnetic poles of magnets repulse each other, and unlike poles attract is the concept behind all electric motors. Electricity moves from the negative to the positive, through a wire, forming a circuit. The wire is now a miniature electromagnet. The positive side of the wire is the north pole and the negative side of the wire is the south pole. Like

poles will repel and unlike poles of north and south will attract. Figure M-2.

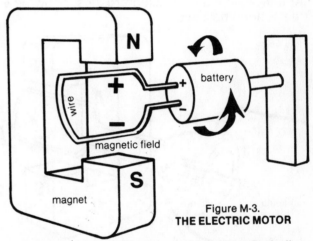

Figure M-3. THE ELECTRIC MOTOR

An electric motor works because of induction. Basically, a motor is a generator working backwards. (The generator converts force into electricity by induction.) (The motor converts electricity into force through induction.)

Here's where the magic begins. Figure M-3.

As long as current runs through the wire loop, a miniature magnet will be formed, and the wire loop will turn *away* from the poles of the magnet. The positive side of the wire will not stay next to the north pole of the magnet. The

For this diagram let us suppose the small magnet is inside the large magnet's magnetic field. In this position, there is no motion because the opposite poles of each magnet attract each other.

But in this position, if we pretend we change the poles of the small magnet, the two magnets start to repulse each other. The small magnet must spin.

In this position, the opposite poles are pulling at each other and the small magnet must spin.

Figure M-2. ELECTROMAGNETISM IN MOTORS

negative side of the wire will move away from the south pole of the magnet causing the wire to twist. When the twisted wire's negative and positive sides are now matched to opposite poles of the magnet, the motion stops. The wire loop and the magnet are now at rest.

COMMUTATOR AND BRUSHES

An ingenious little device called a commutator allows the wire loop to continue flipping around and around.

Figure M-4 explains what the commutator does in basic terms, which is to keep the motor's armature (in this case our single wire loop) rotating in a continuous circle. The dark and light halves of the metal ring and its relationship to the two contacts, called brushes, show how this is accomplished.

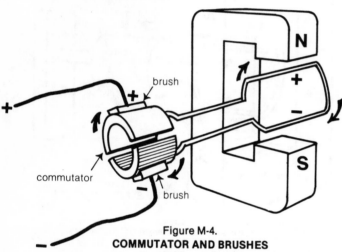

Figure M-4.
COMMUTATOR AND BRUSHES

As the wire loop spins from the repulsion of its magnetic force within the magnetic field of the larger magnet, the power from the battery is switched, through the contacts (brushes) from the light side to the dark side and back again to the light side and so on. In this way, the commutator insures that the (+) positive side of the wire loop is always in the position of repulsion by the north pole of the large magnet. Likewise, the (−) negative side is always in a continuous struggle against the force of the south pole of the large magnet.

As long as we apply a direct current, the loop will continue to spin in continuous motion, because of the commutator and brushes. Brushes can be made out of any good conductor, but generally they are made of carbon, in the form of graphite.

Our theoretical motor has one loop of wire

and a single split commutator. Actual motor construction may vary from a single heavy loop to thousands of wires wound around a soft iron armature, supported by bearings. Commutators in DC motors may have many contact points to effect a smooth transition of power through the brushes.

There are two basic types of motors, AC and DC. Earlier we mentioned that AC is alternating current, and that it moves back and forth in a wave of specific number of cycles. American household electrical current operates at 60 cycles per second.

Electric vehicles in use today generally use DC motors. The controls and other components are simpler in a DC system because battery and energy cells produce direct current. An AC motor must have the DC current converted to AC to be used in an electric vehicle. In DC motors, the basic types are series wound, shunt wound, compound, and permanent magnet.

PERMANENT MAGNET MOTOR

The permanent magnet motor is popular in many lightweight electric vehicle applications, such as bicycle power attachments and trolling motors for small boats. A permanent magnet is like a horseshoe magnet, which needs no electric current to produce magnetic flux. This highly efficient motor can use ceramic or metal magnets and sizes can vary from small motors for toys to larger multi-horsepower motors.

In the diagrams that showed one single loop of wire as a conductor, all used a permanent-type magnet for discussion purposes. We use electro-magnets which create a magnetic field by running electric current through a coil of wire.

THE SERIES MOTOR

The series wound, shunt wound and compound motors all use electro-magnetic field coils to produce a magnetic field. Most automotive starter motors are series wound. The series wound motor is popular in electric trucks, golf carts, winches, cranes and any application that requires high starting torque or "twisting" force. The useable torque and speed of the series motor varies under different load conditions. The heavier the load, the slower the motor speed; the lighter the load, the faster the motor speed. The dangerously high speeds possible under a no-load condition can ruin a series wound motor. Care must be taken to avoid this situation in an electric vehicle.

Figure M-5 is a diagram of a series motor:

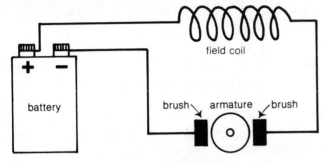

Figure M-5. SERIES MOTOR
In the series wound motor, the field coil is in "series" with the armature. The energy must go "through" the field coil before reaching the armature.

THE SHUNT MOTOR

The shunt motor utilizes a field coil in *parallel* with the armature. This means the current is supplied to both the field coil and the armature at the same time. The current does not have to go through the field coil to get to the armature. The low starting torque of the shunt motor does not lend itself to applications requiring full load start-ups. This motor is very popular for electric vehicle use.

Figure M-6 is a diagram of a shunt motor:

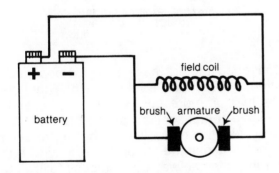

Figure M-6. SHUNT MOTOR
Notice how the field coil (electromagnet) and the armature receive current independent of each other.

THE COMPOUND MOTOR

A compromise between the series and shunt motor is the compound motor. Because it has two sets of field coils, conditions that would cause an absence of field excitation (which could burn out an ordinary shunt motor) do not exist.

The improved speed level, high starting torque, and capability of starting out in series and switching to shunt operation make the compound motor attractive in some applications. Elevators, and other heavy equipment uses are examples of compound motor application.

The compound, series, and shunt motors use direct current.

Figure M-7 is a diagram of the compound motor:

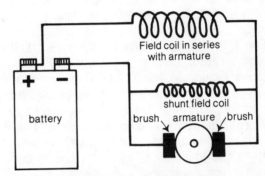

Figure M-7. COMPOUND MOTOR
Notice the two field coils. If a switch were provided to isolate the series field, there would be an even greater flexibility, allowing the unit to start out as a compound and run as a shunt motor.

AC MOTORS

Alternating current or AC motors are manufactured in more shapes, sizes, and for more applications than are DC motors. Household and industrial current produced by utility companies is alternating current; therefore, the majority of electric motors in use today are AC. *Most* AC motors do not need brushes or commutators, which makes them more economical to use and easier to maintain than direct current motors. AC motors have been used in electric cars and trucks by incorporating a device which converts the direct current of the batteries into alternating current.

Motors that will accept both AC and DC current are called "universal" motors.

For purposes of simplicity, we will not discuss all the various types of AC motors, because of their large number and their doubtful application to electric vehicles.

In the simple diagram of the DC motor, the commutator, with its split ring, made the wire loop switch up and back from positive to negative, so the wire loop flip-flopped around continuously when a current was provided.

Alternating current, on the other hand, provides an automatic way of flip-flopping current at a steady beat. Therefore, it is not necessary to do it mechanically with a commutator. The alternating current generators in power stations produce current at a steady alternating beat.

Power stations had many reasons to choose AC instead of DC. The simplicity of the AC generators allowed them to run without commutators and brushes which wear out. By running the AC generators (sometimes called alternators) at a constant regulated speed, a current that alternates at a dependable, steady 60 cycles or 120 flips per second could be maintained.

The first electric utility was the Pearl Street DC generating station in New York, built by Thomas Edison in 1882. As DC power stations proliferated, problems—such as power losses due to the length of the wires needed to reach any great distance—became evident. The lower voltages involved more power losses; the higher voltage possible with alternating current meant much lower power losses.

When AC generators, transformers, and the AC induction motor were perfected, power stations began switching to alternating current. A simple AC motor uses slip rings instead of a commutator to transfer a steady power to the wire loop. Figure M-8

Other AC motors use various forms of converting the alternating current impulses into mechanical force. The other forms are generally based on the use of a phenomenon known as mutual inductance.

An example of mutual inductance is shown in Figure M-9. When Coil B picks up the magnetic field of Coil A, a current is induced in the coil of wire B.

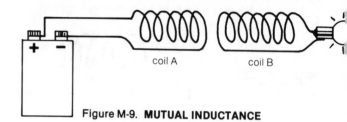

Figure M-9. **MUTUAL INDUCTANCE**

The induction motor was patented in the United States in 1888 by Nikola Tesla. Its basic principle is shown in Figure M-10. The compass needle always follows the bar magnet as it travels around the edge of the compass, because the south pole of the magnet attracts the north pole of the magnetized compass needle. The faster the magnet spins around, the faster the needle will spin.

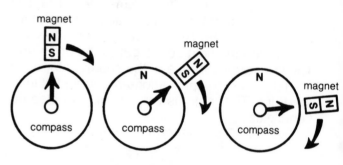

Figure M-10. **BASIC PRINCIPLE OF INDUCTION MOTOR**

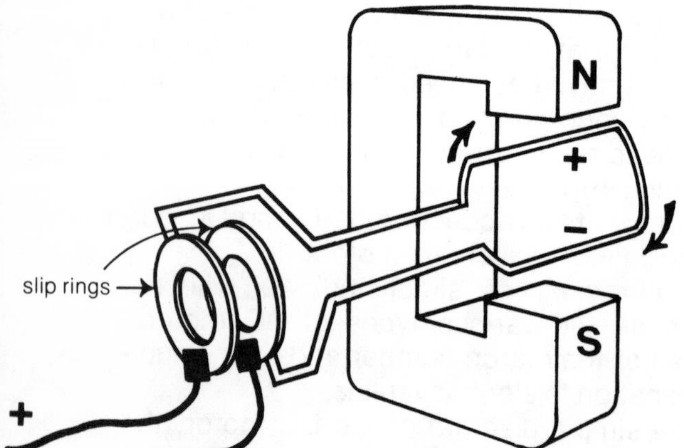

Induction motors have two components. A stationary frame, called the "stator," that contains two or more sets of field coils, and a moveable center section called a "rotor."

The induction motor literally has a "rotating" magnetic field in the stator that reacts with the rotor in the same way our compass follows the magnet. If an induction motor has two poles in its stator and an alternating current of 60 Hertz (cycles per second) is applied, the motor would follow the rotating field at 60 revolutions per second. The speed at which the field rotates is referred to as its "synchronous" speed.

If the number of poles in the stator of an induction motor is increased, the synchronous speed will be slower. A two-pole, 60-hertz motor has a synchronous speed of 3,600 rpm, while a

Figure M-8. **SIMPLE AC MOTOR**
The simple AC motor uses slip rings instead of a commutator, which merely transfers a steady power to the wire loop.

slip rings →

Figure M-11. REVOLUTION OF A MAGNETIC FIELD IN INDUCTION MOTOR

This diagram shows the rotating of a magnetic field in the stator of an induction motor with two sets of poles.

12-pole, 60-hertz motor has a synchronous speed of only 600 rpm.

The main advantage of the simple induction motor is that there is no physical connection between the stator and the rotor, and no electrical contact between the rotor and the power source (such as commutator and brushes on the DC motor). This saves money and time, since there is no need to replace brushes or clean the commutator.

The "mutual inductance" created as the rotating magnetic field of the stator cuts across the rotor's conductive windings, induces a voltage in the rotor's conductors. The interaction between the rotor current and the revolving magnetic field produces motor torque, which turns the rotor in the direction of the magnetic field.

Figure M-11 shows one revolution of a magnetic field in the stator of an induction motor which has two sets of poles.

The rotor of an induction motor never quite keeps up with the stator's revolving field. This is called the "slip," or the difference between the two speeds, and is responsible for the motor's torque. An induction motor whose rotor is in perfect step with the stator's rotating field is called a "synchronous" motor. The accuracy of electric clocks is testimony to the effectiveness of the synchronous motor.

RECENT DEVELOPMENTS IN ELECTRIC VEHICLE MOTORS

Research during the last few years has led inventors and scientists into new realms of motor design. Until recently, little research had been applied toward lighter, more efficient propulsion systems because there was little demand for mass-production of motors for electric vehicle use. Therefore, electric motors generally available for electric vehicles are inefficient at low speeds and disproportionately heavy. Their ostensible design (such as the rewound aircraft generators from World War II used in industrial applications where their weight, size, and "part-load" efficiency were unimportant considerations) did not justify the large capital outlay required to laboratory-develop more efficient designs.

Another consideration relates to inappropriate matching of motors to the transmissions commercially available for electrics. Most of these transmissions are designed for gasoline-engine vehicles and do not utilize the power curve of electric drive systems.

One area the U.S. Department of Energy (DOE) has been analyzing is the improvement of electric vehicle propulsion systems under Public Law 94-413 (see legislation chapter). Under this government program, motor design considerations have been directed to reducing motor weight, cost, and size while improving efficiencies.

Some of the designs the government is reviewing are for pancake, disc, permanent magnet, and higher-speed AC motors. Also reviewed will be a brushless DC motor-power conditioner, a rotary electric wankel-type Japanese design, and an electric motor which *uses no electricity*! These motors are discussed on the following pages.

Variable-Speed Induction Motors

The AC induction motor has been traditionally a fixed-speed device which does not lend itself to electric vehicle use. Vehicle application requires speed variation for efficient power use and driveability.

In recent years much work has been done on variable speed controls for AC induction motors. This has lead to the development of variable speed devices produced by several companies. The advent of high power thyristors, transistors, and control devices with computer logic functions has spurred research.

The induction motor has a high overload capacity which allows it to be used with fixed-gear differentials thereby eliminating, in some cases, the need for a transmission.

General Electric is working on a disc-shaped AC synchronous motor under a DOE contract. It features an iron-free rotor (made of aluminum) into which is set a series of permanent magnets. A thin disc of copper winding supported by epoxy is sandwiched between the aluminum rotor and an iron yoke in an aluminum case.

A Brushless DC Motor

One of the technical papers presented at the EV Expo '80 was a design for a DC motor which uses a solid-state power conditioner to generate the logic necessary to operate without brushes.

The working model was a 15-hp 120-volt, 7600-rpm permanent magnet motor featuring a one-minute peak rating of 35 hp. The prototype used rare earth samarium-cobalt permanent magnets (which would be replaced by less exotic magnets for rproduction models).

The advantages of this brushless version over conventional DC motors relate to efficiency and maintenance. The elimination of brushes, which are the only maintenance-sensitive part of an ordinary DC motor, enables the owner to operate a vehicle with a virtually trouble-free mechanical drive system. And motor weight is reduced—because the brushless motor can run at higher speeds. Because the brushless motor can run at higher speeds, a smaller motor can be utilized, resulting in reduced motor weight.

The "magic" which makes the whole system work is the advent of miniature electronics which enables a power conditioner to electronically compute energy to the rotor and incorporate dynamic and regenerative braking. The energy pulses are directed to a series of terminals which encircle the motor case. The power-conditioner controls motor speed by applying energy in sequence to the terminals. As the signal is increased (and subsequently the power to the rotor), the motor speeds up. The placement of the permanent magnets in the rotor eliminates armature windings and reduces projected manufacturing costs while improving thermal characteristics.

Electromagnetic windings are placed in rows inside the case. As the rows of powerful permanent magnets in the rotor align with the appropriate row of electromagnets, the power conditioner fires the electromagnets causing a magnetic repulsion which spins the rotor.

While the elimination of motor brushes reduces weight and allows higher speeds, the power conditioner adds significant weight to the total propulsion package. The weight of the prototype conditioner was high because of overdesign; however, the production version will undoubtedly be lighter.

The present efficiency of the prototype exceeds 93.4% with an overall motor weight of less than 85 lbs (38 kg). Future plans include more extensive control of motor functions such as torque-speed characteristics to enable the motor to perform some of the duties a transmission would perform in a drive train. The potential of eliminating a transmission is also envisioned with this motor design.

This project was funded by the U.S. Department of Energy under the Electric Vehicle Research Program.

Magnetic Wankel

One experimental DC motor for potential electric vehicle use is a design, by the Japanese firm of Kure Tekko, nicknamed the "Magnetic Wankel."

This motor configuration resembles the internal combustion wankel engine in its use of a single rotor which revolves eccentrically in a cylindrical stator drum. The design differs from conventional motors in that it must be cranked to start.

One model utilizes two separate rotor drums spaced 60 degrees apart. This 45-hp model uses a gear-driven distributor to fire current into the stator electromagnet of each rotor. When electromagnets in the stator are pumped with electricity, they become magnetized and repel each of the three cobalt magnets placed at strategic positions in each rotor. Thus, the rotor is given six power impulses per revolution to kick each of the cobalt segments along. An air-gap between the eccentrically rotating rotor and the stator widens and narrows as the rotor spins.

A small motor is used to crank-start the rotors to 200 rpm; the distributor then energizes the stator coils and allows rotor speeds of up to 5400 rpm.

Magnet-Powered Motor

All the electric vehicle motors reviewed so far have used either AC or DC current. The following is a design which uses *no electricity.*

Anyone who has ever pressed the opposing poles of two magnets together and felt the force of the interaction may have thought it possible to power a motor with that force. Every electric motor, in effect, uses magnetic force, with electricity providing the pulses of electromagnetism required to spin the motor shaft.

A new design (patent #4,151,431; available at your local library) runs a motor on magnet power alone. The inventor, Howard Johnson, has built test prototype motor models and was awarded patent, on appeal, by unanimous vote of eight patent examiners. After demonstration of his working models, the inventor was granted all 28 of his patent claims. The patent office, according to the inventor, has finally acknowledged permanent magnets as a source of energy.

Johnson's prototypes contradict current scientific theories regarding the conservation of energy. The very existence of the working models points up our lack of knowledge of the atomic structure of magnets. Johnson notes that the spinning electrons in rare earth, such as samarium cobalt magnets, weigh only three hundred thousandths of an ounce, yet a one pound magnet can lift 400 lbs (181 kg). To duplicate this feat would require 15 lbs (6 kg) of Alinico (aluminum-nickel-cobalt) magnets.

Johnson has been associated with over 30 patents and has had scientific experience with several large corporations, including atomic energy research at Oak Ridge.

Computers were used extensively to determine magnet stator shape and rotor design. The mathematics generated to calculate the forces in the rotor and stator are monumental. Critical size and shape relationships must be maintained between the fixed stator magnets and the curved magnets with sharp leading and trailing edges used in the rotor. One of the working models is a linear design and another model is a conventional rotary version.

The future of Johnson's magnetic motor will depend upon the development of economical high-power man-made magnets that can compete in strength with samarium cobalt. Johnson claims that there is research and development of such magnets now, with results forthcoming. There will be resistance to change from the scientific community, but we must face the fact that the models *do* work and concentrate on developing production models suitable for commercial applications. If a 15-hp motor could be produced to power a small commuter car, we would be able to revolutionize transportation and the course of history. (An indepth commentary on this motor can be found in the cover article of the spring, 1980, issue of *Science and Mechanics Magazine*, USA.)

Linear Induction Motors

The linear AC motor is one in which the rotor and stator are laid out in a straight line rather than in a circle. When the power is turned "on" the motor produces a linear thrust instead of a rotary motion. If the vehicle or train can be supported by an air cushion or the force of magnetic repulsion, the need for wheels is totally eliminated. The basic purposes of the wheel is to convert rotary motion to linear motion and to support the vehicle above the ground. Eliminating the wheel and its attendant problems of noise, wheel-rail wear, and power loss in bearings, holds great potential value for future high speed mass transit systems. And the most attractive feature of the linear induction motor is that it has no moving parts.

There are two types of linear motors: the linear "induction" and the linear "synchronous." The underside of a linear induction vehicle is lined with electro-magnets facing each other, separated by a rail made of a non- magnetic metal. A magnetic wave is produced by the magnets which push against a "reaction rail" attached to the ground. The undulating magnetic wave motion causes an electric current to be "induced" into the reaction rail. This action pushes the vehicle forward by electromagnetic force.

The linear synchronous motor uses the reaction of a large "on-board magnet" to push against the force induced into the electromagnets buried in the ground under the vehicle. When the magnetic field of the track and the vehicle's magnet are in step with each other, they are "synchronous." A wave of magnetism in the track pushes against the magnetic field of the vehicle magnet, propelling the vehicle along like a wave carrying a leaf in water.

The motor system selected for a particular electric vehicle will obviously depend upon its use. A heavy duty van would use a different motor, control, and battery system than an electric three-wheel recreational vehicle. Expert engineers will design entire systems around the anticipated use of vehicles and incorporate AC or DC motors where suited.

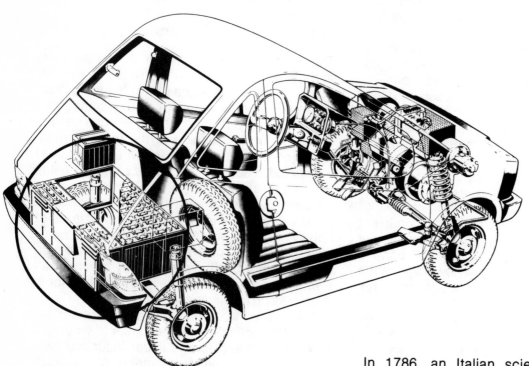

Batteries and Energy Systems

In 1786, an Italian scientist, Luigi Galvani, observed a relationship between electricity and chemistry which became the basis of the electro-chemical battery. During an experiment, he noticed a severed frog's leg twitch when touched to an iron rail and held by a copper hook. Electricity was produced by the interaction of the two metals within the flesh of the frog's leg, causing the muscles to contract.

The first battery was invented by an Italian scientist, Alessandro Volta, in about 1798. Volta's battery, called the "Voltaic pile," consisted of silver and zinc discs separated with cardboard soaked in salt water. A more efficient "primary" cell was conceived by an English chemist, John F. Daniell, in 1836. The first "secondary" battery, a lead-acid storage battery, was invented in 1859 by Gaston Plante, a French physicist.

The ancestor of the modern dry cell, the zinc-carbon cell, was invented by Georges Leclanche, a French scientist, in 1868. The term "Leclanche" is still used to describe this type of cell. For over one hundred years, many scientists have contributed to the steady development of cells and batteries.

In order to understand batteries, we must

first draw our attention to the simple cell, the building block of all batteries. Any "cell" consists of two dissimilar substances called electrodes, placed apart in a liquid called an "electrolyte." The electrolyte is a solution that acts upon the electrodes. It may be an acid, salt, or alkaline solution that will conduct electricity. Chemical action in the cell produces an electric current.

There are two types of cells: "primary" and "secondary." A primary cell is generally unrechargeable, while the secondary cell can be recharged.

PRIMARY CELLS

The flashlight battery is an example of a "primary" cell. The term "battery" in this case is misleading, because a battery is actually a combination of cells.

In the common carbon-zinc flashlight cell, there are three parts:

(1) An electrode of carbon which is placed in the center of (2) a moist paste electrolyte of ammonium chloride (made of water and a salt) contained by (3) a zinc case.

In figure B-1, the carbon rod is the positive electrode (anode) and the zinc case is the negative electrode (cathode).

Ions—electrically-charged atoms—pass from one electrode to another through the electrolyte. This process produces an electric current when the two electrodes are connected together in a circuit through a wire to a "load" such as a light bulb. The circuit is completed within the cell when ions flow in a current through the electrolyte solution.

For practical purposes, we will consider a simple carbon-zinc cell such as the flashlight

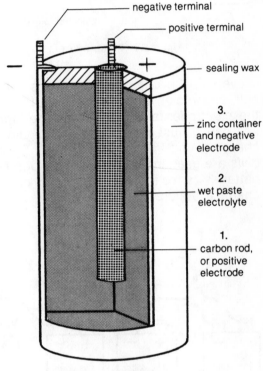

Figure B-1. DRY CELL, CROSS-SECTIONAL VIEW

negative terminal
positive terminal
sealing wax
3. zinc container and negative electrode
2. wet paste electrolyte
1. carbon rod, or positive electrode

battery unrechargeable because when the electrolyte consumes the carbon or zinc electrode, chemical action ceases. The carbon-zinc cell, the oldest type of cell, produces about 1.5 volts of direct current, regardless of its size.

You can make your own primary cells in the experiments shown in Figure B-2.

Primary cells can be connected together to form a battery, which is a combination of cells. Figure B-3.

SECONDARY CELLS

The most unique characteristic of the secondary cell is that electric current can be used to

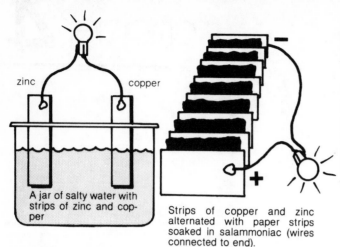

A jar of salty water with strips of zinc and copper

zinc   copper

Strips of copper and zinc alternated with paper strips soaked in salammoniac (wires connected to end).

Figure B-2. **PRIMARY CELLS**

"reverse" the chemical conditions within the cell, and replenish the chemical properties of the electrodes and electrolyte. Therefore, the cell can be used over and over again in discharging and recharging cycles. Secondary cells are used in combinations to form storage batteries, which produce electric current by chemical action.

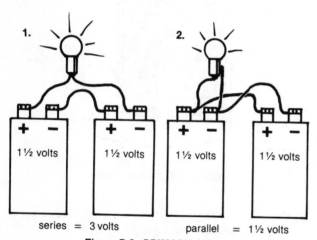

series = 3 volts   parallel = 1½ volts

Figure B-3. **PRIMARY CELLS CONNECTED TO FORM BATTERY**

When cells are connected together they form larger batteries in two ways.

THE LEAD-ACID BATTERY

The most popular storage battery of all time consists of lead-acid cells.

Gaston Plante' developed the rechargeable secondary cell in about 1859. This was the ancestor of the lead-acid battery. Storage batteries became popular in the wake of the Edison electric generating stations, around 1875. Un-

fortunately, the inefficient early lead-acid batteries had to be replaced after a few months of service.

The lead-acid storage battery consists of several identical cells containing two types of lead plates immersed in an electrolyte of sulfuric acid and water. Each cell has two electrodes with positive and negative plates. The positive plates are made of lead dioxide, the negative plates are sponge lead. (See battery cut-a-way view.)

Figure B-4. **CUT-A-WAY VIEW OF A GLOBE-UNION EV-1000 BATTERY SHOWING GRID AND PLATES**

All positive and negative plates are insulated by separators made of an electrically nonconductive material such as porous plastic. Each fully charged cell produces approximately 2 volts. Thus, a 6-volt battery has 3 cells, while a 12-volt battery has 6 cells. The cells are housed in a hard rubber or plastic container called a "battery case." The specific gravity of the electrolyte in a lead-acid battery is used to determine the state of charge of the cells. A fully charged cell has a specific gravity of about 1.30 and a voltage reading of approximately 2 volts.

Specific gravity is used to measure the strength or percentage of sulfuric acid present in the electrolyte. If the specific gravity of a cell in a charged battery is 1.275, the electrolyte is 1.275 times as dense as water. Specific gravity is measured by a device called a hydrometer which consists of a float in a glass tube.

HOW A LEAD-ACID BATTERY WORKS:

Figure B-5, (Illustration #1), shows one cell of a fully charged lead-acid battery. The specific gravity of the electrolyte is 1.275.

The negative plate is sponge lead. The positive plate is lead peroxide. The electrolyte is maximum sulfuric acid with a minimum percentage of water. As we start to discharge the cell (Illustration #2) by attaching a light bulb, the following chemical processes begin:

The ions (electrically-charged atoms) of one electrode pass to the other electrode through the electrolyte and change the composition of the metal electrodes and the electrolyte.

When the cell is fully discharged (Illustration #3), the electrolyte contains a minimum of sulfuric acid and a maximum of water. The specific gravity of the electrolyte is now about 1.110 (or 1.11 times the density of water.)

In the totally discharged cell, the plates cannot produce current because they are both covered with lead sulfate and the electrolyte is weak. The electrolyte is predominantly water instead of sulfuric acid. When we connect the cell to a battery charger, (Illustration #4), the action reverses itself.

This action continues until the cell is fully charged.

Before further discussing the new energy systems, we must define our terminology and methods of rating. To do this, we must turn to the lead-acid battery for examples of each term.

BATTERY CAPACITY

The term "ampere hours" refers to the number of amperes a battery is capable of producing in a circuit for a given number of hours. A lead-acid battery that is rated at 80-ampere-hours capacity is one that can, theoretically:

Maintain 20 amperes for 4 hours
or
10 amperes for 8 hours

When temperatures drop, the lead-acid battery loses capacity. At 0°F, (−18°C), a battery has lost 60% of its power. So a lead-acid battery called upon to start an automobile in cold weather will have less capacity than in warm weather. Also, the car's engine oil, becomes thicker in the cold, further increasing the starting power needs.

Another type of battery rating is "cold-cranking amps." This rating shows the ability of the battery to produce high energy for a brief period, at maximum output. For example, a 95 amp hour battery, such as used in a large automobile, may have 515 cold-cranking amps at 0°F. (−18°C) for 30 seconds.

A relatively new method of rating lead-acid

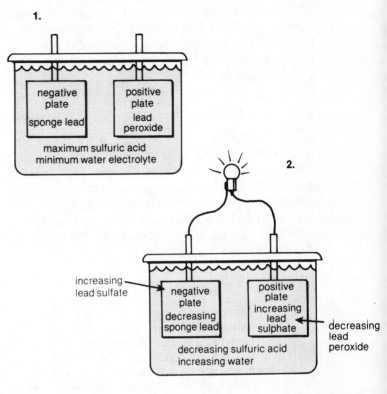

1.

negative plate
sponge lead

positive plate
lead peroxide

maximum sulfuric acid
minimum water electrolyte

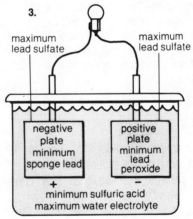

2.

increasing lead sulfate

negative plate
decreasing sponge lead

positive plate
increasing lead sulphate

decreasing lead peroxide

decreasing sulfuric acid
increasing water

3.

maximum lead sulfate

maximum lead sulfate

negative plate
minimum sponge lead

positive plate
minimum lead peroxide

+

−

minimum sulfuric acid
maximum water electrolyte

In the totally discharged cell, the plates can no longer yield useable chemical activity to produce current. Water is predominent in the electrolyte instead of sulphuric acid.

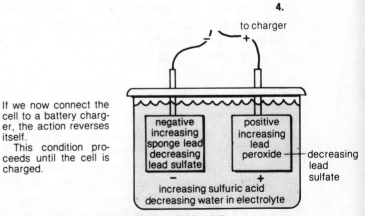

4.

to charger

If we now connect the cell to a battery charger, the action reverses itself.

This condition proceeds until the cell is charged.

negative increasing sponge lead decreasing lead sulfate

positive increasing lead peroxide

decreasing lead sulfate

−

+

increasing sulfuric acid
decreasing water in electrolyte

Figure B-5. HOW A LEAD-ACID BATTERY WORKS

automobile "starting" batteries is the number of minutes a fully charged battery can produce current at a 25 amp discharge rate at 80°F. (27°C). This usually ranges from 50 to 150 minutes, depending on the size or number of plates in the battery.

ENERGY DENSITY

The power a battery can produce for a certain length of time relative to its own weight is called "energy density," or "specific energy." This is expressed in watt-hours per pound (per kg) of battery weight, abbreviated as wh/lb (wh/kg). A lead-acid battery is generally rated at 8 to 19 wh/lb (17.6 to 41.8 wh/kg) at the 3-hour discharge rate.

IMPORTANT NOTE:

Throughout this book, we will compare alternate battery systems to the lead-acid battery as a point of reference. If a new system can produce a 40 wh/lb (88 wh/kg) energy density, for example, we compare it to the 20 wh/lb (44 wh/kg) maximum rating of the lead-acid battery to note an energy storage "twice" as great as the lead-acid type. This means a vehicle can carry half the new batteries to equal an identical range of the lead-acid battery.

POWER DENSITY

Another commonly used term is "power density," expressed in watts per pound of battery weight. This is the power available at any one time (peak power density), or average over a discharge period (average power density). The peak power output is important for acceleration and top speed. A lead-acid battery under prime conditions for a brief period may approach an output of 23-45 w/lb (50-100 w/kg), depending on battery design and test duration.

OPERATING CYCLES

One operating or "deep" cycle refers to a complete discharge of a particular battery system. To determine its maximum range per charge, a fully charged battery is discharged, under load, until drained. However, normal electric vehicle use rarely drains the battery completely due to the danger of cell damage. In tests to determine cycle life, a battery is drained from 70% to 80% depth of discharge, an approximation of extensive everyday vehicle use. An advanced lead-acid electric vehicle traction battery is rated at about 400 deep cycles, but lab tests on smaller modules have demonstrated over 1000 cycles at 70% depth of discharge.

COST

Another important consideration for any battery system to prove worthy of electric vehicle application is the cost factor. We will use the terms "dollars per kilowatt hour" as a guide to the cost of an energy system. This is expressed as $/kwh.

Today's lead-acid batteries have a cost factor of $50-150/kwh, depending upon the battery's intended use.

THE LEAD ACID BATTERY

In electric vehicles, combinations of batteries are used to achieve desired voltages. They are connected together in series or parallel, depending upon the voltage needed.

The design of the lead-acid battery is determined by several factors including the number of plates per cell and the amount of active material per cell. Some batteries have thin plates which provide high specific power because of their lower electrical resistance. Other battery designs use thicker plates which give them a high cycle life and energy because they have a large amount of active material. The active material in each cell determines the specific energy and the total energy.

There are four types of lead-acid batteries in use. The SLI battery (starting, lighting, and ignition), the golf cart battery, the semi-industrial battery, and the industrial battery.

The SLI battery can deliver high power output for a short period of time and at varying temperatures. This type of battery is used to start internal combustion vehicles such as the automobile. The energy available from an SLI battery is less than that of a golf cart battery because the SLI has thin plates which are lightly loaded with active material. The use of thin plates allows high specific power, but also results in short deep-cycle discharge life. Generally speaking, an SLI battery in an automobile is limited to less than 100 deep-discharge cycles but, because the type of discharge normally associated with automobiles is very light

Photo courtesy of S.G.L.
Batteries Mfg., Detroit, Mich.

A "DEEP CYCLE" GOLF CART BATTERY DESIGNED FOR ELECTRIC VEHICLE DUTY.

(less than 10%), the life of an SLI battery may exceed 5000 shallow cycles.

The golf cart battery must be capable of supplying a relatively high power output for long periods of time, while maintaining low battery weight. Battery manufacturers have improved golf cart battery performance to make them more compatible with electric vehicle needs. The golf cart battery has thicker plates than the SLI battery and is designed for a deep-discharge cycle life in the 200 to 400 cycle range. The golf cart battery is used in some small vehicles, such as cars and vans, because of its convenient size and accessibility. Golf cart batteries weigh in about 60 to 70 pounds (27 to 32 kg).

Semi-industrial battery requirements lie between the golf cart and the industrial battery. The semi-industrial battery has a higher specific energy than the industrial battery, yet can deliver energy for a longer period of time than a golf cart battery. The thicker plates yield a high cycle life, yet they are thin enough to maintain high specific energies. The deep-discharge cycle life of the semi-industrial battery can range from 500 to 1,000 cycles.

Industrial batteries are used mainly as a power source for lift trucks, where cycle life and total available energy are important. Industrial batteries may use tubular positive plates instead of the standard pasted plates. Tubular industrial batteries have exhibited long deep-discharge cycle lives of 1,000 to 2,000 cycles. They have a high resistance to abuse, but cannot attain the power density of the golf cart or semi-industrial battery.

The cost of lead-acid batteries depends upon the type. The SLI battery has an initial cost of $50-60/kwh, the golf cart battery an initial cost of $60-75/kwh, the semi-industrial battery an initial cost of $120-150/kwh, and the industrial battery is even more expensive. The SLI battery costs more per deep cycle, compared to the industrial battery.

Meanwhile, lead-acid technology moves onward and upward. For example, the Globe Union Corporation has designed a new lightweight grid which, through a proprietary method, can combine polypropylene plastic with lead. The new plastic/lead grid is superlight and can reduce grid weight by 60% and total battery weight by over 10%. The replacement of heavy lead in non-conductive support structures with lightweight thermoplastics is a significant improvement which can help lead-acid powered vehicles of today.

Engineers at the Japan Storage Battery Company have taken an old idea, an automatic water filling device for use in industrial bat-

Photo courtesy of Lead Industries Association

A truckload of scrapped lead from batteries is hoisted aloft by a hydraulic mechanism that dumps the lead into an outdoor storage area to await processing into recycled lead.

Lead scrap is unique in that most of it comes from batteries, which require more lead than any other end-use application of the metal. For example, in 1973, the battery industry consumed nearly 770,000 tons of lead. Of that total, 645,000 tons were recovered from various forms of scrap, and about 63 per cent of that total came from scrapped batteries.

teries, and modified it for use in their electric vehicle batteries. The new "Quick filler" tops off the water in a battery within 5 minutes, services an entire 36 unit battery set or "monoblock," works when the batteries are level or tilted, and stops automatically. An exhaust system for the explosive hydrogen and oxygen gases, generated during recharging, is also incorporated into the "Quick filler." A one-piece moulded plastic top connects the 36 battery units; the result is a safer low-maintenance battery set with an energy density of 17 wh/lb (38 wh/kg) combined with a 500 discharge/charge cycle life.

Great Britain has also produced improved lead-acid batteries. Chloride technical engineers have substantially improved the performance of their 80-cell experimental battery module by using thin, tubular plates for the positive electrode and light, plastic-coated steel battery trays. Tubular battery plates are not a new idea, but only recently has the technology existed to produce thin tubular plates which have a longer service life than flat plates of the same mass. The improvements to its battery system have increased the range of the test vehicle, the Dodge Silent Karrier Mark I, from 30-34 miles (50-55 km) to 50-55 miles (80-90 km) and improved the energy density of the Silent Karrier's battery pack from 10 wh/lb (23 wh/kg) to 15 wh/lb (34 wh/kg). Chloride technical engineers have also developed an automatic watering system for their battery pack to decrease the necessary maintenance. Anticipated cycle life is 1300 to 1700 cycles.

Considerations for electric vehicle use determine the type of battery to be used. The industrial battery may be too heavy for a vehicle, and not be capable of maintaining the specific power necessary to push the vehicle up to high speed. Yet its cycle life is very attractive. Also, remember that the type of driving to which an electric vehicle is subjected determines both the range per charge as well as the total cycle life of the battery. High speeds and rapid acceleration will dramatically reduce the effective range per charge of a vehicle. The distance the vehicle will travel decreases as the number of accelerations per charge increases.

The total amount of energy that can be removed from a lead-acid battery depends upon the rate at which the energy is withdrawn. Today's lead-acid battery can only deliver 40% of its rated capacity if discharged in a 20 minute period, compared to 100% delivery in a one-

hour discharge period. Therefore, an electric vehicle travelling at high speeds would deplete its batteries much faster than it would if it were driving at moderate speeds.

Low temperature of the electrolyte in a lead-acid battery and the age of the battery can reduce the amount of available energy. When the battery is subjected to low temperatures, the electrolyte becomes more resistant to current flow. The age of a battery affects its performance. A new battery actually will begin to increase its capacity about the first 10 to 20% of its life. Then the energy density peaks and begins to decline. Another factor that determines the longevity of a battery is the type of service to which it is subjected. In cases of deep discharges, the life of the battery is reduced significantly. Therefore, an electric vehicle driven to the point of running out of power will have a lesser number of cycles left in the battery than a comparable vehicle which is driven to only 20 to 40% of its discharge depth.

Battery care is the most important consideration for an electric vehicle. It is in this area that most weaknesses of an electric vehicle will be found. The state of charge and the maintenance of ample water levels in batteries is most important. Attending to corrosion on terminal posts and checking to make sure connections are secure should be considered a routine procedure. Use of proper charging procedures is most critical.

While interim and advanced technology battery systems have other problem areas, sulfation remains the plague of most lead-acid batteries. Sulfation is the formation of sulfate deposits in the plates which can reduce the energy output of a lead-acid battery. One solution to help avoid the effects of sulfation is to keep a battery at the highest charge level possible at all times, without significant overcharging. The wise user of an electric vehicle charges the batteries fully before starting a trip. It is unwise to let a vehicle stand for long periods of time without attaching a battery charger to maintain a full charge when the vehicle is not in use.

Because maintenance will determine a battery's useful life, care must be taken to avoid overcharging, which is wasteful of energy and economically undesirable due to shortening the battery life. Generally speaking, both overcharging *and* undercharging reduce the life of a battery. Undercharging reduces the total energy available so that damage may result due to deep cycling. Also, the simple procedure of a regularly-scheduled topping off of the electrolyte with water as a routine procedure can extend battery life significantly.

ELECTRIC VEHICLE BATTERIES

In the near future, batteries used in electric vehicles will probably be of the lead-acid variety. Even though patents for the lead-sulfuric acid secondary cell ran out around the turn of the century, a million batteries of this type are sold annually for electric golf carts alone. Electric forklifts, automobiles, delivery vans, and other commercial applications significantly increase the number of lead-acid batteries in use.

In order to survive, electric vehicle batteries of the future will have to be lighter, more powerful, durable, economical, and have longer lives. Therefore, the battery of the future will have to be a "superbattery."

A survey conducted by ESB Rayovac Corporation during the Fifth International Electric Vehicle Symposium and Exhibition in 1978 demonstrated that the requirements of 80 percent of today's commuters could be met by state-of-the-art lead-acid batteries. The survey's computer model compared the driver's mileage and varying speed requirements to the energy needs of an electric car with regenerative braking. The computer found that an average commuter trip is 23.5 miles (38 km). Advanced lead-acid automobile batteries capable of producing a range of 100 miles (161 km) are expected by 1984. This would mean that virtually all commuters could drive to work and back with electric vehicles powered by lead-acid batteries.

In the quest for developing the elusive "superbattery," research engineers are trying to reconcile two conflicting goals: a high energy density (wh/lb) and a long cycle life. A higher energy density increases the range of an electric vehicle, and more cycles over the lifetime of the battery reduces the overall cost of the system. Energy density can be increased in a lead-acid battery by using thin electrode plates with a large surface area. These batteries have a greater initial power output, but have short lives resulting from plate corrosion or other undesirable side reactions. These conditions also prevail in nickel-zinc, nickel-iron, and other near-term batteries. Cycle life can be increased by making thicker plates, and heavier battery components and cases. However, the excess weight lowers a battery's energy density.

U.S. Government-funded near-term battery research is aimed toward optimizing both goals: a battery with a specific energy of 25wh/lb (56 wh/kg) and a cycle life of 500 or more deep discharge cycles. This improved model would give today's state-of-the-art electric vehicles a range of 100 miles (161 km). These goals do not seem unreachable. Private industry and governments around the world are spending millions of dollars to insure the development of dependable battery systems that can meet these parameters. Later we will discuss future superbattery prospects with more energetic chemical couples such as chlorine, aluminum, or lithium which can outstrip the energy storage potential of any near-term battery and, as a bonus, produce a longer cycle life.

The list of potential substitutes for the lead-acid battery is impressive. It would take a volume easily as large as this book to delve into the technical characteristics of each of these potential energy systems.

For those who wish to research this subject more intensely, here are the alternatives: batteries using nickel-iron, nickel-cadmium, sodium-sulfur, zinc-chlorine hydrate, lithium-iron sulfide, zinc-air, nickel-zinc, lithium-titanium sulfide, lithium-sulfur, aluminum-air, Iron "Redox", lithium-air and lithium-water, to name a few.

Out of this list, we will discuss eleven systems because they are advanced to the point where construction and operation of a working battery for a vehicle is possible. These candidates are: nickel-zinc, nickel-iron, zinc-air, iron-air, zinc-chlorine hydrate, sodium-sulfur, lithium-iron sulfide, aluminum-air, lithium-air, zinc-bromine, and the Iron "Redox" energy system.

NICKEL-ZINC

The nickel-zinc battery was patented by a Russian inventor in 1901, and introduced in the United States during the 1930's when J. J. Drum developed a rechargeable nickel-zinc railroad battery.

Nickel-zinc batteries have two to three times the storage capacity of conventional lead-acid batteries with a higher specific power output. Therefore, nickel-zinc batteries are capable of delivering more energy and power per charge than lead-acid batteries, conceivably doubling the range of an electric vehicle.

In tests conducted in the U.S. by N.A.S.A. on

The General Motors breakthrough on electric vehicle battery technology is illustrated here in a size comparison between the conventional lead acid batteries in the foreground and the zinc-nickel oxide batteries in the rear. The battery packs have equal energy but the zinc-nickel is only half as large and at 900 lbs., weighs less than half as much as the 2,000 lb. lead acid pack. Discussing the breakthrough are two Delco Remy Division battery engineers, Ralph L. Corbin, (left), senior staff engineer and William B. Wylam, chief engineer, battery systems.

a ¼-ton van powered by nickel-zinc batteries, there was an improvement of 87% in range over golf-cart, lead-acid batteries. At 20 mph (32 km/hr), the nickel-zinc version travelled 54.9 miles (88.3 km), and the golf cart battery version travelled 29.4 miles (47.3 km). Compared to a semi-industrial lead-acid battery in one test, the nickel-zinc showed 75% improvement in a stop-and-go driving cycle.

The nickel-zinc battery however has several problems in spite of its glowing potential. Remember, zinc is used very effectively in primary cells; the problems have always been related to recharging: 1) Zinc dendrites, which are needle-like crystals, grow on the zinc electrode during recharging. The dendrites eventually short-out the battery by penetrating the separator and forming a bridge between the negative and positive electrodes or plates. 2) Another problem is zinc electrode shape

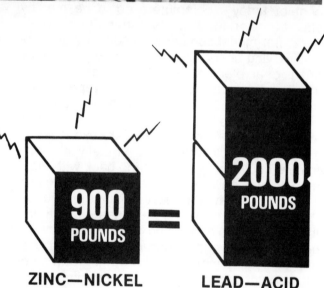

ZINC—NICKEL   **LEAD—ACID**

This illustration shows the size and weight differences between the conventional lead acid battery pack and the new General Motors zinc-nickel oxide battery pack that could power electric vehicles in the future. Both are of equal energy, but the zinc-nickel weighs less than half as much as the old lead acid, and takes up only half as much space.

change; the zinc electrode gradually becomes thicker in the center with repeated recharging cycles. This causes a reduction in surface area and available active material which, in turn, results in lower battery efficiency. Both prob-

Photo courtesy of
Yardney Electric Corporation

YARDNEY NICKEL-ZINC BATTERIES

The Yardney Electric Company of Pawcatuck, Connecticut, U.S.A., has been associated with nickel-zinc batteries since the mid-1960's. Yardney has demonstrated that nickel-zinc can double the range of on-road electric test vehicles over lead-acid batteries. One demonstration used a Sebring-Vanguard Citicar equipped with nickel-zinc batteries. Another used the Fiat X1/23 Electric City Car. The 300 AH 6.4-V battery module shown can provide 2-1/2 times the stored energy of a lead-acid traction battery with the same size and volume.

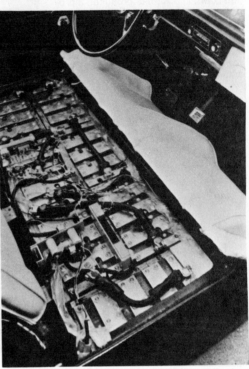

Photo courtesy of Yardney Electric Corporation

MODEL OF A 300AH, 6.4 VOLT NICKEL ZINC BATTERY MODULE

This module would provide 2-1/2 times the stored energy of a lead-acid traction battery of the same weight and volume.

lems have reduced the life of conventional prototype nickel-zinc batteries to between 60 and 100 cycles, which is one-fourth the cycle life of most lead-acid batteries.

An additional problem is the generation of excess heat during discharge for nickel-zinc batteries. Because nickel is an expensive element, the conventional nickel-zinc battery has been both more costly and less efficient than the lead-acid battery.

The ESB Corporation, U.S.A., has been researching the Vibrocel™, a patented vibrating anode recharging system, developed by Tudor, their Swedish subsidiary, which solves several nickel-zinc battery problems. By vibrating the zinc negative electrode at a very low frequency (15 Hz), the Vibrocel reduces zinc dendrite formations and insures an even coating of zinc oxide on the electrode, minimizing the shape-change problem. The stationary nickel (positive) electrode is further protected by a thin plastic netting. A coulometer which measures ampere-hour capacity is incorporated into the recharger. The Vibrocel in early Swedish tests exhibited a life of over 1000 cycles in a 145-amp-hr module. The Vibrocel, however, has limitations of its own. The electrodes must be relatively widely spaced with this system to accommodate vibration; this increases the size and weight of the battery. In addition, the vibration works almost too well, increasing the activity of the zinc electrode and making the underlying metal grid more susceptible to corrosion. With U.S. demonstrations of over 60 deep-discharge cycles (with no dendrite growth), a 23-wh/lb (50-wh/kg) specific energy, and an energy efficiency of 60%, the Vibrocel is a very promising battery system.

EAGLE PICHER NICKEL-ZINC POWERED VEHICLE

The Eagle Picher Company of Joplin, Missouri, U.S.A., has produced a prototype electric recreational vehicle using nickel-zinc battery technology.

The 965-lb (439-kg) two-seater carries 375 lbs (170 kg) of batteries and has a cruise speed of 25 mph (40 km/hr) and a range of 65 miles per charge using a 2-hp motor.

Photo courtesy of Eagle Picher

Energy Research Corp. (ERC), a subsidiary of St. Joe Minerals, has developed the NiVolt™, a 96-volt nickel-zinc battery which is made up of six 10-cell modules connected in series. ERC has developed an effective plastic-bonded nickel electrode containing one third less nickel. This will substantially lower battery cost and make marketing commercially more attractive. In small test modules the ERC nickel-zinc system demonstrated a life of over 1,000 shallow-discharge cycles. In preliminary tests on full-sized units, battery life has been limited to only 76 deep-discharge cycles; however, further improvements are expected. The NiVolt battery uses a semi-permeable separator film to inhibit battery short outs during recharging. This battery is ERC-rated at a capacity of 100 deep-discharge cycles, and a specific energy of 25 to 30 wh/lb (55 to 66 wh/kg) with a theoretical efficiency of 170 wh/lb (375 wh/kg). The ERC NiVolt battery is being used and tested in the Bradley GTE electric fiberglass sport coupe.

The Gould Company, U.S.A., has produced a higher performance 6.5-volt nickel-zinc battery; it has a demonstrated life of 120 cycles in a U.S. government test. In a recent Gould test 220 cycles have been achieved. Gould uses a barrier film in combination with additives to the electrolyte to prevent dendrite growth. The resultant prototype 6.5-volt automobile battery has a higher energy-to-weight ratio. The Gould nickel-zinc battery has an energy density of 30 wh/lb (66 wh/kg) and a peak power output of 70 w/lb (154 w/kg) with a recharge efficiency of 70%. Tests simulating urban driving conditions project a range of 140 miles (225 km) for electric vehicles with regenerative braking.

Other nickel-zinc battery makers are Yardney electronics and Eagle-Picher electronics. "I do believe the zinc-nickel oxide battery has the greatest potential for the near-term for electric vehicles," said Dr. Vincent Puglisi, director of research for Yardney Electric Corp.

At General Motors, design concentration has been in the area of nickel-zinc oxide batteries for the G.M. electric cars to be released in 1985. In June of 1979, Delco-Remy, a G.M. subsidiary, equipped a plant in Muncie, Indiana, to make sealed, maintenance-free, extended-life zinc-nickel oxide batteries. Full size zinc-nickel oxide batteries having a 300-cycle life have been reported by G.M. Now rated at 27 wh/lb (60 wh/kg), the G.M. goal is a battery with an energy of 32 wh/lb (70 wh/kg).

THE NICKEL-IRON BATTERY

Thomas Edison had developed a battery for the electric vehicles of his day known as the "Edison Cell," which was a nickel-iron storage battery. This battery was used extensively in early electric cars. Patents for the "Edison Cell" ran out before the First World War, but some vehicles continued to use them thereafter with remarkable longevity. Because the Edison cell produces only 1.2 volts, a ten-cell battery is needed to equal 12 volts. This system may well yet be a contender for the next generation of electric vehicle batteries.

The nickel-iron battery has a life of over 1,000 cycles and reported power density of 45 w/lb (99 w/kg) and specific energy of 20 w-hr/lb (44 w-hr/kg) at a 2-hour rate. Costs of $70-140 per/kwh are projected for this battery. Actual price estimates for nickel-zinc and nickel-iron systems are difficult to estimate because of variable mass production costs. A point in favor or these systems is the possibility of reclaiming the nickel.

One Japanese developer reported a nickel-iron performance of 38 w-hr/lb (84 w-hr/kg) at the 5 to 7-hour rate of discharge and a life of 500 cycles.

Recent studies by Eagle-Picher Industries on 5-cell, 6-volt batteries with improved, thicker, sintered iron-plaque electrodes have shown an energy efficiency, comparable to lead-acid batteries, of 70 to 80%. Eagle-Picher nickel-iron batteries have a specific energy level of 22 wh/lb (50 wh/kg) with goals of 27 wh/lb (60 wh/kg). Tests on electrodes have demonstrated a specific power rating of 50 w/lb (110 w/kg) and 1300 deep discharge cycles for nickel-iron batteries.

Historically, because of their 10 to 15 year life and low maintenance, nickel-iron batteries have been used for lighting rail cars and operating deep-mining vehicles. Future applications, in addition to electric vehicle use, include stand-by submarine power and back-up units for solar energy cells.

Westinghouse is also testing nickel-iron prototype batteries. Their goal is to improve the battery and, at the same time, lower the cost. Therefore, the focus has been on the nickel electrode which is not only the most expensive component of this system, but the life-limiting one as well.

To increase surface area and reactivity, the Westinghouse battery incorporates sintered steel wool in both electrodes. The positive electrode is nickel-plated. The resulting battery has a demonstrated specific energy of 21 wh/lb (48 wh/kg), a specific power of 45 w/lb (100 w/kg) and a 300-500 + cycle life. This translates into a

predicted range of 96 miles (154 km) in electric vehicles with regenerative braking which is 36 miles (58 km) more than the range achieved by conventional lead-acid batteries and about 20 miles (32 km) more than "improved" lead-acid batteries.

The nickel-iron battery system is not efficient during recharging, compared with a lead-acid battery. When charging, the nickel-iron battery stores only 50 to 60% of the current compared with 75% efficiency for the lead-acid battery.

When charging, the nickel-iron battery gives off more hydrogen than a similar lead-acid battery. This causes loss of water from the electrolyte.Therefore, charging not only requires cooling for the system, but care must be taken that hydrogen is properly vented to avoid combustion.

METAL-AIR BATTERIES

Four metal-air batteries under consideration for long-term development are the iron-air, zinc-air, lithium-air and aluminum-air varieties. Tests indicate a 300 to 400% improvement in specific energy ratings over lead-acid systems with a cycle life of nearly 300 cycles and energy densities ranging from 38 to 55 wh/lb (84 to 121 wh/kg).

The metal-air systems have a relatively high specific energy level and are lightweight because air reacts directly with the metals, but they are limited in peak power output and energy efficiency. Therefore, they are being considered in electro-chemical hybrid-battery systems for vehicles. Hybrid batteries incorporate the high specific energy of one battery system with a second battery system designed to produce high peak power. In operation, the high specific energy battery—that is, the zinc-air or iron-air—provides the energy necessary for cruising. When the need for acceleration or passing is required, the load is transfered to a high current battery, which is connected into the system. A relatively small high current battery, such as a lead-acid type, can meet the peak demand that is needed and can be recharged from the energy of the battery pack when acceleration is not required.

Both zinc-air and iron-air batteries were combined with high power lead-acid batteries in hybrid configurations in tests made in Japan. The Daihatsu Lightweight Passenger Automobile powered by an iron-air/lead-acid hybrid system travelled 162 miles (260 km) at 25 mph

(40 km/hr). Two other vehicles, one automobile and one truck, with hybrid zinc-air/lead-acid batteries had ranges of 283 miles and 308 miles (455 and 496 km) respectively, at the same speed.

ALUMINUM-AIR BATTERIES

Another metal-air system of interest for the distant future is the aluminum-air battery.

The Lawrence Livermore Laboratory of the University of California and Lockheed Missiles and Space Company's Research Laboratory, Palo Alto, California, under U.S. Department of Energy contracts, have explored lithium-air, calcium-air, magnesium-air and aluminum-air batteries.

Of these, the aluminum-air battery seems to enjoy the most optimistic position due to recent developments which have produced proprietary aluminum alloys of high efficiency. The new alloys give the aluminum-air battery superior performance over earlier aluminum-air batteries where efficiencies were low due to the aluminum becoming inactive or corroding in liquid electrolytes.

Aluminum-air batteries have extremely high energy density and, although lithium-air batteries have enjoyed a successful development and lithium itself exceeds aluminum in energy-to-weight ratio, aluminum is easier to handle and store, more abundant, and is produced by an established, mature industry with a large domestic production capacity.

The aluminum-air battery operates as a fuel cell by adding aluminum anode plates and water. During discharge, the aluminum and water react with air to produce electricity and a reaction product, a dry powder called hydrargillite. The trihydrated alumina hydrargillite is periodically removed about every 250 miles (400 km) and demineralized water is added. After about 1000 miles (1600 km), the aluminum plates are totally consumed and new aluminum anodes are installed in the vehicle.

The advantage of this system lies in the potential of the vehicle to attain both internal combustion engine vehicle performance (due to the remarkably high potential energy density of the aluminum-air battery) and utilize rapid refueling by mechanically charging the cells. The recharge time required would be no more than a few minutes to add water and remove the hydrargillite powder. The hydrargillite powder is then returned to the aluminum production plant to be reprocessed back into aluminum anode plates. An alternate system would allow the vehicle to travel 1,000 miles (1600 km) between aluminum anode changes and merely store the hydrargillite when taking on water every 250 miles (400 km).

Although the aluminum-air cell has a high energy-density of 136-181 wh/lb (300-400 wh/kg), it does not have the comparable power-density at this time to provide adequate vehicle performance. (*Projected* power density is 79 w/lb (175 w/kg)). It is believed, however, that, by incorporating an aluminum-air battery with a flywheel storage system to provide peak power requirements, a vehicle could compete with internal combustion automobile acceleration.

There are several problems which must be studied and overcome before the aluminum-air battery will power our 21st century automobiles. Some of these problems are associated with lowering the cost of the air cathode and preventing its fouling by road dirt and carbon dioxide. Other considerations will involve matching a complete propulsion system to the relatively low power-density of the cell and designing a battery compartment to accommodate a physically large battery pack.

When and if these problems are solved, the aluminum-air battery will take its place among the most potent of the new "super-batteries."

ZINC-CHLORINE HYDRATE BATTERY

The high specific energy potential of the electro-chemical coupling of chlorine and zinc has been recognized since its discovery by Sir Humphrey Davy in 1811. While the energy couple was attractive, there was a need for a safe and practical method of storing chlorine, which is a toxic gas. The solution was the evolution of the zinc-chlorine hydrate battery system by Energy Development Associates (EDA), a subsidiary of Gulf & Western. In this system, chlorine is stored as a solid hydrate (chlorine-water compound) and chilled to 48°F (9°C) by an on-board refrigeration unit. Chlorine in the form of chlorine-hydrate is safe for storage and can be easily recycled into chlorine gas when returned from the storage area to the battery stack, the energy-producing section of the system.

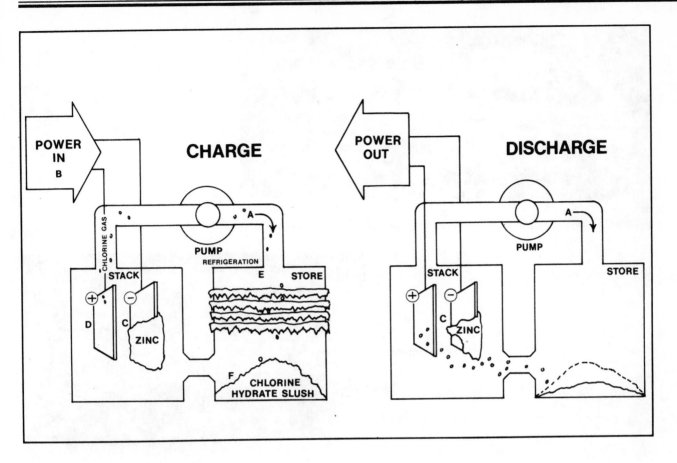

HOW THE ZINC-CHLORINE HYDRATE SYSTEM WORKS

1. During the charging mode, a pump moves the electrolyte (a solution of zinc chloride in water) through the battery system. (See A.)

2. As DC current is passed through the battery from an external source (B), zinc metal is electro-deposited on the negative electrode plates. (See C.)

3. During this charging sequence, chlorine gas is generated on the positive plate in the stack area, and carried away by the circulating electrolyte. (See D.)

4. The mixture of chlorine gas and electrolyte is now pumped into the storage area (See E.) of the system, where it is chilled to 48°F (9°C) and the pale yellow, solid zinc-chlorine hydrate is formed. (See F.)

5. The battery is fully charged when the hydrate store is full and excess electrolyte is returned to the stack.

6. During discharge, the circulating electrolyte carries the chlorine to the positive graphite plates in the stack, permitting current, which powers the car, to be withdrawn from the battery. The electro-reaction of the zinc metal at the negative electrode forms zinc ions and the electro-reaction of chlorine at the positive electrode forms chloride ions.

7. During discharge, zinc chloride is formed and dissolves in the circulating electrolyte. The electrolyte passes once more from the stack and transfers heat to the store, causing more chlorine to be dissolved in the electrolyte as the chlorine-hydrate decomposes. Electrolyte returning to the stack carries chlorine to sustain current withdrawal. When the chlorine-hydrate is dissipated in the store, the battery is totally discharged.

The graphite plates in the stack are stable and do not deteriorate with recycling of the cell. In four years of continuous testing, the cell performed over 1,400 charge/discharge cycles—the equivalent of 200,000 miles of vehicle

EDA VOLKSWAGEN RABBIT

EDA MINI-VAN

travel. The zinc-chlorine hydrate system has a demonstrated specific energy of 30 wh/lb (66 wh/kg) with a much higher level projected for vehicle use.

In an early test using a converted Chevrolet Vega, a range of 150 miles (240 km) at 50 mph (80 km/hr) was reported.

Recent test vehicles included a mini-van and a Volkswagen Rabbit. Both vehicles have been adapted to house the G + W ELECTRIC ENGINE™. The Rabbit has achieved acceleration of 0 to 30 mph (48 km/hr) in 9.8 seconds with a range of 150 miles (240 km) at 55 mph (88 km/hr) on a single charge. Systems are being designed to power fully sized commercial vans which will yield a 100-mile (161-km) range at 55 mph (88 km/hr).

EDA predicts an urban 4-passenger vehicle could have a 150-200 mile (240-320 km) range at 55 mph (88 km/hr) and a battery life of 100,000 miles (161,200 km) with a $40/kwh battery cost in a developed market.

One of the major projected uses for the zinc-chlorine hydrate system is the bulk storage of off-peak energy for electric utilities. Effective load leveling with deep-discharge capability and long cycle life (10 year/2500 cycles) for utilities is an important goal for this battery system.

ZINC-BROMINE

Exxon's approach to the zinc-bromine battery is a practical one. In order for the electric car to compete with a gasoline car, the range and the cost must be comparable. The zinc-bromine energy density of 29-32 wh/lb (65-70 wh/kg) would be wasted if the cost of the system was prohibitive. However, Exxon's prototype 52-cell battery stack operates without expensive metal separators or metal electrodes and the projected cost is only $30-40/kwh if mass produced.

One of the problems inherent in circulating electrolyte batteries is uneven charge distribution due to shunt currents which cause uneven plating on the electrodes and premature cell failure. Shunt currents are "rogue" currents which escape into the battery case rather than travelling from electrode to electrode. Exxon's Shunt Current Protection is a small electrical charge deliberately fed into the battery case, precluding rogue currents and the side effects associated with them.

The Exxon battery incorporates a bromine reservoir which insures long-term charge retention, a pump to circulate the electrolyte (an aqueous solution of zinc bromine and a complexing agent), and, of course, Shunt Current Protection. Although design and development are in the early stages, a full-sized test module with Shunt Current Protection has been successfully recharged 75 times during a three-month period (with tests continuing) and no sign of zinc dendrite growth. In contrast, a cell without Shunt Current Protection shorted out after only 12 hours in operation and had extensive zinc dendrite growth.

HIGH TEMPERATURE BATTERIES

For electric vehicle use, the sodium-sulfur battery lies in the more distant future. This high temperature system could make it possible for a vehicle to travel 200 miles (320 km) on one charge. Laboratory tests using single cells have approached specific energy of 45 w-hr/lb (99 w-hr/kg). This is almost four times the energy density of a lead-acid battery. In this system the sodium and sulfur must be in liquid form, which requires an operating temperature of 570 degrees to 750 degrees F (300 degrees to 400 degrees C). The electrolyte is solid and made of ceramic or glass-fiber material.

A prototype vehicle using a sodium-sulfur battery was tested in 1973 by the Electric Council in England. The electric van was capable of travelling more than 100 miles (160 km) on a single charge.

Another sodium-sulfur battery is being developed by the Ford Motor Company which uses molten sodium and sulfur electrodes; the electrolyte is a sodium ion conductive ceramic. Prototype single-cell designs range from slightly over one-half pound to nearly two pounds (.247 kg to .878 kg). These relatively small cells can produce a maximum power of 143 watts each and promise a power density of 74 w/lb (163 w/kg) with an energy density of 68 wh/lb (150 wh/kg).

Like standard lead-acid batteries, these cells are designed to be used in battery packs instead of as single cells. Sodium-sulfur batteries will place the range of an electric vehicle closer to that of its gasoline-powered counterpart if thermal management problems can be overcome.

Before a successful sodium-sulfur battery pack is developed, however, several heat-related problems must be solved. One heat problem pertains to the liquid electrodes which will "freeze up" at ambient (or room) temperatures. Methods must also be found to: 1) heat the battery cells prior to start-up, 2) maintain a high internal temperature while the vehicle is in the cruising mode, and 3) conversely, cool the cell during long periods of peak power output. Improved insulation and heat (temperature) balance are crucial. If one individual cell becomes hotter than the rest, that cell produces more current, internal resistance decreases, and the cell becomes even hotter— a process which can damage the cell. Therefore, even heat distribution is another critical design goal. Because today's fibrous insulation is so bulky, sufficient insulation requires more space than the volume of the cell itself.

Ford engineers are studying "super" insulations which alternate layers of reflective foil with advanced thermal insulators.

A lithium-iron sulfide battery cell, originally developed by the Argonne National Laboratory, is now being actively pursued by Eagle-Picher Industries, Gould, and General Motors. The prototype cell operated for over 250 deep discharge cycles. This battery cell uses solid lithium-aluminum particles in the negative plate, solid iron sulfide particles in the positive plate, lithium chloride-potassium chloride eutectic salt as the electrolyte, and boron nitride fabric as the electrode separator. This molten salt battery operates in the range of 750 to 900° F (400 to 480° C). The cell can hold as much energy as five lead-acid cells; GM designers believe that the lithium-iron sulfide battery could increase the range of a lead-acid powered commuter vehicle from 30 to 200 miles (48 to 322 km) per charge. Like the sodium-sulfur battery, its high temperature operation requires careful thermal management and insulation. Unlike the sodium-sulfur battery which contains vibration-sensitive ceramic electrolyte (beta-alumina), the lithium-iron sulfide battery is rugged in construction and is particularly suited for traction application. The development of the lithium-iron sulfide battery is still in an engineering prototype stage, with production expectations five years away.

THE IRON-REDOX ENERGY STORAGE SYSTEM

The GEL iron-redox energy system is an electrically rechargeable electrochemical device based upon aqueous iron chemistry.

This solid/liquid energy converter stores fuel

in a solid form in cartridges within the negative electrode structure of its reactor. The "fuel" is electrodeposited iron.

An oxidizing liquid in the form of a water solution of ferric chloride salt is circulated from a tank through the reactor by an electric pump. During discharge, the iron in the reactor is oxidized to ferrous ions solubilized and carried into the liquid stream with the recirculating oxidizer, the ferric chloride. As the system discharges, the concentration of ferric chloride diminishes as the ferrous chloride increases. To recharge, the ferrous chloride is electrolyzed back to ferric chloride and iron is electrodeposited on the negative electrode. The key to this system is the utilization of the electrolyte "oxidizer" tank which can be removed and replaced with a fresh tank of regenerated fluids. The cartridge, in the form of a reactor electrode array, contains enough fuel to equal several refillings of the oxidizer tank. The system can be recharged electrically or mechanically. When recharged electrically, the ferrous chloride is reconverted to ferric chloride and iron is redeposited on the negative plates. When recharged mechanically for the purpose of quick charging, the tank can be drained of ferrous chloride solution and refilled with ferric chloride solution or a fresh oxidizer tank can be installed. It will also be possible to install fresh negative plate (iron) cartridges which would dramatically increase the range.

The GEL prototype system operates at ambient temperature and has a projected energy density of 30 wh/lb (66 wh/kg) and a projected power density of 40 to 60 w/lb (88-132 w/kg).

GEL Laboratory tests have demonstrated a cell life of over 1,000 cycles which could represent up to 150,000 miles (241,350 km) in a suitably designed electric vehicle.

The New Resources Group of Sanford, North Carolina, is fitting an Iron Redox Storage System into a Hummingbird Hybrid Van prototype from Electric Passenger Cars and Vans, San Diego, California.

FUEL CELLS

Recently, there has been great interest in the concept of the fuel cell for vehicle use. This renewed interest began with fuel cell innovations used in the space program. The NASA Gemini program was the first practical use of a fuel cell; General Electric designed the Gemini fuel cell.

The Gemini system did not use an aqueous (liquid) electrolyte. Instead it used a special polymer membrane, much like a sponge, which eliminated certain electrolyte container problems. This special type of hydrogen oxygen cell used platinum in the electrodes and may not be practical for electric vehicles on earth. Although their excellent power-to-weight-and-size ratio make them ideal for electric vehicle use, they are far too costly.

A fuel cell produces electricity by utilizing a fuel and an oxidizer. The fuel can be hydrogen or hydrocarbons such as natural gas, methanol, or even gasoline. The fuel is combined with an oxidizer such as air or oxygen slowly in a controlled manner to produce electric current in the presence of a catalyst. (A catalyst is something that causes a chemical reaction without being itself consumed in the process.) Platinum, silver, or nickel are examples of catalysts used in fuel cells. Although fuel cells are subject to some heat loss, they have efficiencies of 84% at room or "ambient" temperatures.

By far the most popular fuel cell is the hydrogen-air and hydrogen-oxygen type which is being developed in a number of countries by many companies using various combinations of catalysts, electrodes and electrolytes. The hydrogen-oxygen cell produces emissions that do not cause pollution because combining hydrogen and oxygen results in the formation of pure water.

Because hydrogen and oxygen in combination are used as rocket fuel, storage is a sensitive area. Care must be taken to avoid sparks that could cause an explosion. The use of pressurized tanks or super-cooled (cryogenically) stored liquid hydrogen and oxygen suggest two storage possibilities.

Another method for storing hydrogen is called the metal-hydride system. This system is accomplished by pumping hydrogen into specially designed tanks that contain metals (such as a combination of iron and titanium alloy) into which hydrogen is chemically absorbed. The difficulties of cryogenic storage, which requires complicated hardware to lower the temperature sufficiently to liquify hydrogen, are overcome to an extent with the hydride system. The advantages of ambient temperatures and the lack of high pressure and safer storage, make the hydride system attractive. Because hydride storage can absorb hydrogen about 75% as well as cryogenic methods, this type of system will probably be used extensively in the future.

Virtually all internal-combustion-powered vehicles can be converted to burn hydrogen-air or hydrogen-oxygen mixtures. Experimental automobiles have been built using this concept. There is a strong probability that we will see hydrogen used in some form in the vehicles of tomorrow. Perhaps the future use of the fuel cell (and of hydrogen in general) will be oriented to large utility companies that produce electric power. The advantages of the fuel cell for mass electrical production will probably be associated with the excess energy from nuclear generating stations. These stations must operate at high capacity in order to retain efficiencies. Also, there is a lower demand for electric power during off hours, when electric consumption is moderate. By producing hydrogen through electrolysis during these off-peak hours, the energy normally wasted could be stored as hydrogen to be used later as required in fuel cells or sold directly to natural gas companies.

CONCLUSION

While the lead-acid battery represents the state of the art for electric vehicle batteries of today, work is being done in many countries to improve its performance and life. The lead-acid batteries of today can provide enough range in advanced vehicle designs to fill many of the functions necessary for an electric vehicle.

Argonne National Laboratory made a study to determine the acceptable range of an electric passenger automobile. The study showed that a 100 mile-per-day range would meet most of the needs of the U.S. driver. In order to accomplish this, a vehicle battery system would require an energy density of about 25 wh/lb (56 wh/kg) and a capacity of 30 kwh at a cost of about $60/kwh. Today's lead-acid batteries have energy densities of about 10 to 14 wh/lb (22 to 31 wh/kg). The range of the lead-acid powered vehicle is about 25 to 70 miles (40 to 112 km) per charge with the cost for current lead-acid batteries in the $50 to $150/kwh range. Reports from battery manufacturers indicate possible energy densities of advance lead-acid designs of 20 to 25 wh/lb (44 to 55 wh/kg) in the near future. Also, a number of improvements can be made to reduce weight without power reduction.

All of the new battery systems that are under consideration have specific energies which are

COMPACT BATTERY CELL
Under development at General Motors Research Laboratories is the "lithium/iron sulfide" battery, a high performance battery that may someday greatly extend the range of electric vehicles—to 200 miles or more between recharges.

Here, GM senior research engineer Thompson G. Bradley works on an experimental battery cell housed in a nonreactive helium atmosphere. The battery is cooled down from its normal operating temperature of 870°F, about that found in a home "self-cleaning" oven.

higher than those of lead-acid batteries. But problems involving limited life, charging difficulties, complexity of systems, and high costs have prevented their use in vehicles. Although they are presently under development and available at great cost it may be three to five years before we see the nickel-zinc and nickel-iron batteries in production at a commercially acceptable cost. Other batteries will be adopted as their technologies progress in the distant future.

We have discussed some of the various battery approaches to power storage for an electric vehicle. Perhaps hybrids of more than one type of battery may eventually be used in a single vehicle. Certainly, the advantages of the long life nickel-iron and the power density of an advanced lead-acid battery could be combined in a way that would utilize the strengths of each system. The new system that can stand the test of practical daily use, ease of operation, and marketing acceptability will obviously be the winner.

The projected evolution of a true electric vehicle system comprised of super-energy-efficient motor, controller, suspension, transmission, tires, and aerodynamics will provide more range for *any* battery system including lead-acid.

When an energy source such as the zinc-chlorine hydrate system, which has proven its value for both utility load power levelling and test vehicle use, is placed in our super-efficient automobile, we may find commonplace a cruising range of 200 miles (320 km) or more per charge. Since 96% of all round trips made in today's automobile are of 100 miles (161 km) or less, such an advanced electric automobile and light delivery van will be quickly assimilated into world transportation.

The anticipated development of the futuristic aluminum air cell, with a 1000-mile (1600-km) range and five-minute mechanical refueling, will relegate conversation about the range of electric vehicles to the nostalgia of a bygone era.

COMPARISON OF THREE BATTERY TECHNOLOGIES

The three battery cells shown here have the same energy storage capacity. At left is a conventional lead-acid battery. The next two are experimental batteries under development at General Motors Research Laboratories, Warren, Mich. In the center is the zinc/nickel oxide battery, about ⅓ the size and weight of the lead-acid; at right is the lithium/iron sulfide, about ⅙ the size and weight.

ELECTRIC VEHICLE BATTERY CHART

System	Electrolytes	Temp °C	wh/kg (3-5 Yr)	w/kg (Peak)	Life (Cycles)	Cost $/kwh	wh/kg	w/kg (Peak)	Life (Cycles)	Cost $/kwh
				Current				Projected		
	Near Term									
Lead-Acid	Aq*. Sulfuric Acid	Room Ambient	41	140	300	—	50	150	>1000	60
Nickel-Iron	Aq. Potassium Hydroxide	Room Ambient	50	130	400	—	60	150	>1000	120
Nickel-Zinc	Aq. Potassium Hydroxide	Room Ambient	65	150	200	—	70	150	> 800	70-100
Zinc-Chlorine Hydrate	Aq. Zinc Chloride	30-50°	50	70	100	—	80	90	>1000	100
	Intermediate Term		**(5-10 Yr)**							
Lithium-Iron Sulfide	Lithium/ Potassium Chloride	400-480°	100	120	250	—	150	250	>1000	100
Sodium-Sulfur	Beta-Alumina	300-350°	90	100	200	—	150	200	>1000	100
	Long Term		**(Over 10 Yr)**							
Zinc or Iron-Air	Aq. Potassium Hydroxide	Room Ambient	80-120	40	150	—	90	80	>1000	100
Zinc-Bromine	Aq. Zinc Bromide	Ambient	—	—	75 +	—	65-70	80	>1000	50-100
Aluminum-Air	Aq. Sodium Hydroxide	60°	—	—	—	—	300-400	150	—	50-100
Iron-Redox	Aq. Ferric Chloride	Ambient	—	—	—	—	66	88-132	>1000	

*Aq. stands for Aqueous

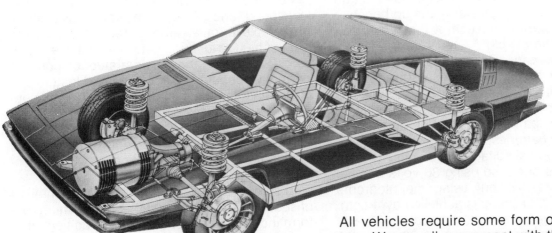

chapter 5

Electric Vehicle Controls

All vehicles require some form of control system. We are all conversant with the controls of a conventional automobile, which include the accelerator, brake, shifting mechanism, and steering. The motorized cranes used in construction have a great number of controls to perform a variety of complicated duties. Electric vehicles need controls that will extract the most power and range from an energy system.

Historically, electric cars contained controllers that would isolate various segments of a battery pack. Electric cars such as the Milburn and the Baker used mechanical relays and resistors placed between the batteries and motor to control speeds. This method varied the voltage going to the motor by using a combination of "parallel" or "series" battery connections to obtain desired voltages. The first speed might combine all batteries in parallel to produce 12 volts, other speeds would use all batteries in a different combination to produce 24 to 36 volts, and higher speeds would be obtained by placing the batteries in series to produce 48 volts or more, depending upon the number of 6-volt batteries the vehicle could carry.

The type of switch used to interconnect batteries is called a relay or solenoid. The solenoid is nothing more than a very heavy duty switch that can accept the high load requirements of electric vehicle power. Inside the solenoid is a coil of wire wrapped around an iron piston type device which, when electrically activated, causes the piston to close a switch electromagnetically. Combinations of solenoid relays can yield a variety of voltages for electric vehicle's speed requirements.

Unfortunately, the surge of power from the lowest voltage selection causes undesirable starting because of the tendency to jerk from a standstill. To lessen this problem, a resistance is provided by placing resistors in the circuit for the first speed. The use of resistors is an inefficient expedient. The resistor heats up because it is diverting some of the energy that would normally propel the vehicle.

A contemporary electric automobile, the Sebring-Vanguard CitiCar, uses a three-speed voltage regulation method. The first speed is achieved by parallel combinations to obtain 36 volts from the battery pack, which consists of eight 6-volt batteries. A nichrome resistor reduces the actual voltage to 18 volts. The second speed is achieved using 36 volts parallel again, this time without using the nichrome resistor. The third speed is achieved by a combination of series connections to obtain 48 volts for the maximum top speed of 38 mph (61 km/hr).

"While the series-parallel voltage switching is a throwback to the turn of the century, it is a proven control method in many modern vehicles."

Today, many electric vehicles use solid state systems, the most common of which is the SCR (silicon controlled rectifier.) Another type of solid state control is the "thyristor" which is similar to the SCR, in that it is an electronic device using semi-conductor material. The SCR, the most popular semi-conductor controller, is commonly referred to as a "chopper" because it quite literally chops the battery current into pieces to be fed to the motor as speed requirements dictate.

Up to 1,000 power pulses per second switch the motor on and off repeatedly. Depending upon the controller, the pulse "on" time and the frequency of "on" times are varied. These power pulses to the motor can theoretically produce smooth acceleration up to top speeds. Unfortunately, some tests indicate that in actual use, at very low speeds, the chopper produces a shuddering effect as the battery current is pulsed in nominal amounts to the motor. Work is being conducted to design ever-improving control systems using solid state technology.

Early electric choppers have been SCR units exclusively, because transistors have not been capable of handling the larger currents required for vehicle use. New transistorized systems are being developed that will be able to meet vehicle needs. One advantage of transistors over SCR or thyristors is that while the SCR can pulse up to 1,000 times per second, the transistor can pulse up to 20,000 times per second. This could alleviate the shuddering at lower speeds.

For electric vehicles which have short range, low speed, and moderate power requirements, the simple parallel-series, stepped controllers are the best solution. Lightweight vehicles such as golf carts find the cheaper stepped controls perfectly adequate. But heavier and faster vehicles need the flexibility of the 97%-efficient solid state devices. The separately excitable field and armature of the compound wound or shunt wound DC motor currently offer benefits of high flexibility in conjunction with SCR chopper control.

In some cases, the power regulation method of speed control is not suitable for optimum performance. In these cases, the addition of a multiple-speed mechanical transmission may be needed. This depends upon the design of the vehicle and its intended use. Generally speaking, a multi-speed transmission is desirable in an electric vehicle because it can reduce the high current drain needed for difficult terrain. While it is true that a transmission is unnecessary for moderate-use vehicles, the needs of a versatile electric car are more demanding.

The high cost of SCR controls have rendered them impractical for some forms of electric transportation. Such is the case in electric bicycle conversion kits, which use a single forward speed on-and-off switch for control. The cost of SCR controls will become more economical as more are manufactured.

Another area of controls which deserves attention is braking. All electric vehicles are equipped with mechanical brakes, whether they be disc or drum, mechanical or hydraulic. But there is another type of braking which can extend battery life by using the force generated by the stopping vehicle to partially recharge the battery system. This type of braking is called "regenerative". The SCR chopper control can be used to strengthen the field current of a shunt- wound motor during deceleration. The motor is now converted into a generator and current is delivered to the battery.

Regenerative braking is designed to provide an extended range of the vehicle. Theoretically, 10 to 40% energy retrieval is possible. Driving cycles with frequent acceleration and deceleration benefit the most from regenerative braking. Another benefit of regenerative braking is that it improves penetration of the electrolyte into the grid material of a lead-acid battery. Effectively, battery life and efficiency are increased.

A regenerative braking system used on the Mars II made by the Electric Fuel Propulsion Company of Detroit uses an alternator attached to the drive motor. This regenerative system alone can stop the vehicle in about 500 feet (152 m) from a speed of 30 mph (48 km/hr).

One forklift manufacturer noted that substantial driver training was necessary to achieve desired regenerative braking yields. Vehicles designed with regenerative braking often have a dual brake system where the first position of the brake pedal yields regeneration and subsequent pressure provides both regeneration to its maximum and the application of mechanical brakes. Also a deceleration sensation can be incorporated into the design by engaging regeneration when the driver's foot is removed from the accelerator pedal.

Another form of braking which is occasionally used is "dynamic" braking. This basically has the effect of regenerative braking, except that the voltage produced by the motor acting as a generator does not have to be greater than the battery voltage. So braking action can be extended to a lower speed than with normal regenerative braking. The energy produced by dynamic braking is dissipated through a resistor bank which requires very large resistors. Because this system does not offer the recovery of kinetic energy and because it adds to the vehicle's complexity, it is generally not recommended as an auxiliary braking system.

Whether the mechanical brakes which must be incorporated into any vehicle design are drum or disc, either shoe or disc pad retractors must be used to prevent drag and useless energy waste.

In some control systems "free wheeling" or coasting is used to extend range. In this case the motor is disconnected. Free wheeling ceases when the brake is applied. The regenerative braking circuit is then energized followed by the engagement of the mechanical brakes.

The future control system for all electric vehicles will be based on space-age microprocessor technology. Several vehicles have been built using the concepts of superminiaturized computers, including two U.S. Government-funded electric cars (see Legislation chapter). Eventually, all vehicles will be using this control system.

This inevitable course of action is due primarily to the almost infinite flexibility of microprocessor controls. With this system, the computer "brain" monitors every vehicle function including speed control, regenerative braking, charging, load differentiation, motor protection, temperature control of components, and a host of other passenger-related vehicle duties. Well within the province of this system is the ability to monitor and protect a weak battery within a battery pack from overcharging, overheating, or overloading. The constant monitoring of vital vehicle functions will enable the electric vehicle to stretch every last ounce of energy from any battery system.

FUTURISTIC INSTRUMENT PANEL
A comprehensive electronic map display on the passenger's side is the basis for extremely precise trip monitoring.

Vehicles of the Present

There are few forms of transportation that can compare with the quietness, grace, and elegance of an electrical vehicle; a phenomenon matched only by sailboating, skydiving, and skiing.

Electric vehicles in use today are not as rare as one might expect. Many mass transportation systems use electric trains, which are efficient and pollution-free. The passenger of any office building elevator is actually riding in an electric vehicle, and most people are unaware that cross-country diesel trains are actually electric powered. Their diesel engines are used to run generators that produce electricity and supply power to electric motors which drive their wheels. The average person unknowingly comes into contact with electric vehicles every day.

The manner in which electric vehicles affect the lives of the people of the world is evidenced by their diverse functions. While electric automobiles remain an oddity in the contemporary transportation structure, certain fields are definitely the domain of electric power. Two examples are the electric forklift (which outnumbers its internal combustion counterparts), and electric golf carts.

chapter 6

In many urban situations, electric automobiles of even the most modest levels of development can meet today's acceleration and cruising speed requirements. Because much of urban traffic operates in the 10 to 20-mph (16 to 32 km/hr) range, a 60 or 70-mph (97 or 113 km/hr) top speed seems unnecessary. An electric vehicle with a 30-mph (48 km/hr) top speed can accelerate with conventional vehicles without becoming an obstruction to traffic or safety. The controls of an electric vehicle are similar to those of a modern automobile. There is no problem adapting the operator to new driving habits. However, the owner of an electric vehicle will have to adopt a style that is conservation-oriented, because electricity cannot be stored in abundance. Practice and familiarity with this problem will allow the driver to adapt with no more discomfort than the difference between moving from a luxury sedan to an economy model.

The modern vehicle designer is faced with problems that were unheard of a decade ago. He is conscious of dwindling energy reserves and aware of restrictive federal requirements for safety, emissions, and performance. Today's electric vehicle technology is adequate to meet many of these requirements.

When I first began researching this subject, I noticed that electric vehicles had been abandoned by a number of companies during the 1920's era. It seemed odd that one company after another had fallen victim to the proliferation of the gasoline vehicle. A company had to divert its efforts to internal combustion models or face bankruptcy. Unfortunately, I observed a similar recurrence when I tried to contact electric vehicle companies which had operated businesses within the past five years. A significant number of my letters were returned with the notation "Address Unknown" or "Moved." It seems the entrepreneural nature of electric vehicle production is a rocky road. These business ventures included efforts that range from sports cars, vans, and electric motor scooters to commercial vehicles.

Even well-publicized production vehicles, such as the Sebring Vanguard CitiCar, and the Elcar, an Italian import produced by Zagato, have not received high public acclaim. Although it remains true that any electric car will still draw a sizeable crowd of "gawkers," the fact remains that the average person, spoiled by the large luxury passenger automobile replete with air conditioning, power steering and brakes, electric seats and other accoutrements, will not accept a small commuter electric vehicle as an interim solution to gas shortages, even as a second car.

In truth, the small, four-cylinder import that achieves 35 to 40 miles (56 to 64 km) per gallon on the highway still provides economy, handling, and creature comforts which are difficult for an electric automobile manufacturer to match. There are no production electric automobiles that can equal the acceleration, economy, cruising speed, and general wherewithal of a Volkswagen Rabbit. Development of the Rabbit is a result of many millions of dollars invested in research and production.

The plight of a new electric commuter vehicle is, therefore, to be compared against tried and true, successful, and publicly-accepted vehicles that have endured more than twenty years of automotive history.

Any interim design that is to be embraced by the public will need a strong impetus to warrant participation. Perhaps gasoline prices in the

United States of two dollars per gallon may trigger a public awareness of economy and conservation and thus may contribute to electric vehicle acceptance.

One manufacturer has oriented his designs toward the luxury vehicle market shared by Mercedes and Rolls Royce. The "Transformer One" electric, luxury, sports sedan which sells for over $30,000 brings to mind the golden days of the expensive electric carriages designed to service the very wealthy. But the optimum electric vehicle must be an economy-oriented, four-passenger commuter sedan, priced in the $4,000 to $5,000 range, to be competitive in those markets secured by Toyota, Datsun, Honda, and Volkswagen.

Our "Vehicles of Today" chapter does not include every vehicle produced in the world currently. Every year new prototypes and designs for production vehicles emanate from the United States, England, Japan, France, Germany, and other countries interested in this growing field. By the time this book goes to press, there may be production vehicles offered to the public that will differ greatly from those listed. However, the reader will be in a position to appreciate the coming of a new generation of vehicles.

One thing is certain—even as I write this, somebody out there will be putting the finishing touches on a prototype in hopes of attracting financial backing to enter the market. The texture of this new field will be determined by those companies that fulfill the public's need. No one can predict which company will be chosen by the public as its standard bearer. Solutions may come from the small dynamic producer geared expressly for electric vehicle design, or it may

be an offshoot of the "Big 3" automakers in the United States. Or possibly a Japanese manufacturer, who will unveil a completely-tested entry, boxed and packaged for immediate consumption.

ELECTRIC AUTOMOTIVE DEVELOPMENT IN AMERICA

Sebring-Vanguard

Only a few thousand electric automobiles have been produced and sold in the United States. One of the most popular of these vehicles is the Sebring-Vanguard CitiCar, the first mass-produced electric automobile in America. The Sebring Vanguard Company was based in Columbia, Md., and had been producing electrics for over three years. This vehicle received much publicity after its introduction in 1974 and for a time was selling as many as could be produced.

The CitiCar looks a little bit like a cross between a golf cart and a telephone booth and is a courageous effort to enter into an infant market with a fully functioning product.

Energy storage for the CitiCar is accomplished by eight 6-volt traction deep cycle batteries. Power is transmitted through a series-wound DC General Electric motor, producing 3.5 horsepower. One test report of the 1,250 pound (567 kg) CitiCar yielded a zero to 30 mph (48 km/hr) time of 13.9 seconds and a top speed of 38 mph (61 km/hr).

The CitiCar I uses a combination of voltages to the motor to achieve various speeds. The first speed uses 24 volts parallel (all batteries) with a nichrome resistor. The second speed uses 24 volts parallel without the nichrome resistor, and the third speed uses 48 volts series. The forward-reverse control is on the dashboard and is operated by a toggle switch with a safety neutral position. The city driving cycle is rated at an electricity consumption of 3.5 miles (5.6 km) per kilowatt hour. Maximum range of the CitiCar is 40 to 50 miles (64 to 80 km). The maximum range per day with intermittent charging is rated at 100 miles (161 km).

The CitiCar was also available as a CitiVan which is a lightweight utility truck conversion. The CitiVan uses a 6-hp 4,100-rpm air-cooled, series-wound DC motor. The power source is eight 6-volt deep-cycle batteries with a total rated voltage of 48 volts. The projected battery cycle life is 400 to 600 full recharges. The body

---

PLEASE NOTE: Vehicle specifications have been obtained from the manufacturer or from other published sources. Because we have not formally tested each vehicle shown, we must rely upon the manufacturers' good intentions regarding published specifications.

Inquiries regarding specific vehicles should be directed to the manufacturer.

We have been unable, in a number of instances, to obtain photographs of some prototype and production vehicles which are scheduled for public introduction.

CITICAR
Photo courtesy of
Sebring Vanguard

is a rust and corrosion proof impact resistant plastic; the frame is aluminum. Total curb weight is 1,360 lbs. (618 kg) with a suggested list price of about $4,000.

The CitiVan and CitiCar are both ideal for duty such as mail delivery. One CitiVan was sold to the U.S. Postal Service R. & D. Center at Rockville, Md.

The Long Island Lighting Company of New York began an electric vehicle demonstration program on April 4, 1977, to test and evaluate the practicality, performance and efficiency of the electric vehicle for meter reading and as "second car" transportation. In addition, this program was designed to encourage other vehicle fleet owners to use electric automobiles for duties such as meter reading, patrols by police, security, and delivery. Long Island Lighting Company purchased two CitiCars initially and their success has prompted an order for eighteen additional vehicles.

Another experiment is the Salt River Project (SRP) which is the power utility for Phoenix, Arizona. The three CitiCars were used in a demonstration during July, August and September of 1976, during which time 7,300 total miles (11,748 km) were driven by SRP employees in a variety of service duties.

Mr. Robert Beaumont of Sebring-Vanguard acknowledges that, although improvements have been made since the CitiCar's introduction in 1974, there is still room for more

development. He also pointed out that eighteen years elapsed between the development of Ford's Model T and Model A (although one must remember that over fifteen million Model T's were produced versus the CitiCar's 2,000).

One CitiCar owner, John Hoke, in the National Capitol Park Region in Washington D.C., surpassed the 35,000-mile (56,315-km) mark with his 1974 CitiCar.

In an effort to learn more about his vehicle's performance, Hoke collected data on power consumption, mileage, and service costs. During the initial year of recordkeeping, an average power consumption of 0.346 kilowatt hour per mile or about 3.5 cents, including maintenance costs, was established. At a later date, when steps were taken to prevent overcharging and the associated loss of energy, power consumption was even lower.

Searching for methods to further conserve energy, Hoke changed his driving habits. By utilizing less rapid acceleration, coasting when possible, and avoiding braking by anticipating traffic light changes, kilowatt use per hour was finally reduced to only 0.232. After two years, Hoke's rather thick and "tight" performance log prompted the staff of Jet Propulsion Labs to request a copy of the base data and findings. The evaluation of this material was published in a 1978 U.S. Department of Energy report.

JOHN HOKE AND HIS CITICAR

Photo courtesy of
General Engines, Inc.

COMUTA-CAR

The Comuta-Car,
Comuta-Cab, and Comuta-Van

Though the Comuta-Car, Comuta-Cab, and Comuta-Van resemble the original Sebring-Vanguard models, significant improvements have been made. The front and rear bumpers are constructed of shock-absorbing materials and the braking system has been redesigned. The suspension system has been re-engineered and the frame is fully gussetted.

Performance specifications for the three vehicles are identical. Each carries eight 6-volt lead-acid batteries which supply power to a 6-hp General Electric DC motor. The 1460-lb (662-kg) vehicles can accelerate to 30 miles per hour (48 km) in 15 seconds, have a maximum speed of 35 mph (56 km/hr) and a cruising speed of 35 mph (56 km/hr). A special Commuter Vehicle field-weakening controller and direct drive are standard components of the vehicles.

As of 1979, the Commuter Vehicles Division of General Engines, Inc., has established a dealership network in the United States. For more information, contact General Engines Company, Commuter Vehicles Division, P.O. Box 1479, Sebring Air Terminal, Sebring, FL 33870.

ELECTRO-SPORT

Photo Courtesy of General Engines, Inc.

The Electro-Sport

The General Engines Co. also offers a full scale electric replica of a 1929 Mercedes-Benz roadster called the Electro-Sport. This custom sports runabout is built to order as a limited production model.

The Electro-Sport uses a 4-speed manual shift, 72 V. series wound D.C. motor and carries twelve 6 V. "deep cycle" golf cart batteries weighing 62 lbs (28 kg) each. Top speed is 50 mph (80 km/hr) with a 45 mph (72 km/hr) cruising speed. Range is 50 miles (80 km) per charge. Vehicle weight is 1690 lbs (768 kg).

For more information contact: General Engines, Inc., Commuter Vehicles Division, 591 Mantua Blvd., Sewell, New Jersey, U.S.A. 08080

E.V.A. "CURRENT FARE"

"CHANGE OF PACE" WAGON

METRO

E.V.A.

Electric Vehicle Associates, Inc., Cleveland, Ohio (EVA), manufactures electric vehicles for fleet and individual use. A previous model, the Metro, was based on the Renault 12 TL body and powered by nineteen 6-volt batteries. The vehicle had a cruising speed of 55 mph (89 km/hr, with a range of 30 to 55 miles (48 to 88 km) per charge. This compact, 4-door sedan had automatic transmission, power steering, and power disc brakes. The control system was a SCR solid-state control with battery and motor protection. Vehicle weight was 3150 lbs (1429 kg), including battery charger.

Another successful vehicle was the "Change of Pace" electric station wagon and sedan. Basic American Motors production Pacer models were converted to electric power and had a top speed in excess of 55 mph (88 km/hr) and a range of more than 40 to 60 miles (65 km and 97 km) per charge. Zero to 30 miles (0 to 48 km) per hour performance was 12 seconds. The curb weight of the vehicle was about 4150 lbs (1882 kg) carrying an onboard 110 or 240-volt battery charger.

The EVA early vehicles were successfully incorporated for fleet and individual use and are still used today. Many of the vehicles were sold to fleet operators where they were tested in "sheltered" environments.

The EVA "Current Fare"

Electric Vehicle Associates' "Current Fare" is available in several popular Ford production models. A four-door sedan, two-door coupe, sedan delivery and station wagon are among those offered.

Each has a 4-speed manual or 3-speed automatic transmission enabling them to exceed speeds of 55 mph (88 km/hr) and accelerate from 0 to 30 mph (0 to 48 km) in 12 seconds. Driven by a 30-hp DC traction motor with forced air ventilation, the vehicles are equipped with SCR solid-state speed controls with optional regenerative braking.

The range of the 4000-lb (1814-kg) vehicle is 35 to 60 miles (56 to 96 km) per charge, depending on speed, gradients, and number of stops. City driving averages 40 miles per charge.

The Current Fare is available for individual and fleet use and meets all Department of Energy and Federal Safety Standards. For more information, contact Electric Vehicle Associates, Inc., 9100 Bank Street, Cleveland, OH 44125.

Amectran Exar-1

The Exar-1 is a pre-production prototype. This five-passenger 2-door electronic-powered automobile is the result of research compiled since 1973.

The company, under the direction of Edmond X. Ramirez, Sr., has developed a unique manufacturing and marketing concept which would result in the construction of many small factories located adjacent to urban areas.

The steel-bodied prototype was designed by the famous Italian master designer, Pietro Frua. Molds are being made in the U.S. by a tooling expert in this field. Production models are scheduled to be constructed of acrylic-reinforced Kelvar plastic on a 4130 chromalloy steel chassis.

Performance details of the 3,000 lb (1360 kg) production plastic-bodied Exar-1, according to Amectran, are a top speed of 85 mph (136 km/hr) with acceleration from zero to 60 mph (96 km/hr) in 12 seconds. Cruising range at 55 mph (88 km/hr) is stated at 75-100 miles (120-161 km).

The power train consists of an 1,800 lb (816 kg) lead-acid battery pack, 19-hp series wound GE motor weighing 225 lb (102 kg) and modified combination Cableform and GE controller with regenerative braking. A 4-speed semi-automatic transmission completes the drive-train.

An on-board computer controls and monitors nearly all vehicle systems. The microprocessor is used to optimize electricity flow to the motor, and monitor motor temperature, battery water level, battery state-of-charge, all instrumentation including volt-meter, tachometer, speedometer, ammeter, clock and accessories. The mini-computer will also set the battery charging cycle, adjust the proper cabin temperature and provide a digital anti-theft combination number readout ignition locking device.

The steel-bodied prototype weighs approximately 5000 lb (2268 kg) but production Exar-1 models will weigh about 3000 lb (1360 kg) due to plastic construction, and are designated to include as standard equipment: AM/FM stereo with tape player and 40-channel CB, air conditioner, heater/defroster, computerized diagnostic system, and more. According to Mr. Ramirez: "The overall idea of this design is to combine the roominess of a mid-sized automobile, the compactness of an efficient, practical commuter vehicle, and the futuristic design and aerodynamic soundness of an expensive sport car." When production of the Exar-1 commences we may see an electric automobile which blends futuristic styling and outstanding performance at a price competitive with mid-sized internal combustion automobiles.

For more information regarding price and anticipated vehicle availability, contact American Ecological Transportation (Amectran), 8585 North Stemmons Freeway, 900 Twin Towers South, Dallas, TX 75247.

AMECTRAN EXAR-1

BRADLEY GT II ELECTRIC

Bradley Electric

Bradley Automotive manufactures four Turn-key production electric vehicles. The four models are the GT Sport Electric, the GT II Electric, the MGT Electric and the '34 Mercedes Marlene Electric. Each vehicle uses a standard Volkswagen chassis and transmission.

All models are powered by the Tracer I Electric Propulsion System which consists of a rear-transaxle-mounted General Electric 20.9-hp direct drive series traction motor, 16 six-volt lead-acid batteries and an EV-1 SCR controller. Performance of all vehicles is 0-30 mph (48 km/hr) in 8 seconds, a top speed of 75 mph (121 km/hr) and a range of 85 miles (137 km).

Each vehicle chassis is a lightweight fiberglass design of under 2700 lbs (1224 kg). The styles range from the classically elegant to the sleek and sporty.

The Bradley GT Sport Electric and the GT II Electric are both two-passenger gull-wing sport coupes. The MGT Electric is a replica of the British Leyland 1952 MGTD and the Bradley Marlene Electric is a replica of the classic 1934 Mercedes Benz. Both have retractable convertible tops.

The vehicles are sold as fully assembled production models only. For further information and prices, contact Bradley GT Turnkey Electric Vehicles, 14414-21st Avenue North, Plymouth, MN 55441.

BRADLEY GT SPORT ELECTRIC

BRADLEY MGT ELECTRIC

BRADLEY MARLENE ELECTRIC

JMJ Electracar

The Citation Electracar is one of the latest models developed by JMJ Electronics Corporation of Oklahoma City, Oklahoma. JMJ produces a family of internal combustion engine conversion models and has adapted the Citation using the same basic techniques incorporated into its Omni Electric and Rabbit Electracar. Both the Omni and Rabbit have four-speed manual transmissions and offer an optional power controller with regenerative braking.

The JMJ Omni Electracar

The Omni Electracar, available for both individual and fleet use, has a 50-mile (80-km) range with a maximum speed of 70 mph (113 km/hr) and a cruising speed of 55 mph (88 km/hr). The two-passenger electric Omni Sedan accelerates to 30 mph (48 km/hr) in 12 seconds. The vehicle carries 12 6-volt lead-acid batteries with a total weight of 800 lb (363 kg). Power is supplied to a 12-hp DC motor.

The JMJ Rabbit Electracar

The Rabbit Electracar in many respects is similar to JMJ's other conversion vehicles. With a cruising speed of 50 mph (80 km/hr) and maximum speed of 60 mph (97 km/hr) using a 12-hp DC motor, the 3240-lb (1409-kg) sedan accelerates from zero to 30 mph (0 to 48 km/hr) in 12 seconds. The weight of the battery pack,

JMJ CITATION ELECTRACAR

JMJ OMNI AND RABBIT ELECTRACARS   Photo: Sandra Kraus & Associates, Inc.

consisting of twelve 12-volt batteries, is 852 lb (386 kg).

For more information, contact JMJ Electronics, 4415 Highline Blvd., Oklahoma City, OK 73108.

Hummer Electric Automobile

The Hummer is a two-passenger experimental automobile which has a top speed of 55 mph (88 km/hr) and a range of 40 miles (64 km) at 45 mph (72 km/hr). Acceleration from zero to 30 mph (48 km/hr) requires less than 12 seconds.

The 1,752-lb (794-kg) vehicle prototype is powered by eight 12-volt lead-acid batteries which are connected in series. The batteries

are centrally mounted in a backbone configuration which can provide fast battery exchange.

Power is controlled by a transistorized pulse-width modulator to a pair of 3.5-hp series-wound 48-volt DC motors mounted at each of the rear wheels. A 5:1 motor-to-wheel belt drive ratio provides power and eliminates the need for a gear differential. This prototype uses tires with low rolling resistance and incorporates glass-reinforced plastics in the body and much of the chassis.

Although much public interest has been expressed in the Hummer and its performance is acceptable for many city driving needs, Hummer does not plan to enter production at this time. Further information can be obtained by contacting Hummer Incorporated, a division of Kreonite, 715 E. 10th Street, P.O. Box 2099, Wichita, KS 67201.

EFP History

In 1970, the EFP Electric Hornet won the Electric Class of the Clean Air Car Race which was a seven day event. Also, the components of the Electric Fuel Propulsion Corporation were used in the CalTech Vehicle from the Great Electric Car Race as noted in the History Chapter.

The electrified Hornet used a 20-hp electric motor, 24 batteries and had a top speed of 79.2 mph (128 km/hr). The vehicle weighed 5,500 lbs. (2495 kg) and utilized a solid state controller.

An earlier Electric Fuel Propulsion Vehicle was called the Mars II and was a converted Renault R-10 weighing 3,640 lb (1651 kg) which carried 1,700 lbs (771 kg) of batteries. The car featured a regenerative braking system and utilized a 15-hp direct-current motor which could accelerate from zero to 40 mph (64 km) in 10 seconds and reach a top speed of 60 mph (97 km/hr) with a 70 to 120 mile (113 to 193 km) range from lead-cobalt batteries. Recharge cycles claimed for the lead-cobalt batteries were 800, which would be the equivalent of driving up to 90,000 miles (144,840 km) per battery set. Normal cruising speed was 45 to 55 mph (72 to 89 km/hr). In a test, on October 6, 1967, the Mars II traveled 2,000 miles (3219 kg) across the U.S.

EFP MARS II   Photo courtesy of Electric Fuel Propulsion, Inc.

EFP ELECTRIC HORNET   Photo courtesy of Electric Fuel Propulsion, Inc.

TRANSFORMER 1   Photos courtesy of Electric Fuel Propulsion, Inc.

Transformer I

The Transformer I is a $30,000 luxury electric-powered automobile produced by Electric Fuel Propulsion Corporation (EFP), Detroit, Michigan. Features such as leather interior, air conditioning, stereo tape deck, powered seats, power brakes and electric windows are among the accessories available. The Transformer I has a top speed of 70 mph (113 km/hr) and cruising speed of 55 mph (88 km/hr). Acceleration is zero to 30 mph (48 km/hr) in 8 seconds. Power is stored in a 180-volt tri-polar lead-cobalt battery system. A 32 volt DC motor is used with a solid-state electronic controller.

The lead-cobalt battery system is patented by Mr. Robert R. Aronson, inventor, founder and president of Electric Fuel Propulsion Corporation. It is claimed that the lead-cobalt battery has more than twice the energy per pound than ordinary lead-acid batteries and can store new energy six times faster. The lead-cobalt battery can be charged to 80% capacity in approximately 45 minutes using a "fast- charge" system. Normal lead-acid batteries could not survive constant fast recharging at this rate, but the cobaltous sulphate with other chemicals enables quick charging of 400 to 500 amps DC without harmful oxidation or production of toxic gases. EFP rates their battery at a 50,000-mile (80,467-km) life and an 18-watt- hours/lb (40-wh/kg) rating, which is attractive by today's standards. Battery replacement is estimated at $1,500 at today's prices, and the electric motor has a projected life of over 20 years.

For long trips, a trailer-mounted gasoline-powered generator is an optional piece of equipment. The five-passenger car uses a standard General Motors two-door mid-sized body. Future model considerations include a Transformer II four-door sedan, based on the Cadillac Seville.

Research accumulated from the Transformer I has led to the development of the Electric Limousine and Silver Volt produced by the Electric Auto Corporation, which has acquired the rights to patents and technology of the Electric Fuel Propulsion Company through a licensing agreement.

Mobile Power Plant

A mobile generator makes it possible to cover hundreds of miles of expressway driving an eight-hour day with a quick booster charge at lunch time. By hitching the EFP mobile power plant, the Transformer I can yield up to 1,100 miles (1,770 km) a day (equalling 22 hours of driving at 50 mph (80 km/hr) with two hours for refueling. Normal driving range is stated as 100 miles with an occasional midday supplemental charge.

E.A.C. ELECTRIC LIMOSINE

E.A.C. Electric Limousine

The super luxury, six-seater Electric Limousine was produced as a companion car to the Silver Volt and uses the same basic technology. This vehicle is produced in limited numbers for an exclusive clientele and should only be considered by those who can afford a Rolls Royce.

The onboard Auxiliary Power Unit (APU) provides power for accessories such as air conditioning, heating, power brakes, windows, and seats while extending range, as a series hybrid,

E.A.C. SILVER VOLT

to 85 miles (137 km) under normal driving conditions. Range at a constant 30 mph (48 km/hr) is 120 miles (193 km) per charge.

Top speed for passing is 70 mph (113 km/hr), cruising speed is 55 mph (88 km/hr), and acceleration is zero to 30 mph (48 km/hr) in 7 seconds. (The author has test driven this vehicle and can attest to its tremendous power.)

For more information, contact The Electric Auto Corporation, 2237 Elliot Avenue, Troy, MI 48084.

E.A.C. Silver Volt

The Silver Volt is a four-passenger station wagon which includes a three-speed automatic transmission with lockup torque converter, air conditioning, power steering, electric windows, power brakes, and other accessories as standard luxury features.

The 5,900-lb (2675-kg) prototype carries a 2,543-lb (1153-kg) 150-volt patented lead-cobalt, fast charge battery pack with automatic watering, venting, and heating systems.

The vehicle can travel 65 to 100 miles (104-161 km) on pure battery power with an additional range of 100 miles (161 km) assisted by an on-board generator. The use of the auxiliary power unit (APU) allows the Silver Volt to operate as a series hybrid. Power is directed from the battery pack through a high-power electronic SCR chopper, with regenerative braking, to a 100-kw (max), 150-volt DC motor. Top speed is 70 mph (112 km/hr), with a cruising speed of 55 mph (88 km/hr). Acceleration from zero to 30 mph (48 km/hr) is 8 seconds. In a test conducted by Detroit Testing Lab, Inc., a Silver

Volt travelled 307.5 miles (495 km) in 12 hours at an average speed of 43.3 mph (70 km/hr) with intermittent fast charges. The APU was not used during this test. In a similar test, the vehicle travelled 212.4 miles (341 km) in 8 hours.

The vehicle's performance is due to the lead-cobalt battery which can be recharged to 80% of its capacity in 45 minutes. The lead-cobalt battery differs from a conventional lead-acid battery in two basic ways: 1) All positive and negative plates are connected in three places compared to only one point of connection. According to E.A.C., "these multiple interplate electrical connections greatly enhance the ability of the cell to accept and deliver currents at high rates." Also, 2) Cobalt is added to the electrolyte "to act as an anti-catalyst, both prolonging plate life and inhibiting the formation of harmful stibine gas." Company tests have produced 50 continuous months of electric vehicle use on lead-cobalt battery packs which is the equivalent of up to 50,000 miles (80,450 km) driving. E.A.C. rates its energy density at 17 wh/lb (37.6 wh/kg) at the 6-hour rate and 12.5 wh/lb (27.6 wh/kg) at the one-hour rate, and 800 life cycles.

The heart of the "Fast Charge System" is to establish a network of Electric Auto Charge Stations equipped with three regular charge outlets and one fast-charge outlet.

The Silver Volt is being developed into a volume production automobile with licensed dealerships. Full production will commence upon completion of testing in Fort Lauderdale, Florida. For more information, contact The Electric Auto Corporation, 2237 Elliott Avenue, Troy, MI 48084.

Photos courtesy of Unique Mobility

UNIQUE MOBILITY ELECTREK HATCHBACK

Unique Mobility

UNIQUE MOBILITY produces two electric automobile models available to the general public, named the "ELECTREK UNCAR." The 2 + 2 sedan or two-seat hatchback has a top speed of 75 mph (121 km/hr) and accelerates from zero to 30 mph (48 km/hr) in 9 seconds. Cruising range at a constant 40 mph (64 km/hr) is 100 miles (161 km).

The two-seat hatchback has a 20 cubic foot (.57 cubic meter) to 35 cubic foot (.99 cubic meter) carrying capacity, depending upon the use of the second seat. The body, made of fiberglass reinforced plastic (FRP), was de-signed and built from the ground up as an electric automobile.

The mechanical features include a specially-designed solid state controller, four-speed manual transmission and a 32 hp separately ex-cited DC motor. The 2650-lb (1202-kg) vehicle carries a 1014-lb (460-kg) battery pack con-sisting of sixteen 6-volt lead-acid batteries. Energy costs are estimated to be 1¢ per mile.

For more information, contact UNIQUE MOBILITY, 3730 So. Jason, Englewood, CO 80110.

Lektrikar II

The "LEKTRIKAR II" is a 4-passenger electric car produced by Western Research Industries. This 3200-lb (1451-kg) sedan has a maximum cruising range of 70 miles (112 km) and a top speed of 75 miles per hour (120 km/hr). Power from the 1260-lb (571-kg) 108-volt lead-acid bat-tery pack is directed through an SCR controller to a series-wound 22-hp motor. Acceleration is zero to 30 mph (48 km/hr) in 8 seconds with a cruising speed of 55 mph (88 km/hr). Energy consumption is rated at .16 kwh/mile at 45 mph (72 km/hr) with a 500-cycle projected battery life.

The "LEKTRIKAR II" is a production automobile available to the general public from Western Research Industries, 3013 West Sahara Avenue, Las Vegas, NV 89102.

LEKTRIKAR II   Photo courtesy Western Research Industries

ELECTRIC BY SOUTH COAST TECHNOLOGY

Photo courtesy of South Coast Technology, Inc.

Electric by SCT

South Coast Technology, Incorporated, produces the "ELECTRIC BY SCT," a 2-passenger electric automobile that uses the Volkswagen Rabbit body. The 3100-lb (1410 kg) sedan has a top speed of 65 mph (105 km/hr), a cruising speed of 55 mph (89 km/hr), and an acceleration rate of zero to 30 mph (48 km/hr) in 10 seconds. A 70-mile (112-km) maximum range is based on a steady moderate speed of 45 mph (72 km/hr) with only occasional stops. The transistor chopper and 17-kw separately-excited motor are matched to a 4-speed manual transmission. Power is supplied by 18 ESB 6-volt lead-acid batteries.

This vehicle is marketed to the public in limited quantities and will be available with additional VW body styles, including pick-up trucks. For price and delivery information, write South Coast Technology, Inc., P.O. Box 3265, Santa Barbara, CA 93105.

Utopia GL

The Utopia GL is a four-passenger production electric automobile which is built with a modified Ford Pinto two-door coupe body. Stated range for the 2700-lb (1224-kg) sedan is 120 miles (193 km) at 20 mph (32 km/hr), 96 miles (154 km) at 35 mph (56 km/hr) and 42 miles (67 km) at 55 mph (88 km/hr). Acceleration is zero to 30 mph (48 km/hr) in 15 seconds and top speed is 55 mph (88 km/hr).

Sixteen lead-acid batteries weighing 880 lbs (400 kg) supply power to a pair of 96-volt 6-kw motors through a "mechanical logic" controller equipped with regenerative braking.

As an option, the company offers a one-wheeled trailer with an on-board generator which provides unlimited range for the Utopia GL.

Present research efforts include work on a new controller which will allow the use of AC induction motors.

UTOPIA GL

For more information regarding vehicle price options and local availability, contact Utopia Electric Vehicles, Inc., P.O. Box 9308, Tampa, FL 33674.

CHEVROLET ELECTROVETTE

This is a clay model study of an electric car concept which General Motors is pressing ahead with in its Electric Car Project Center.

Chevrolet Electrovette

The Electrovette is a General Motors electric prototype which has been introduced in two versions. The original Electrovette was a two-passenger sedan powered by twenty lead-acid batteries weighing 920 lb (417 kg).

The front-wheel drive prototype weighed 2,950 lb (1338 kg) and had a top speed of 53 mph (85 km/hr) with acceleration from zero to 30 mph (48 km/hr) in 8.2 seconds. Range was 50 miles (80 km) at 30 mph (48 km/hr).

In September, 1979, a second version of the Electrovette was introduced with a zinc-nickel oxide (nickel-zinc) battery pack. The 3,050 lb (1383 kg) vehicle uses a 240-volt DC motor with an on-board computer which serves as a signal control processor or "brain" of the system. Motor speed is regulated by a solid-state chopper and yields a top speed of about 50 mph (80 km/hr) with a range of 100 miles (161 km). Anticipated battery life is estimated at 30,000 miles (48,270 km) with improved nickel-zinc batteries.

The original Electrovette used lead-acid batteries rated at 12 wh/lb (26 wh/kg), while their new nickel-zinc rating is 27 wh/lb (60 wh/kg) with a goal of 32 wh/lb (70 wh/kg).

In January, 1980, General Motors established a new Electric Passenger Car Project Center in Warren, Michigan, to design and engineer an electric commuter car. This idea center will involve many divisions to enable GM to realize its goal of introducing to the public a production urban electric with a top speed of around 50 mph (80 km/hr) and a range of 100 miles (161 km) by the mid-1980's.

The next generation GM electric vehicle power system is the lithium-iron sulfide battery which has been under development at GM for many years. The high temperature (800° F) system cell has been tested to 16,000 hours and more than 750 cycles. At the four-hour discharge rate the energy density was 41 wh/lb (90 wh/kg) or about 3½ times that of conventional batteries.

While the lithium-iron sulfide battery promises a significant improvement in vehicle performance, it must be considered a long-term solution.

The Solar Surrey

Lawrence Livermore Laboratories, operated by the University of California for the Department of Energy, has built the Solar Surrey to test the reliability of a variety of solar cells. Scientist Guy Armantrout (pictured) tests the vehicle, which is powered by 484 silicon solar cells. It can travel up to 6 miles (9.6 km) at speeds to 11 mph (17.6 km/hr) on one sunny day's charge of electricity. The solar cell array, which is similar to those used in space satellites, is placed over the cab of the vehicle.

EKECTRICAR I   Photos courtesy U.S. Electricar Corporation

LECTRIC LEOPARD I (MODIFIED RENAULT)

LECTRIC LEOPARD (VOLKSWAGEN CHASSIS)

LECTRIC LEOPARD (FIAT STRADA)

U.S. ELECTRICAR CORPORATION

The U.S. Electricar Corporation of Athol, Massachusetts, was formed in March, 1978, by Chandler H. Waterman to manufacture electric passenger automobiles for public and fleet use. The founding company, C. H. Waterman Industries, is responsible for a number of on-road electric models such as Datsuns, Pintos, DAFS, Renaults, and others in daily use since 1971.

Currently the company offers three electric passenger models called the "Lectric Leopards." One model, the Lectric Leopard I, uses a modified Renault LeCar body and chassis. This 2580-lb (1170-kg) four-passenger sedan has a top speed of 55 mph (88 km/hr) and a range 60-80 miles (96-128 km) per charge under average driving conditions. A DOE test made in 1978 yielded a 117 mile (188 km) range at a constant speed of 25 mph (40 km/hr). This vehicle carries 16 lead-acid batteries weighing 1050 lbs (476 kg) and uses a 16-hp Prestolite compound wound motor through a two-step contactor control or an optional SCR solid state controller. Acceleration is zero to 30 mph (48 km/hr) in 15 seconds.

The Lectric Leopard I uses the basic power train system used in all Lectric Leopard models except for a 20-hp motor in the Lectric Leopard II which is modelled after the Fiat Strada. The Strada models weigh 500 lbs (226 kg) more than the Le Car-based Leopard I.

The Lectric Leopard II has a custom-designed fiberglass body on a Volkswagen chassis and uses the same drive components and battery configuration of the Leopard I. A newer version of this model may use a Fiat chassis.

The U.S. Electricar Corporation is forming a growing dealership network as production capability increases with expanded manufacturing facilities. Long term corporate goals indicate that additional new models will be introduced using other FIAT body styles.

For information about availability from local dealerships, contact The U.S. Electricar Corporation, 250 South Main Street, Athol, MA 01331.

Free-Way Electric

The Free-Way, an electric vehicle that is capable of freeway speeds, has been developed by H-M-Vehicles, Inc. of Apple Valley, Minnesota. The first prototype of the three-wheeled hatchback won the Twin Cities Great Economy Race in 1977 and 1978.

The Free-Way comes in five basic models: two electric and three gasoline-powered. The electric version has a cruising range of 50 miles (80 km) at 40 mph (64 km/hr), with a maximum range of 75 miles (121 km). Top speed is over 55 mph (88 km/hr), and acceleration is zero to 30 mph (48 km/hr) in a brisk 7 seconds. The 600-lb (272-kg) vehicle uses a 4-hp permanent magnet motor and is powered by four 12-volt batteries. This lightweight car, with two wheels in front for greater stability, has been designed for op-

Photos courtesy H-M-Vehicles, Inc.

timum range at freeway speed. Although the Free-Way is basically designed for one person, a passenger can be carried behind the driver.

All models of the three-wheeled Free-Way have a variable-speed automatic transmission, regenerative braking, and steel-frame chassis covered with fiberglass. The Free-Way is sold completely assembled, batteries included. For more information regarding prices, delivery and how to obtain their book *High Mileage Vehicles a New Technology*, contact H-M-Vehicles, Inc., 6276 Greenleaf Trail, Apple Valley, MN 55124.

Die Mesh Spider

The experimental Die Mesh Spider is based on a 1972 converted FIAT 850. Three 3.2 hp electric motors produce a top speed of 55 mph (88 km/hr). The power pack of 18 lead-acid batteries provides a 42 mile (67 km) range. Total vehicle weight is 2850 lbs (1292 kg).

Die Mesh has been involved with electric vehicle research since 1968. One development is an infinitely variable traction transmission which permits continually variable output speeds from a constant input speed.

DIE MESH SPIDER   Photo courtesy of Die Mesh Corp.

ELECTRIC PASSENGER CARS

ELECTRIC PASSENGER CARS AND VANS

For many years, Electric Passenger Cars and Vans, Inc. of San Diego, California, has produced a number of innovative electric and hybrid vehicles under the direction of Peter Rubie.

The original "Hummingbird I" was a prototype which used the Volkswagen 181 "Thing" body.

A second development prototype, the "Hummingbird II," uses the Volkswagen Rabbit body. This model weighs 2570 lbs (1165 kg) and uses 12 6-volt lead-acid batteries and a 15-hp series-wound motor to yield a range of 50 miles (80 km) at 40 mph (64 km/hr) with a top speed of 52 mph (84 km/hr).

Another production prototype, the "Hummingbird Hybrid MK IV," is a four-passenger electric hybrid automobile which uses a converted Pinto sedan or station wagon body with internal combustion components removed (including gas tank).

The MK IV is a series hybrid with a 7.5-kw gasoline generator supplying energy which has been extracted from the batteries during vehicle operation. Recharging is accomplished in the hybrid mode or, while the vehicle is stationary, by using the on-board generator or built-in charger. Performance capabilities are said to be a range, on level ground at 50 mph (80 km/hr), of at least 40 miles (64 km) without hybrid and 58 miles (93 km) in hybrid mode. Acceleration from zero to 30 mph (48 km/hr) is 11 seconds. Mechanical components of the MK IV include 16 6-volt Trojan T135 batteries with power directed to the 22-hp Prestolite series motor from a Cableform controller with regenerative braking. Curb weight of the hybrid is 3150 lbs (1428 kg). A Hummingbird KSV (Kinetic Safety Vehicle) body was displayed at the Electric Vehicle Expo in 1978. The vehicle uses a patented crash resistant body, developed by Vicom International, which is designed to give small cars the safety of larger vehicles.

The Hummingbird Hybrid Van is a conversion of a VW "Kombi" with the internal combustion engine components removed. In operation and recharging, the Hybrid Van is similar to the MK IV Hybrid. The 3500-lb (1588-kg) van uses virtually all of the same drive components as listed for the MK IV. Top speed is 55 mph (88 km/hr) and acceleration from zero to 30 mph (48 km/hr) is 15 seconds. Range on level ground at 50 mph (80 km/hr) is said to be at least 35 miles (56 km) without using hybrid power and 62 miles (100 km) in the hybrid mode. City range without hybrid operation is at least 50 miles (80 km) and 100 miles (161 km) in hybrid mode.

The Hummingbird Van is now being fitted with an Iron Redox Energy System which is expected to increase range and performance (see battery chapter).

For current vehicle availability, price, and delivery information, write Electric Passenger Cars and Vans, Inc., 5127 Galt Way, San Diego, CA 92117.

ELECTRIC PASSENGER VAN

HENNEY KILOWATT

MURRILL MOTOR'S 3XE

B&Z ELECTRA KING

Henney Kilowatt

The origins of Henney Kilowatt date back to 1961 when vacuum cleaner manufacturer Eureka Williams converted a Renault Dauphine to electric power. The current manufacturer, Design Innovations, purchased forty of these vehicles at a distress sale, and made improvements upon the vehicle design and performance. Henney Kilowatt has been available to the public since October, 1978.

The two-passenger vehicle has a cruising speed of 40 mph (64 km/hr) and a cruising range of 60 miles (97 km) at 35 mph (56 km/hr). The 2545-lb (1154-kg) Henney Kilowatt carries 14 6-volt lead-acid batteries and is powered by a 7-hp DC motor.

For more information, contact Robert Steven Witcoff, Design Innovations, 46 Kirkwood Drive, Glen Cove, NY 11542.

Murrill Motor's 3XE

The two-passenger 3XE convertible carries six 6-volt batteries. Propulsion is provided by two 2.5-hp DC motors. The 950-lb (431-kg) vehicle can accelerate to 30 mph (48 km/hr) in ten seconds and has a cruising speed of 45 mph (72 km/hr). The plastic bodied convertible has a cruising range of 100 miles (161 km) at 40 mph (64 km/hr). Drive train features include direct drive from the motors with motor switching to provide reverse motion and an A.G.E. solid state controller without regenerative braking.

Company plans include vehicle production for sale to the public. For more information, contact Murrill Motors, P.O. Box 41588, Sacramento, CA 95841.

B & Z Electric Car

The B & Z Electric Car Company of Signal Hill, California, U.S.A., produces the B & Z electric car, which is a three- or four-wheel, two-passenger, two-door coupe. They also produce a "Rancho," 1/4-ton pickup truck, a "Long Rancho" 1/2-ton pickup and the four passenger "Surrey." Each vehicle is custom made.

The B & Z car has a top speed of 18 to 32 mph (29 to 52 km/hr) depending on the horsepower of the motor selected. Motors range from 1 to 3-1/2 horsepower. The standard battery pack is 336 lbs (152 kg) with additional battery packs available. The range is 22 to 56 miles per charge (35 to 90 km), depending on battery selection.

EP-10A ELECTRIC MINI-CAR

3-E Vehicles

By no means a stranger to the field of electric vehicles, 3-E Vehicles has a history of contributions. Formerly producer of a mini-car kit, the company, under the direction of Paul Shipps, is currently developing several production prototypes. Shipps has written several publications, home-built manuals, and technical papers, as well as a report to the U.S. Department of Energy on the performance of various power systems for small electric vehicles.

3-E Vehicle's new models, which may be available as moderate-cost production vehicles in 1982, are derived from the XEP-100 Sport Commuter. These models are referred to as "Neighborhood Safety Cars," which are three-wheelers with styling similar to the Sport Commuter. The fiber-reinforced plastic-bodied vehicles are noted for their safety features, including a bumper system designed to protect the operator and pedestrians or cyclists. Two of the three models can be registered as motorized bicycles. The models differ in weight and power. The first model is the lightest and least expensive. With a curb weight of 550 lb (249 kg)

the three-wheeler houses 4 deep-cycle, 12-volt batteries and is geared for a maximum speed of either 25 or 30 mph (40 km/hr or 48 km/hr). The second model is essentially the same, but uses six heavier, 6-volt batteries. The third model is planned to have a curb weight of about 765 lb (347 kg) and a more powerful motor and battery pack which will allow speeds of 45 to 55 mph (72 km/hr to 88 km/hr).

As noted previously, another service offered by Shipps and 3-E Vehicles is the preparation of detailed engineering manuals and supplements for home-built conversions of various subcompact automobiles to electric power. The manual, "Engineering Data-Electric Vehicle Conversions—the 1980's," describes basic technical data associated with the mechanics and operation of vehicles powered by electricity. Topics covered within the manual include the basics of road loads, minimizing drive train losses, minimizing power circuit losses, DC motors and their installed performance, control systems and efficiencies, batteries and their installed performance curves, battery life and cost table with selection curves, vehicle weight minimization and distribution, and a set of engineering data work sheet forms to simplify the selection of a battery pack and gear ratios to optimize range, speed, climbing, and acceleration appropriate to the converter's needs. The basic manual treats several conversion variations of the Ford Pinto and Fiat 128 as examples.

Specific supplements to the manual are also available which review technical details of conversion vehicles such as: Chevette, Honda Civic, Datsun 210, Ford Fiesta, VW Rabbit, VW Beetle, Toyota Corolla, and Renault 5/LeCar.

For information regarding vehicles, manuals or supplements, contact Paul R. Shipps, President and Technical Director, 3-E Vehicles, P.O. Box 19409, San Diego, CA 92119.

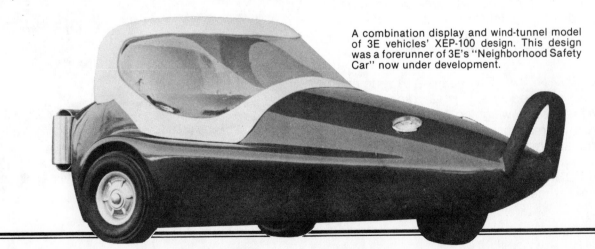

A combination display and wind-tunnel model of 3E vehicles' XEP-100 design. This design was a forerunner of 3E's "Neighborhood Safety Car" now under development.

SEARS "XDH-1" RESEARCH CAR

Photo courtesy of Sears Roebuck and Company

Sears, Roebuck and Co., U.S.A.— "XDH-1"

In the early days of automobile pioneering, the Sears Roebuck Company produced a variety of motor carriages which competed for the market of gasoline-powered cars. Eventually, the company divested itself of their automobile production division because they found there was more money to be made selling parts for Henry Ford's "Model T."

In 1953, Sears introduced the "Allstate." This automobile was a version of the Kaiser "Henry J" compact model, and was the last attempt for a Sears bid into the automobile production industry.

Today, Sears has put its name on an experimental electric automobile—not for the purpose of introducing a new model, but as a means to promote its line of "DieHard" batteries.

The "XDH-1," which means "experimental DieHard number one," is a reconstructed Italian Fiat 128-3P weighing 3,110 lbs (1411 kg).

Sears claims no intention of marketing an electric automobile in the forseeable future, and has no ties with the Fiat company.

The XDH-1 is powered by twenty Sears Die-Hard experimental electric vehicle batteries.

This front-wheel-drive vehicle carries five batteries in front and fifteen in the rear. Cruising range is 90 miles (145 km) at 47 mph (76 km/hr). A four-speed transmission with clutch allows speeds of up to 75 mph (121 km/hr) using a compound-wound 120-volt World War II airplane starter motor rated at 40 hp peak. Other features include a solid state controller and regenerative braking.

Photo courtesy of Sears Roebuck and Company

KESLING YARE

Photos courtesy of Dr. H.D. Kesling

Kesling Yare

The Yare is a totally streamlined, $60,000 proto-type vehicle built by Dr. H.D. Kesling, of Westville, Indiana, U.S.A.

It has an elongated, egg-shaped appearance and its four wheels are arranged in a diamond pattern. The front and back wheels, centrally located, are used for steering; power is applied to

KESLING YARE POWER PLANT

the side wheels, which are just slightly rear of center. As the vehicle steers, the body tilts in one direction, which results in one side being six to ten inches higher than the other. This feature also allows easy entrance to the vehicle.

The "Yare" is a nautical term, meaning complete, eager, lively, prepared, fit to move, easily worked, manageable and active.

Performance yields a 55 mph speed (88 km/hr) in 12 seconds from a 12 hp motor. The 72-volt battery pack produces a range of over 50 miles (80 km) per charge. The total weight is 2,300 lbs (1043 kg), with a height of only 52 inches (130 cm).

Dr. Kesling believes that if this car were put into production it would sell for about $4,000, and that it would conceivably be produced by a boat manufacturer rather than an auto maker.

The twelve 6-volt golf cart batteries are positioned in the frame as shown. The power plant of the vehicle is a tricycle formed by the two side wheels and the rear wheel, which can be disconnected in a few minutes from the body. Seating arrangement makes it possible for three adults and two children to ride comfortably in the "hull."

COPPER DEVELOPMENT CAR

Photo courtesy of
Copper Development
Association

COPPER ELECTRIC RUNABOUT

Photo courtesy of
Copper Development
Association

Copper Development Association

Copper Electric Town Car is a dramatic, stream-lined electric vehicle of advanced prototype design conceived by the Copper Development Association, Inc., the copper and brass industry's advanced market development arm.

The electric Town Car has a range of 103 miles (165.8 km) at a cruising speed of 40 mph (64 km/hr) and a 73.3 mile (118 km) range in start-and-stop city driving. Acceleration is a brisk zero to 30 mph (48 km/hr) in 8.8 seconds, with a top speed of 59 miles per hour (95 km/hr). The two- seater hatchback model uses existing components and innovative technology, and is designed for optimum range. The 2,952 lb (1339 kg) vehicle carries approximately 1,200 lbs (544 km) of batteries with battery weight expected to be reduced when state-of-the-art batteries become more efficient. To minimize mechanical friction, radial tires and other measures were used. To assure low wind resistance, a stream-lined shape, smooth underpan, flush windows and windshield wipers concealed by a flush panel were incorporated into the design.

The eighteen 6-volt lead-acid storage batteries can be recharged overnight. The motor is specially wound, separately excited, and matched to a control system which provides the highest possible efficiency using production components.

The Copper Development Association, Inc., produced this vehicle to keynote the unique properties of copper in electric vehicle production. Copper and copper alloys are used in motor windings, battery cables, and a variety of components which are a valuable contribution to the production considerations of electric vehicles.

Copper alloy tubing used for hydraulic brake lines and copper alloy brake drums are used in all four wheels. This vehicle also incorporates regenerative braking. In a suburban cycle of two stops per mile, reaching 35 mph (56 km/hr), the range without regenerative braking was 68.7 miles (110.6 km) per charge, compared to 73.3 miles (118.0 km) per charge with regenerative braking.

Copper Electric Runabout

To date, the Copper Development Association has conceived six electric vehicle projects, the latest of which, the Copper Electric Runabout, is a new four passenger automobile with several distinct advantages over the Town Car.

The Runabout's most noteworthy feature is the four passenger, three door design configuration, with the rear-seat occupants facing rearwards. This vehicle can be described as "short but roomy," and built tall to eliminate the psychological feeling of smallness.

The body is constructed of fiberglass reinforced polyester. The chassis includes a "backbone" design which houses the batteries in the center of the vehicle. The 12 advanced lead-acid batteries are manufactured by Globe-Union and weigh 822 lbs (373 kg). Total vehicle weight is 2,152 lbs (980 kg), which is about one third lighter than the Copper Electric Town Car.

The 14 hp (1 hour rating) motor can accelerate the vehicle from 0-30 mph (48 km/hr) in 8.6 seconds. Top speed is 59 mph (95 km/hr), and the cruising range is 72 miles (116 km) at a constant 40 mph (64 km/hr). A city driving cycle of two stops per mile with a 35 mph (56 km/hr) maximum speed between stops yielded a 79 mile (127 km) range.

G.E. CENTENNIAL ELECTRIC

Photo courtesy of the General Electric Company

G.E. Centennial Electric

The Centennial Electric was built to honor the 100th birthday of the General Electric Company. This sleek, low-slung, experimental four passenger sedan will serve as a test bed for General Electric products. Although the company does not plan to market the vehicle, it is prepared to supply automobile manufacturers with G.E. motors, solid state controllers, and other essential components.

The front-wheel drive subcompact was designed "from the ground up" using commercially available off-the-shelf components and battery systems.

A 24 hp G.E. motor and 18 Globe-Union advanced lead acid batteries, mounted in a centrally located chassis tunnel, supply the power through a G.E. Solid-State controller. The vehicle features a stainless steel underbody and chassis and a hatchback for rear seat passengers. Total weight, including batteries, is 3,250 lbs (1500 kg).

The stop-and-go range is 45 miles (72 km) based on the SAE-J227a/D driving cycle. At a constant 40 mph (64 km/hr), the vehicle can travel 75 miles on a single charge. Accelleration is 0-30 mph (48 km/hr) in nine seconds, and top speed is 60 mph (97 km/hr).

The Centennial Electric was built to G.E.

specifications by Triad Services of Dearborn, Michigan, USA. Triad Services is an engineering design company headed by Michael A. Pocobello, who is responsible for many electric vehicle prototypes including the Copper Development Van and the Copper Electric Town Car.

Photo courtesy of the General Electric Company

Eighteen Globe-Union advanced lead-acid batteries, weighing 1,225 lbs (555 kg), are stored in a movable trolley in the centrally located chassis tunnel.

THE ELECTRIC AUTOMOBILE, IMMEDIATE FUTURE—AN EXPERT OPINION

There are few men in the world today that possess more experience in electric vehicle design and development than does Robert McKee, president and founder of the McKee Engineering Corporation in Palatine, Illinois. McKee has experience in development and engineering design that began over sixteen years ago, and has developed vehicles ranging from Formula A and Can-Am designs to the Howmet Turbine Cars that currently hold six international records.

McKee Engineering has contributed a myriad of innovations to all forms of vehicle development. For over nine years, concentration has been directed toward electric vehicles. McKee is the pioneer of the backbone frame concept. In this system, the batteries are situated in the center of the vehicle, surrounded by frame members. This provides easy access to the batteries, which roll out on a tray. Several prototype models use this system, which permits battery exchanges in less than five mintues.

Globe-Union Endura

The "Endura" is a four-passenger fiberglass experimental prototype built by McKee Engineering for Globe-Union, Milwaukee, Wisconsin. Globe-Union, a major battery manufacturer, produces batteries under many trade names including Sears, Ford, Jeep, Caterpillar, NAPA, AMC, Interstate, Farm & Fleet, and Gibson.

GLOBE-UNION ENDURA

The Endura carries 20 Globe-Union lead-acid electric vehicle batteries weighing a total of 1300 lbs (590 kg). A 25 hp series-wound DC motor with a rear-wheel-powered transaxle is regulated by a solid-state controller from the 120-volt battery pack.

The vehicle weighs 3,200 lbs (1,451 kg) and features a fiberglass shell with integral steel roll cage for strength. The chassis is lightweight aluminum with backbone frame to house batteries and provide a low center of gravity. A removable rear quarter panel converts the Endura from a 2 + 2 coupe into a station wagon.

Top speed is 60 mph (97 km/hr); acceleration is 0 to 30 mph (48 km/hr) in 8.7 seconds. Range is 115 miles at 35 mph (185 km at 56 km/hr).

Globe-Union Maxima

The Globe-Union Maxima is a prototype five passenger station wagon designed as a test bed for Globe batteries.

Top speed is up to 75 mph (120 km/hr) using a 20 hp General Electric Motor and 240 volt electrical system consisting of twenty specially formulated deep cycle 12 volt batteries. Total vehicle weight is 4,350 lbs (1978 kg).

Globe-Union, Inc. is the world's largest manufacturer of "replacement" automotive batteries.

The Maxima was designed and built by Globe-Union.

GLOBE-UNION MAXIMA
Photo courtesy of Globe-Union, Inc.

McKEE "SUNDANCER"

Photo courtesy of McKee Engineering

Corporations such as ESB, Inc., (Electric Storage Battery Company), Barrett Electronics, Victor Comptometer, McCulloch, Westinghouse, Autodynamics, Electric Fuel Propulsion, Linear Alpha, and Globe Union have used the capable skills of McKee Engineering. In each case, the design and implementation of the prototype vehicle was suited to individual needs. McKee Engineering has designed, built, and tested more "on-road" experimental electric vehicles than any company in the United States.

McKee SUNDANCER

The "Sundancer" is an experimental, two passenger prototype built by McKee Engineering, Palatine, Illinois, U.S.A., for the ESB Corporation, Philadelphia, Pennsylvania. ESB (Electric Storage Battery), a major battery manufacturer committed to the advancement of battery and electric vehicle technology, commissioned the construction of two Sundancers to serve as test beds for batteries, controllers and motors.

Features of the Sundancer are: rear mounted 8 hp motor with two speed transaxle, fiberglass body and backbone frame with front loading battery tray.

Top speed is 60 miles per hour (96 km/hr); range is 80 miles (130 km) city and 120 miles (193 km) at a steady 30 mph (48 km/hr). Acceleration is 0 to 30 mph (48 km/hr) in 9 seconds. Weight is 1600 lbs (725 kg) of which 850 lbs (386 kg) is batteries.

Photo courtesy of McKee Engineering

SUNDANCER BACKBONE FRAME

Mr. Robert McKee, president of McKee Engineering, demonstrates the operation of the Sundancer's front-loading battery tray. A fresh set of batteries can be installed in less than five minutes.

The backbone frame, a McKee innovation, allows for a low center of gravity and isolates batteries from the car's occupants.

U.S. ELECTRIC TRUCKS

Today, there is a large potential market for electric pickup and delivery trucks. Commercial vehicles can begin to reduce the consumption of gasoline and lower urban pollution in the immediate future.

The economics are better for fleet ownership than individual ownership in the electric truck industry. Fleet-size operations using ten or more vehicles and delivery circuits with stop-and-start driving of forty to fifty miles (64 to 80 km) per day are best suited for this application. The upkeep necessary for these vehicles would be accomplished by the same facility now used for an existing fleet. Maintenance would largely serve battery needs, while the mechanical maintenance should be low as indicated by the dependability record of electric vehicles in general.

Some applications most suited include wholesale/retail deliveries, food processors, parcel and mail delivery, rental trucks, gas and electric utility service, and small business applications such as bakeries, florists, and pizza delivery.

GoLIAth Program . . . . Lead Industries Assn.

In the U.S., one of the leaders in the promotion and dissemination of electric vehicle information to the industry and public has been the Lead Industries Association (LIA). LIA has mounted a continuing effort to build a market and, more importantly, an acceptance of electric trucks, buses, and cars by both the commercial and public sectors.

As early as 1974, LIA started a program to provide needed electric vehicle information—a program that examined in depth some of the problems faced by on-the-road electric delivery vehicles.

To implement this program, LIA joined forces with the electric utility industry and one of its own trade groups, the Electric Vehicle Council (EVC). The LIA brainchild manifested itself in the form of a lightweight, battery-operated truck appropriately named GoLIAth.

LIA's GoLIAth was designed as a test bed around lead-acid batteries to exhibit the appropriateness of this type of energy system for short-haul multiple stop, pick-up, and delivery services. Data was also designed to include personal transportation routes and commercial/industrial applications.

January, 1974, marked the beginning of a year-long tour for GoLIAth. Starting in New York City and including 25 major cities in the U.S. and Canada, GoLIAth proceeded to fulfill the four major objectives of the LIA program:

1. To educate industry and important segments of the commercial market that a lead-battery powered vehicle can do the job and is available now.

GoLIAth Photo courtesy of Lead Industries Association

2. To determine the role that lead-acid batteries play in the developing electric vehicle industry.
3. To determine the parameters of work-service situations which lend themselves to electric vehicle use.
4. To help determine the effect of electric vehicle delivery use on the load of electric utilities.

During the 2500-mile (4000km) tour, GoLIAth performed a variety of demanding tasks that included delivery of parcels, newspapers, sewing machines, mail, and tools. It carried men and machines for park maintenance, and transported people and equipment. Demonstrations of the vehicle's capabilities were provided for environmental agencies, city, state, and Federal officials, and for business and industry representatives.

NATIONAL PARK SERVICE VEHICLES

Photo courtesy Dave Goldstein

The Electric Vehicle Program of the U.S. National Park Service

One of management's goals for the nation's capital parks in Washington, D.C., has been to evaluate conservation techniques to discover better and more economical ways to service and maintain grounds. The electric vehicle has emerged as a means to provide energy-efficient service and avoid the environmental problems associated with conventional park transportation.

As far back as 1973, the National Park Service's National Capital Region (NCR) has been modifying electric vehicles to suit park needs.

John Hoke, NCR's Urban Park Specialist, explored ways the parks could benefit from electric-powered transportation. By the end of 1979, NCR could boast of the most diverse fleet of vehicles powered by electricity with new applications expanding daily.

Another promising concept which offers the potential solution to these problems is "hybridization." By incorporating an onboard gasoline-powered generator, vehicle range is significantly extended. Also encouraging is the use of a Stirling engine generator assembly and nickel-zinc batteries which store 2.5 times the reserve energy of conventional lead-acid batteries. A successful 180-mile (290-km) test run was performed on a small electric golf cart equipped with these features. Hoke has sought industry cooperation to help package his innovative concepts.

Due to their experience, NCR is now in a position to offer other government agencies guidance in developing similar programs. Numerous articles and reports published by NCR have attracted national and international recognition. The NCR effort has helped the electric vehicle earn a permanent role in park operations and recognition as one solution to the challenge of improved resource management.

U.S. POSTAL SERVICE ELECTRIC VEHICLES   Photo courtesy of AM General Corp.

The United States Postal Service Electric Vehicle Program

In the future, one major user of electric vehicles will be the U.S. Postal Service. If the current electric vehicle demonstration program now in effect continues to prove electric vehicle superiority, as many as 30,000 conventional vehicles (trucks, vans, and passenger cars) will be converted to electric power.

If these plans become a reality, there will be a large ongoing market for electric vehicles, with up to 15,000 new vehicles required each year.

Studies for electric postal vehicles began in 1971, using an English Harbilt Electric Van. In a Cupertino, California, operation, Harbilt trucks were in continuous use for two years, exhibiting about 1,800 vehicle-days of service with a total of only 33 days down time, as of September 1, 1977. In this test the vehicles were on the street less than five hours a day with about eleven miles per day average. Nevertheless, this constituted an annual mileage of about 3,200 miles (5,149 km).

The Harbilt Vans in the Cupertino test operated on 1.3 kilowatt hours per mile (.8¢ kwh/km). At 2.8¢ per kilowatt hour, fuel costs equalled about 3½¢ per mile (2.1¢ per km) compared to almost 6¢ (3.7¢ per km) for a comparable gasoline-powered vehicle. As gasoline prices go up, the disparity in price becomes more pronounced.

Because of the success of the Cupertino pro-gram, the U.S. Postal Service has purchased 350 additional electric vehicles built by A. M. General Corporation, which is a subsidiary of American Motors. The converted "Jeep type" vehicles were delivered from May, 1975, to March, 1976.

Of the 350 Jeeps 300 are operating in southern California, which is one of the nation's most severe smog areas. Other vehicles were placed in diverse climates for testing purposes.

To date, the vehicles are performing with few problems and data will soon provide the program with annual costs based on fuel and maintenance.

Not all U.S. Post Office routes are suited for electric vehicles. However, a review by the post office indicates that at least 30,000 routes could be serviced by this type of vehicle.

Reports indicate the possible acquisition of 750 additional electric vans by the postal service. Specifications will be issued and bids taken as soon as the cost analysis is cleared by the board of governors.

Let us hope that the future plans of the post office will include more of these electric vehicles, because they are ideally suited to many of the problems of the postal service and also reduce smog and emissions. Their use by the postal service would be a well-placed step forward as a foothold for the budding electric vehicle industry.

AM GENERAL POSTAL VAN

Photo courtesy of AM General Corp.

AM General Corporation

AM General Corporation is a subsidiary of American Motors located in Wayne, Michigan. In 1974, the company received a $2 million contract from the U.S. Post Office to design and produce 350 Electric Postal Delivery vehicles called the Electruc with a 500 lb (227 kg) payload capacity and top speed of 33 mph (53 km/hr). An Electruc can make 300 stops in five hours within a 20 mile (32 km) range. Maximum range is 30 miles (48 km). Cruising speed is up to 40 miles per hour (64 km/hr).

Eleven Electrucs were sold to divisions of American Telephone & Telegraph (AT&T), five of which operate at the telephone division of New York Bell. Other Electrucs were tested in Indiana and Minnesota, and one Electruc is in a demonstration program at Bell Laboratories in Murray Hill, New Jersey.

AM General Corporation is the first major U.S. company to produce electric vehicles in significant numbers.

Grumman Postal Truck

Grumman Allied Industries has designed a prototype light-duty delivery truck to meet the requirements of the United States Postal Service and the U.S. Department of Energy.

The design incorporates features such as sliding doors to conform with regulations governing postal vehicles.

A production program will be instituted to service test several of the 500-lb (227-kg) payload capacity vehicles. The current design features an 18-hp Prestolite DC motor, Globe-Union lead-acid batteries, and a General Electric EV-1 SCR controller.

The manufacturer, Grumman Allied Industries, is located at 445 Broad Hollow Road, Melville, NY 11747.

U.S. POSTAL SERVICE TRUCK

JET INDUSTRIES ELECTRICA 007

JET INDUSTRIES 600 VAN

JET INDUSTRIES

Electrica 007

Jet Industries' Electrica 007 is a sleek two-passenger vehicle based on a Dodge Omni sport sedan. The 3625-lb (1643-kg) vehicle reaches a maximum speed of 60 mph (96 km/hr) and has a cruising range of 55 miles (88 km) at 35 mph (56 km/hr).

The Electrica 007 carries a 1320-lb (598-kg) battery pack containing 20 6-volt lead batteries with propulsion provided by a 20-hp DC motor through an SCR controller.

Electra Van 600

The Electra Van 600 was Jet Industries' first battery-powered vehicle. The company now produces five other models. The Electra Van 600 is fashioned after a Subaru van which has five doors for convenient cargo handling. Seating is for two or four passengers.

The 600 has a top driving speed of 55 mph (88 km/hr) and accelerates from 0 to 45 mph (0 to 72 km/hr) in 15 seconds.

The 2690-lb (1219-kg) vehicle carries an 1122-lb (508-kg) battery pack. Propulsion is provided by a 20-hp DC motor through an SCR controller.

Electra Van 750

The Electra Van 750 is one of Jet Industries' 2-door pickup trucks. The vehicle has a cruising speed of 40 mph (64 km/hr) and a top speed of 55 mph (88 km). Batteries account for 1320 lbs (598 kg) of the vehicle's total weight of 3790 lbs (1718 kg). The pickup is powered by a 20-hp DC motor through an SCR controller.

Electra Van 1000

With the introduction of Electra Van 1000, Jet Industries increased carrying capacity by converting a Dodge-bodied van to electric power. This two-passenger commercial vehicle has the same rate of acceleration and maximum speed as its predecessor, the Electra Van 600.

The 4- to 6-door, 4760-lb (2158-kg) van carries 24 6-volt acid-lead batteries which weigh a total of 1584 lb (718 kg).

Propulsion is provided by a 37-hp DC motor through an SCR controller.

The Electra Van 1000 is among a number of vans incorporated into everyday use as part of a U.S. Department of Energy program.

Electra Van 1000P

Jet Industries' Electra Van 1000P is a wider version of the 750 pickup truck with a larger carrying capacity. Capable of accelerating from 0 to 30 mph (0 to 48 km/hr) in 10 seconds, the ''1000P'' can reach a maximum speed of 55 mph (88 km/hr). The 4790-lb (2172-kg) vehicle carries a 1584-lb (718-kg) battery pack consisting of 24 6-volt lead-acid batteries.

The 37-hp DC motor provides propulsion through an SCR controller.

Electra Van 1400

The Electra Van 1400 window van carries eight passengers and is specially designed to transport people to and from convention facilities, hotels, and airports.

The Electra Van 1400 weighs 5460 lbs (2476 kg), uses a 37-hp DC motor and carries 1584 lbs (718 kg) of batteries.

For more information write to Jet Industries, Inc., P.O. Box 17184, Austin, TX 78760.

Battronic Minivan

The Battronic Truck Company, a division of Boyertown Auto Body Works, Boyertown, Pa., U.S.A., has produced the Minivan in conjunction with the Electric Vehicle Council (EVC).

The EVC is a non-profit association dedicated to the proliferation of electric power for transportation. Its membership includes electric power producers, manufacturers of related products, university members, and individuals involved in government and research organizations in nineteen countries throughout the world.

One of the EVC functions is the development of a vehicle which could demonstrate the effectiveness of electric transportation. The Battronic Minivan, a 1/4-ton (227 kg) battery-operated truck, was produced and distributed to 64 U.S. utilities in 32 states. A total of 110 Minivans have accumulated over 100,000 aggregate miles (160,934 km) of on-road experience. The EVC is using this demonstration to gather and tabulate data for research purposes.

The specifications of the Minivan include: an electronic SCR controller, series-wound 112-volt motor and a patented quick-change battery system. Maximum vehicle weight with load is 6,800 lbs (3084 kg); top speed is about 60 mph (97 km/hr).

BATTRONIC MINIVAN   Photo courtesy of Lead Industries Association/Battronic, Inc.

The Volta

The Volta, an electric pick-up truck by Battronic Truck Corporation, has a convenient, patented quick-change feature for battery packs. Volta power packs can be replaced in less than five minutes or about the same time it takes to fill up at the pump. The actual transfer time involved, as determined by independent testing, is three minutes, 42 seconds. A special Battronic Lift is used to simplify the task of changing batteries.

The 4850-lb (2199-kg) Volta has a top speed of 60 mph (95 km/hr). Vehicle acceleration is zero to 30 mph (48 km/hr) in 12 seconds, with a range of 65 miles (105 km) at 25 mph (40 km/hr)

or 35 miles (56 km/hr) at 45 mph (72 km/hr). The Volta meets all U.S. Department of Energy performance requirements.

The 1600-lb (725-kg) battery pack consists of 24 six-volt lead-acid batteries. A 38-hp series-wound DC motor propels the pick-up truck through an SCR controller.

Three battery systems include: 1) electric vehicle batteries with 750 cycles, 2) golf cart type batteries with 300 cycles, and 3) industrial type batteries with 1500 cycles.

For more information, contact Battronic Truck Corporation, Third and Walnut Streets, Boyertown, PA 19512.

VOLTA BATTRONIC PICK TRUCK

COPPER DEVELOPMENT VAN
Photo courtesy of
Copper Development Association

Copper Electric Van IIIB

The Copper Development Association (CDA) sponsored the construction of the CDA Electric Van for the sole purpose of accumulating "in-use" data of electric truck application.

The CDA Van has been leased to the Water Meter Department of the City of Birmingham, Michigan, since November 13, 1973. It has been in daily use on assignments which relate to servicing water meters. The daily mileage ranges from 10 to 60 miles (16 to 96 km), totaling about 7,000 miles (11,250 km) per year.

Features of the experimental van include front-wheel drive, a 22-hp GE DC series motor, automatic transmission, fiberglass body and 1000 lb (454 kg) payload capacity. Top speed is 53 mph (85.3 km/hr); range is 95 miles (152 km) at a constant 40 mph (64 km/hr) at full payload.

Vehicle curb weight is 5,100 lbs (2,312 kg), of which 2,340 lbs (1,064 kg) is lead-acid batteries. The vehicle manufacturer is Antares Engineering.

GMC Electric Van

The GMC Truck & Coach Division has built a limited number of electric vans as part of a U.S. Department of Energy demonstration project. In this program, the 8100-lb (3682-kg) vehicles are designed to meet the fleet requirements of the American Telephone and Telegraph Company.

The electric vans will be used in Southern California for limited range utility operation on a fixed daily downtown or suburban schedule with overnight charging. This type of sheltered operating environment is the perfect "near term" use of electric power for commercial transportation.

Power is supplied from a 2500-lb (1134-kg) lead-acid battery pack through a solid state controller to a 50 hp series-wound DC motor. Acceleration is from zero to 30 mph (48 km/hr) in 12 seconds. Top speed is 50 mph (80 km/hr) and range is 40 miles (64 km) per charge.

The demonstration program vans are the first electric trucks produced by GMC since 1916.

**GMC BATTERY POWERED
COMMERCIAL VAN**

Gould Electric Van

Two electric vans were produced by Gould in 1979. One van is designed for service and delivery duty, the other is directed toward personal use with a 12 passenger capacity.

The vehicles are designed to meet or exceed the DOE performance standards for state-of-the-art electric vehicle technology. For commercial vehicles, these requirements are as follows: the vehicle must accelerate from 0 to 31 mph (50 km/hr) in 15 seconds, and be able to maintain a speed of 46.5 mph (75 km/hr) for 5 minutes. Range can be no less than 31 miles (50 km) per charge.

GOULD ELECTRIC VAN

EVA PICK-UP TRUCKS

Photos courtesy of EVA Corp.

EVA ELECTROVAN

The EVA ElectroVan

The Electric Vehicle Associates of Cleveland, Ohio, have a prototype design for inner-city delivery and shuttle vans. Each van can handle a 500-pound (227-kg) payload with a range of 40 miles (64 km) per charge. A 96-volt 200-amp-hour battery pack is exchanged through side access doors. Duties of the EVA ElectroVan include light hauling, personnel carrying and postal service. For more information write EVA, 9100 Bank St., Cleveland, Ohio 44125.

ELECTROBUS

Photo courtesy of EVA-Chloride

The EVA ElectroBus

The Electric Vehicle Associates, Inc. (EVA) produce and market the ElectroBus, a heavy-duty electric mass-transit vehicle.

Originally, the ElectroBus was developed by the Otis Elevator Company, which divested itself of on-road electric vehicle operation in 1976, selling all rights to EVA. Eleven ElectroBuses have been in transit operation for three years with an excellent performance record, including low operating and maintenance costs. The ElectroBus has been well received by the public.

A new ElectroBus development by EVA incorporates greater passenger capacity and efficiency. The Electrobus is ideally suited for short haul, feeder, and shuttle operation. Power is supplied from a 156-volt traction battery through a thyristor (SCR) control, to a 65-kw heavy-duty traction motor. No transmission is used, because the motor is directly coupled to the differential. Acceleration is zero to 15 miles (24 km) per hour in six seconds and zero to 20 miles (32 km) per hour in ten seconds, with a full passenger load. The vehicle also uses regenerative braking, which reduces brake wear and returns recovered energy back to the batteries.

The 72-volt battery system averages 50 miles (80 km) at a cruising speed of 35 mph (56 km/hr) before recharging.

For more information contact EVA, 9100 Bank Street, Cleveland, OH 44125.

**BATTRONIC
ELECTRIC BUS**

Photo courtesy of Lead Industries Association

Battronic Electric Bus

The Battronic Corporation of Boyertown, Pa., produces various electric buses. Two Battronic buses began serving a bus line in Montevideo, Minnesota, in June, 1978. Each 22-passenger vehicle operates over a 42 mile (67 km) route during a 6½ hour working day.

ELECTRIC-POWERED CYCLES

One of the simplest electric vehicle applications is the two- and three-wheeled cycle configuration.

The electric bicycle was patented in 1895, therefore the concept cannot be considered modern. Unfortunately, the early electric bicycles required heavy batteries and, consequently, heavy frames, wheels, and motors. Yet, some electric two-wheelers had highly ingenious designs, such as motors built into the wheel hub, thus eliminating belt or chain drive.

Modern application of battery and motor design now produces efficient, roadworthy, and economical products. Because of the moderate speeds and the lack of a cumbersome body, the electric bicycle can provide transportation at low cost and high kilowatt-per-hour efficiency.

The "fair weather" aspect of the electric bicycle complements the problems associated with poor battery performance during winter months. Electric bicycles are stored or unused during harsh weather, in the same manner as motorcycles.

And, finally, they are the least expensive of all electric vehicles. A low-cost electric kit which bolts onto a conventional bicycle is well within the budget of anyone. Senior citizens can attach a "helper" electric kit to their three-wheel trikes, and become free to shop and travel.

While there have been many electric-kit manufacturers in the last five years, the following companies have continued to produce and service their products. The companies mentioned can be contacted by those interested in electric kits. New kit manufacturers are occasionally advertised in the science magazines which are written for the general public.

SOLO ELECTRA SCOOTERS   Photo courtesy of Solo Motors, Inc., Newport News, Va.

Solo Electra

The German Solo Electra is a pedal-assisted electric scooter with a top speed of 16 mph (25 km/hr) and a maximum range of 25 miles (40 km) per charge. (Higher speeds are achieved with larger sprockets.) The Bosch 500-watt 24-volt permanent-magnet motor transfers power from two 12-volt, 40-ampere-hour batteries via a two-step vee belt and chain transmission with automatic centrifugal clutch. Front and rear drum brakes and shock absorbers are featured, with a tubular steel and epoxy plastic body.

The Solo Electra is distributed in the U.S. by the Odyssey Company, 112 Main Street, New Canaan, Conn. 06840, U.S.A.

General Engines Company

General Engines Company of New Jersey, U.S.A., has developed and marketed a line of electric mopeds and electric bicycle kits.

Their line of "Electropeds" also includes a three-wheeled trike for senior citizens or factory use.

For further information regarding the latest models and prices, contact General Engines Co., Electric Products Division, 591 Mantua Blvd., Sewell, N.J. 08080, U.S.A.

"Pedalpower" #50 Kit

The basic "Pedalpower" electric drive kit #50 uses a .5 hp permanent magnet motor with a friction drive that is designed to disengage for pedaling. The weight of the motor unit is 12 lbs (5.4 kg). Range for the model #50 is 25 miles (40 km) per charge. Another kit, the model #100, uses a 1 hp motor. A standard 12-volt light-utility battery supplies power.

"PEDALPOWER" #50 KIT Photo courtesy of General Engines Co. Inc., Electric Products Division

Electroped 6X2000

The Electroped 6X2000 utilizes a folding frame, which is ideal for campers. Features include a mono-shock, sealed-beam headlight, front-drum/rear-coaster brakes and a .5 hp friction-drive motor which yields a 25 mile (40 km) range. Total vehicle weight with battery is only 70 lbs (32 kg).

ELECTROPED 6X2000

Photo courtesy of General Engines Co. Inc., Electric Products Division

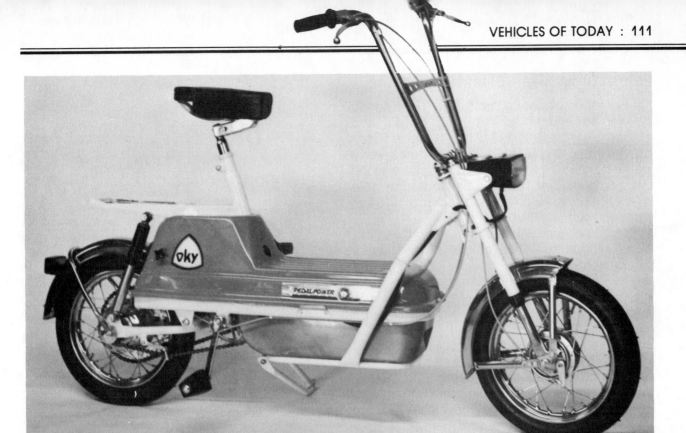

ELECTROSCOOTER

Photo courtesy of General Engines Co. Inc., Electric Products Division

"Electroscooter"

The "Electroscooter" features a 1.5 hp motor and variable belt transmission, which yields a top speed of 20 mph (32 km/hr) and range of 25 miles (40 km) per charge. Other features include front and rear drum brakes and telescopic shocks. Weight is 125 lbs (57 kg).

"Grocery Getter"

The "Grocery Getter" is a pedal trike with a 1 hp friction-drive motor. Range is 25 miles (40 km) per charge; speeds are 8-1/2 mph (19 km/hr) with no pedaling; 14 mph (23 km/hr) with motor and pedaling combined.

GROCERY GETTER

Photo courtesy of General Engines Co. Inc.,
Electric Products Division

Palmer Industries—Electric Cycle Kits

Palmer Industries of Endicott, New York, began developing electric drives long before the energy crisis of 1973-1974. The "Electra Ride" Kit, invented by Jack Palmer, features easy installation on over 100 various models of bicycles. Adaptation requires only an adjustable wrench and screwdriver and is accomplished without modifying the bicycle.

The 12-volt permanent-magnet, weatherproof motor is rated at 75% efficiency and disengages from the wheel to allow coasting. The friction-drive unit with clutch has only one moving part. A vinyl-coated steel battery case is designed to allow for battery maintenance without removal.

The Series-3 Kit features a 3/4-hp motor, a 17-mph (27-km/hr) speed and a 15-mile (24-km) range without pedal assist, using a light utility battery. The kit includes everything needed to convert a bicycle or adult tricycle to electric power, and carries a one-year warranty. Trike speed is 12 mph (19 km/hr).

"Happy Wanderer"

The Palmer "Happy Wanderer" is an outdoor

PALMER "ELECTRA RIDE" SERIES 3 KIT

electric three-wheeler designed for handicapped or elderly use. Features include two forward and one reverse speed with single hand control. Range is 15 to 20 miles (24 to 32 km)

"HAPPY WANDERER"

EXECUTIVE MARK II

with speeds of 3 and 7 mph (5 and 11 km/hr). This vehicle is designed to operate on dirt or paved roads, wet or dry grass.

Executive Mark II Kit

The Executive Mark II model for bicycles and tricycles uses an industrial-rated 3/4-hp, ball-bearing, permanent-magnet motor with a two-year warranty.

Palmer Industries also makes a "basic" electric-drive kit using a 1/4-hp motor for those who wish only occasional use on flat terrain. In 1976, they also introduced an electric three-wheel industrial vehicle.

For more information and price list, contact Palmer Industries, P.O. Box 707, Endicott, N.Y. 13760, U.S.A.

LYMAN ELECTRIC BIKE

Lyman Electric Bike

The Lyman Electric Bike is an advanced design electric motorcycle with a top speed of 40 mph (64 km/hr) and a cruising range of 40 miles (64 km) per charge.

Three type 27 12-volt lead-acid batteries transfer power to a 36-volt series motor through a 3-speed controller or optional solid state motor control (available only with optional high torque motor). Vehicle weight is 375 lbs (170 kg) of which 150 lbs (68 kg) is the battery pack.

All of the products shown in this two-page section are available to the public from Lyman Metal Products, Electric Division, 15 Meadow Street, South Norwalk, CT 06856.

Lyman Electric Platform

The Lyman Electric Platform is an electrically-powered material mover designed for any industrial application which requires a clean, quiet, pollution-free vehicle.

The three wheeler, which has a payload capacity of 750 lb (340 kg), is powered by two ½ hp, 24-volt permanent magnet motors which drive both front wheels through vee-belts. Two speeds are controlled by an air-activated series/parallel switch: 3½ mph (5.6 km/hr) in the 12-volt mode and 7 mph (11 km/hr) in the 24-volt mode. Range is 50 miles (80 km) per charge.

Options include a solid state controller, fiberglass front fenders, and hard rubber tires.

LYMAN ELECTRIC PLATFORM
Photos courtesy Lyman Metal Products

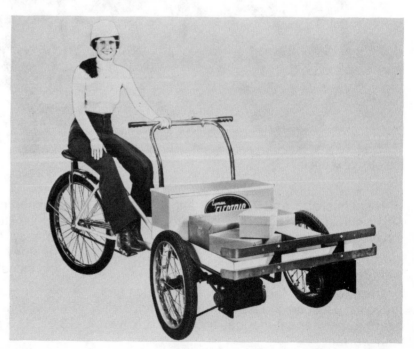

LYMAN ELECTRIC QUAD

LYMAN ELECTRIC TRYCYCLE

Lyman Electric Quad

The Lyman Electric Quad is an electrically powered 4-wheel bicycle for two with pedal assist designed for shopping, beach, estates, trailer camps, and retirement villages.

Power from the two type 27 12-volt, 95-amp hour batteries is directed to the rear wheels via a vee-belt drive from dual ½ hp 24-volt permanent magnet motors.

A series/parallel 12-24 volt, 2-speed air switch (activated through a nylon tube) provides a top speed of 9 mph (14 km/hr) in the 12-volt mode and 18 mph (29 km/hr) in the 24-volt mode. Range is 40 to 50 miles (64 to 80 km). Options include a surrey top with frame and a solid state controller.

Lyman Electric Tricycle

The Lyman Electric Tricycle is a heavy duty three-wheeler designed for industrial plants, resorts, estates, institutions, and trailer camps.

Power from the type 27 12-volt battery is controlled by a one-speed switch through a ½ hp, 12-volt permanent magnet motor to a vee-belt drive to the right rear wheel. Top speed is 7 mph (11 km/hr) and range is 25 miles (40 km) per charge.

Lyman Electric Super-Trike

The Super Trike uses a 1 hp 24-volt permanent magnet motor to provide 7 mph (11 km/hr) in the 12-volt mode and 15 mph (24 km/hr) in the 24-volt mode. Range is 40 to 50 miles (64 to 80 km). Options include dual motors with dynamic electric brakes and three-speed control.

LYMAN SUPER-TRIKE

American Microcar

The American Microcar Company of Farmingdale, N.Y., produces the Microcar in gasoline-powered and electric models.

Both Microcar models are designed to perform short trips common to metropolitan areas. The electric version weighs only 300 lb (136 kg) and has three moped-style wheels.

This functional compact car has a range of 30 miles (48 km) and cruising speed of 20 mph (32 km). The Electric Microcar is designated as a "local use vehicle" thereby enabling it to operate under most existing moped laws. An integrated polyethylene convertible body can be enclosed with snap-on vinyl roof and side panels.

For more information regarding price and local distribution contact American Microcar, Inc., 115 Florida Street, Farmingdale, NY 11735.

Electric Bicycle with Pancake Motor

Patscentre International's electric bicycle has a unique front wheel "pancake" motor with all-electronic controls which provide regenerative braking and coasting. In the regenerative mode, the motor automatically converts into a generator and feeds power back to two lead-acid batteries mounted on the rear axle.

The pancake motor is designed with 18 magnetic poles instead of the usual two, thereby allowing easy starting and low motor speeds.

When the throttle is closed and twisted forward, it works as an electromagnetic retarder to bring the bicycle to a gradual stop. Manual braking is only necessary for sudden stops.

The electric bicycle's pancake motor is rated at ½ hp. It is self-starting without brushes and can deliver high torque at low speeds. Top speed is 18 mph (28 km/hr) and cruising speed is 15 mph (24 km/hr) with a range of 40 miles (64 km) per charge.

For further information, contact Patscentre International, Melbourne, Cambridge, England.

Photos courtesy
Patscentre International

TRANSITRON 1 MOTORCYCLE   Photo courtesy of Transitron

Transitron I Motorcycle

The Transitron Company, formerly Charger Hawaii, has developed the Transitron I motorcycle as a test bed for new drive systems.

A new design-prototype automobile is now being finished which will include a "liquid battery recharging system" which allows for recharging in three minutes. The new Transitron electric car will not weigh more than five percent of a comparable piston-engined vehicle. The company claims that the vehicle will be a significant "breakthrough" upon completion.

The present Transitron I test motorcycle uses lead-acid batteries and weighs about 580 lbs (263 kg). A transistorized controller feeds power from 230 lbs (104 kg) of batteries to a separately excited motor. Top speed is 60 mph (97 km/hr). Range with conventional batteries is about 40 miles (64 km) per charge.

Information regarding vehicles should be directed to Transitron, Suite 412, 745 Fort Street, Hawaii Building, Honolulu, Hawaii 96815.

Eagle Picher 3-Wheel Motorcycle

The Eagle Picher Company of Joplin, Missouri, U.S.A., has produced this electric "trike" to demonstrate the energy density of their "silver-oxide-zinc" batteries, which have been used extensively in the U.S. space program in vehicles such as the "lunar rovers."

The vehicle carries less than 200 lbs (91 kg) of silver-oxide-zinc batteries and can travel 150 miles (241 km) at about 35 mph (56 km/hr). Two 1.5 hp permanent-magnet motors are used with a step-voltage-switching control.

The cost of silver batteries for a production vehicle is generally considered impractical; however, they are ideal for special non-transportation duties.

Agrati-Garelli Corporation

A limited number of Garelli electric-powered mopeds were produced as prototypes by the Agrati-Garelli Corporation of Italy, a leading producer of gasoline-powered mopeds. Although Garelli believes there is a market for electric mopeds, none are under production at this time.

AGRATI-GARELLI MOPED   Photo courtesy Agrati-Garelli Corp.

EAGLE PICHER "TRIKE"   Photo courtesy of Eagle-Picher Company

HYBRID ELECTRICS

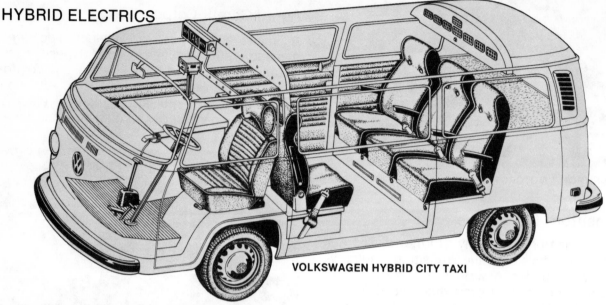

VOLKSWAGEN HYBRID CITY TAXI

In the battery chapter, we mentioned "hybrid batteries," which combine more than one battery to produce a system which utilizes the strong points of each individual battery type.

The most commonly accepted hybrid electric vehicle is powered by an internal combustion or heat engine combined with a battery-electric system, such as the Volkswagen City Taxi described later. (See page 138).

In this combination, the electric motor provides additional power for rapid acceleration and other peak power demands while a comparatively small heat engine is used to enable the vehicle to cruise at higher speeds. The hybrid system is attractive because energy requirements at high speeds for a pure electric vehicle are quite high, while acceleration of a heat engine produces high pollution. In hybrid combination, these two systems can complement each other. The end result is lower pollution and a more efficient use of energy.

Another benefit is battery life. In a hybrid, there can be a higher battery cycle life because of the relatively shallow discharge cycles necessary to maintain operation of the vehicle.

All battery-hybrid-heat-engine vehicles are grouped into two classes: series and parallel. The series system takes the net power output of the heat engine and converts it into electricity through a generating system. The electric power is then converted to mechanical power via an electric motor connected to the drive wheels. The vehicle is then controlled as one would drive an ordinary electric vehicle. In this application the engine operates at a constant speed and load for maximum fuel economy. If the engine power output is greater than the vehicle's need at the time, the excess power is used to charge batteries. The use of regenerative braking can also capture kinetic energy otherwise lost.

In the parallel class of hybrids, power is delivered from the heat engine directly to the wheels through a transmission. Excess power is then used to charge the batteries. The electric motor in this type of system is driven by the heat engine to become a generator. When stopping the vehicle, the motor is used for regenerative braking. This type of system allows the use of gasoline power on the highway and all-electric power for city use. The parallel hybrid is more expensive to construct than the series, due to the mechanical transmission necessary for the gasoline or heat engine.

An application of the parallel system is to take a conventional automobile, fill the trunk with batteries, and attach an electric motor directly into the differential. The vehicle could then use a much smaller engine, perhaps a 4-cylinder instead of a V8. This system would give excellent acceleration due to the high torque provided by the electric motor from a standing start, and unlimited range due to the cruising capability of the heat engine.

An example of a series hybrid would be to attach a fuel-powered generator to an existing electric automobile, such as the Sebring Vanguard. The generating set would charge the battery pack while the vehicle was in use. At a standstill in traffic, the batteries would be charging while not in use.

The heat engine for a hybrid can be small. A

MERCEDES-BENZ HYBRID-ELECTRIC BUS

MAZDA TITAN HYBRID TRUCK

20-horsepower engine would be sufficient for a compact car while a 60-horsepower engine would be suitable for a van.

The diesel engine is highly efficient and has a high continuous power and long potential life. Perhaps it will be a candidate for hybrid vehicle use.

The rotary engine is another potential candidate for hybrids. It operates at a high rotational speed and can be coupled directly into a high-speed electric generator without a transmission. It is light, compact, and simple—and the durability of the rotary engine is at least as good as conventional piston engines because, with no valves, camshafts, and springs, there are fewer moving parts. In the United States, Europe, and Japan, new versions of rotary engines are being studied which are expected to have lower fuel consumption, lower emissions, and the ability to use a variety of fuels.

Another candidate is an external combustion type called the Stirling engine, which theoretically has high efficiency, low emissions, and is capable of using various fuels. The Ford Motor Company has fitted and test-driven vehicles with Stirling engines. United Stirling of Sweden has a series of five engines under development that vary in power output from 40 to 150 horsepower.

Gas-turbine engines are light, compact, durable and have low emissions. In aircraft use, gas turbine engines are highly developed; however, smaller versions, such as auxiliary power units, find their minimum fuel consumption too high for automotive applications. More work is being done in this area, and perhaps after additional research and development is accom-plished, we will see a gas turbine in a hybrid vehicle.

Six types of hybrid urban buses have been built and several are in operation in Europe and Japan. As a result of successful operation, many hybrid buses are now on order for delivery during 1978-1980. These buses will be powered by both diesel and electric drive systems, using batteries, overhead trolley wires, or both. The hybrid concept for urban buses is appealing because of stop-and-go driving patterns, and because the space for batteries and drive system in a large bus is abundant.

Hybrids are generally regarded as unlimited-range vehicles because their range is determined by the size of their fuel tanks, which can be refilled. Unfortunately, range is limited when driven in the all-electric mode; however, the general concept of a hybrid is attractive, because most hybrids have been designed to have performance comparable to a conventional automobile. With the ability to accelerate, climb hills, and pass other vehicles at high speeds, hybrids break away from the generally accepted pattern of an electric vehicle. Some people feel that the electric hybrid is a stepping stone to pure electric vehicles. However, we must remember that hybrids are relatively expensive vehicles because of the components required to make them feasible. If the consumer price of a hybrid becomes astronomical, their market will be proportionately small. If hybrids can be made economically, they will be assimilated into the transportation market before all-electric automobiles, because of their speed and range advantage.

Briggs & Stratton Gasoline/Electric Hybrid

The Briggs & Stratton Company of Milwaukee, Wisconsin, is one of the world's oldest manufacturers of portable power sources. The prototype 6-wheel electric hybrid was built to demonstrate the applicability of their 18-hp gasoline power plant for vehicle use. Briggs & Stratton air-cooled engines have been in service powering lawnmowers, washing machines, and a host of home and industrial applications for over 40 years.

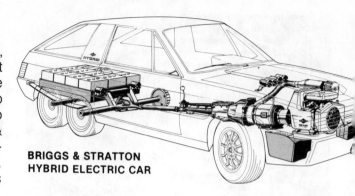

BRIGGS & STRATTON HYBRID ELECTRIC CAR

The vehicle, designed by Brooks Stevens Associates to carry two adults and two children plus groceries, uses a modified Marathon C-360 six-wheel chassis (see Canada section). The parallel-hybrid design allows the use of either gasoline or electric power or both. Cruising range on electric power is 30 to 60 miles (48 to 96 km) depending upon driving conditions, while the range is up to 280 miles (450 km) in the gasoline-powered mode. The use of gasoline and electric combined can yield up to 150 miles per gallon (63 km/L), and 25 to 40 miles per gallon (11 to 17 km/L) when using gasoline power alone. The obvious advantage lies in the ability to use electric power in urban areas and have a 55 mph (88 km/hr) highway capability plus the extended range of gasoline power for interstate travel.

The 6-wheel design provides a captive trailer that houses the 1000-lb (453-kg) Globe-Union battery pack on the rear two wheels. The engine/motor combination powers the middle two wheels while the front wheels are used for steering.

A 20-hp series-wound DC motor powers the 3200-lb (1451-kg) vehicle through a 4-speed manual transmission.

The Briggs & Stratton Company has no plans to produce automobiles. This experimental model was built to demonstrate the practicality of their hybrid design and to attract the interest of vehicle manufacturers.

Battery Charger

Creative Automotive Research of Whittier, California, has designed the Battery Charger, a gasoline/electric hybrid passenger car using a 1975 Dodge Charger body. Built as a production prototype, the Battery Charger has a top speed of 45 mph (72 km/hr) and a range of 800 miles (1287 km) at 45 mph (72 km/hr). The 4320 lb (1981 kg) vehicle accelerates from zero to 30 mph (48 km/hr) in 10 seconds. The Charger uses nine 6-volt, lead-acid batteries which weigh a total of 450 lb (204 kg).

Propulsion is provided by a 15-hp DC motor through a controller equipped with regenerative braking to a four-speed manual transmission. Additional propulsion, when operated as a parallel hybrid, is obtained from an Onan two-cylinder, 25-hp gasoline engine.

Hybrid Hornet

The Hybrid Hornet, a converted American Motors model, is another gasoline/electric hybrid prototype produced by Creative Automotive Research.

The 3500-lb (1587-kg) Hornet accelerates from zero to 30 mph (48 km/hr) in 6 seconds. The 850-lb (385-kg) six-volt lead-acid battery pack consists of 16 batteries with power directed through a six-step electric relay controller to a 20-hp DC motor.

A 12-hp auxiliary power gasoline engine, used in combination with electric power, produces a 320 mile (514 km) cruising range at 22 mph (35 km/hr).

For more information about the Hornet, Charger, or a set of plans and diagrams for each vehicle, write Creative Automotive Research, Suite G, 8136 Byron Rd., Whittier, CA 90606.

ANTSER INSTRUMENT PANEL

Lincoln-Mercury Antser

The Mercury Antser is a concept car to demonstrate the type of vehicles we can expect to find in the late 1980's. If built, the four-passenger 1200-lb (544-kg) hybrid would use two power cells to provide DC power to drive all four wheels. A compact power generator would continuously recharge the energy cells. The computer-operated dual power system would be virtually pollution-free and permit extended cruising range.

An electronic instrument panel would provide a variety of computer-controlled information while allowing the driver electronic operation of all vehicle functions. A comprehensive electronic map, programmed by a computer cassette, would allow precise computer-based trip monitoring.

Hybrid Chevette

This converted General Motors Chevette prototype is capable of operating as a "parallel-hybrid" in three modes: gasoline, electric, or a combination of both. The cruising speed in the electric mode is 25 mph (40 km/hr), while the cruising speed in the hybrid gasoline-electric mode is 40 mph (64 km/hr). Cruising range is 40 miles (64 km) at 25 mph (40 km/hr) while powered electrically and is limited to the amount of gasoline carried, 12.5 gallons (47.3 liters), when used as a hybrid.

HYBRID CHEVETTE

The 2700-lb (1225-kg) prototype vehicle carries eight 12-volt lead-acid batteries which provide power to a 22-hp DC motor in the electric mode. Drive train features include direct drive from the motor and either automatic or manual transmission connected to the standard 80-hp water-cooled, gasoline-powered Chevette engine.

For more information contact: Lyon Laboratory, 1200 Orchard Ridge, Bloomfield Hills, Mich. 48013

HYBRICON CENTAUR

Photos courtesy Hybricon, Inc.

The Hybricon Centaur

The Centaur is a parallel hybrid prototype which operates on gasoline and/or electric power. While commuting at city speeds, up to 35 mph (56 km/hr), the Centaur runs on electric power using two G.E. motors, with electric clutches, connected to the rear wheels. Seven six-volt golf cart batteries, weighing 441 lbs (200 kg), provide about one hour of continuous driving in the "all-electric" mode.

The original vehicle was a Honda 600 sedan. The 32 hp aircooled internal combustion engine and front wheel drive have been retained to provide the components for gasoline powered operation.

For optimum economy, the vehicle starts out on electric power and shifts to gasoline power at about 30 mph (48 km/hr). This is an efficient use of the electric motors which operate more economically at low speed rather than high cruising speeds. Top speed under full gasoline power is 70 mph (113 km/hr).

During the gasoline driving mode, the motors are engaged, and act as generators to recharge the battery pack. One hour of driving at 50 mph (80 km/hr) under gasoline power will recharge the batteries up to 80% of a full charge. Additional driving will complete the recharging process, but at a slower rate. Combined range is 160 miles (257 km) per 4 gallons (15 liters) of gasoline.

The body of the 2,180 lb (990 kg) four passenger hybrid was styled by the famous automotive customizer, George Barris. The pro-

totype vehicle was designed to attract a manufacturer who would produce the car in large quantities.

For more information, write: Hybricon, Inc., 11489 Chandler Boulevard, North Hollywood, California, 91601, USA.

The NRG Nitrogen-Electric Hybrid

The NRG Company of Peoria, Illinois, USA has designed a unique hybrid-electric truck. The electric motor is connected to a manual trans-

THE NRG NITROGEN-ELECTRIC HYBRID PICK-UP TRUCK.

mission, and a battery pack is located under the front hood. A tank in the rear holds cryogenically stored liquid nitrogen under low pressure.

The basic advantage of this series-type hybrid is the elimination of conventional overnight battery recharging. The batteries are continuously charged, as the vehicle is driven, by a small vane-type air turbine which is powered by the nitrogen as it expands when changing from a cryogenic liquid into a gas.

The nitrogen lines are directed: from the tank, around the motor case and through pipes, (which also serve as the connecting cables for the batteries), and finally to a turbine pump motor. The turbine is connected, with a V-belt, to a 35 ampere alternator.

As the nitrogen expands from a liquid to a gas with the assistance of the heat generated by the motor and the battery cables, it turns the pump which runs the alternator that recharges the batteries. This patented system allows the flow of electricity to be almost resistance-free when travelling through super-cooled cables. In addition, the motor runs longer and more efficiently in a cooler mode. The batteries, operating under very shallow discharge cycles, will last longer then similar batteries which are constantly subjected to "deep discharging."

After the nitrogen passes through the air turbine, it can be directed to other pumps to do additional work, such as power steering and brakes. The cryogenic nitrogen is, of course, a natural air conditioning system. Through a heat-exchanger, the nitrogen can also supply heat for the passenger compartment.

Nitrogen itself is an inert gas, totally non-flammable, non-volatile and non-toxic. Large volumes of nitrogen are now produced as a by-product of oxygen and argon manufacturing. Most of this nitrogen is unused and is returned to the atmosphere, although some is retained for commercial use such as cooling for cross-country food trucks. Currently, liquid nitrogen is about one fifth as expensive as gasoline in the U.S. The limitless source of nitrogen exists in two-thirds of the air we breathe. After it is expelled by the vehicle, it will return to the atmosphere, undiminished and unpolluted.

The range of a vehicle would be related to the amount of nitrogen carried and, of course, the weight of the vehicle and batteries. Conventional highway speeds could be maintained, and refilling the nitrogen tank, in a typical automobile, would take about as long as a gasoline fill-up, about every 500 miles.

The NRG Company claims that the Self-Charging System could be used to convert any conventional automobile, light truck, forklift or industrial application. Other uses would include boats, wheelchairs, emergency generators, and the conversion of conventional electric vehicles.

(See page 124 for another "NRG" system).

The nitrogen "plumbing" of the NRG truck shows the harness which carries the nitrogen through the battery compartment. The heat generated at the battery terminals helps liberate the nitrogen from a cryogenic liquid into a gas. When in use, the battery cables are covered with frost as the nitrogen cools the terminals allowing for reduced electrical resistance.

The NRG low-pressure liquid nitrogen tank is situated in the rear of the vehicle. In automotive use, a smaller tank could be stored in the trunk, taking up about as much space as a conventional gasoline tank. This tank can be filled at a truck stop in the same time as a gasoline powered vehicle. Nitrogen itself is inert and non-combustible insuring a high degree of safety in handling.

Cryogenics Unlimited Corporation

Another unusual vehicle propulsion system, developed by the inventors of the "NRG System," is the method by which a cryogenic "expansion system" powers a turbine connected directly to a transmission.

The unique 72-lb (33-kg) turbine-drive assembly uses no combustible fuel. Instead, the driven member of the turbine is powered by the expansion of either cryogenically-cooled liquid nitrogen or liquid air which is returned to the atmosphere to be used again—with no depletion of the resource which forms the basis of the fuel medium. By utilizing the immense potential energy stored in liquified atmospheric gases, the turbine in effect becomes the "engine" which powers the vehicle. The advantages of liquid nitrogen and liquid air are numerous (see NRG article) and are compounded by the potential construction of liquification plants in virtually any location. The cost of transporting a "base fuel" to the production plant is eliminated because the "fuel" is extracted from the atmosphere.

While it is true that liquified atmospheric gases power the vehicle directly, it is also true that the gases are not a "fuel" in the sense that they are not "prime energy sources" such as gasoline. Instead, they serve as an interface between the prime energy source and the vehicle. In the case of an oxygen liquification plant, the

A prototype of the Cryogenics Unlimited Corporation was displayed at the EV EXPO 80 in St. Louis, Missouri, in May 1980. The basic vehicle was a Volkswagen chassis conversion "kit-car" using a fiberglass body replica of an early M.G. sportscar. The basic vehicle was modified to accept the turbine to transmission drive system and house the cryogenic storage tanks.

prime energy source could be coal, oil, gas, or hydroelectric power, for example. While liquified-gas-powered vehicles are not directly "electrified," they do avail themselves of the electricity generated to liquify the atmospheric gas. Therefore, the interface would not exist without the electricity necessary to produce liquid nitrogen or liquid air.

Liquid nitrogen and air vehicles have a place in the transportation mix of the future and offer a pollution-free option to internal combustion engine vehicles. For more information, contact Cryogenics Unlimited, Inc., 2513 Avenue Q½, Galveston, TX 77550 USA.

Cryogenic tanks are stored behind driver's seat while a "heat-exchange" device, in the form of serpentine tubes, is located under the front hood. The purpose of the "heat-exchanger" is to expand and pressurize gas by raising its temperature.

The turbine drive unit is bolted to the standard Volkswagen transaxle.

SPECIALIZED ELECTRIC VEHICLES

E-Z GO GOLF CART
Photo courtesy of E-Z-Go

E-Z-Go

The Polaris E-Z-Go Division of Textron, Inc., P.O. Box 388, Augusta, Georgia 30903, U.S.A., produces the E-Z Go. This is the latest generation of vehicles designed by a company which claims to be the largest producer of golf carts in the world. E-Z-Go golf carts have carried golfers over 400 million miles (644 million km) in the last two decades.

The basic E-Z-Go can be used as a golf cart, airport baggage or passenger carrier, and for maintenance, security, or a variety of industrial uses. Features include a weight of 960 lbs (436 kg) with batteries and a four-passenger capacity. Conversion kits can transform the basic E-Z-Go into a flatbed truck.

Electronic Leisure Industries, Inc. Electrocart®

Electronic Leisure Industries, Inc. has introduced the Electrocart® which is the world's first mass-produced electric racing cart.

The Electrocart is powered by two 12-volt, 105 amp-hour, deep-cycle batteries and has a top speed of 45 mph (72 km/hr) with a range of 25 miles (40 km). At 25 mph (40 km/hr), the Electrocart has a range of 40 miles (64 km).

This recreational vehicle uses a one-hp, high-torque motor and space-age electronic circuitry. A pulse width modulation controller, manufactured by Power Controller Corporation, Marblehead, Mass., is the heart of the system. A patent-pending control package is the brain of the system; it has a key entry with a fully programmable, lap counter/speedometer system that features memory recall, battery indicator, dead man switch, and LED display panel.

The Electrocart's molded, high-impact fiberglass body is available in 57 colors. As safety features, Electrocart incorporates a spring-loaded, all-around bumper system, roll bar, hydraulic brakes, 4-point shoulder harness, and a padded head rest, steering wheel, and seat.

Electronic Leisure Industries is planning to construct indoor recreational centers featuring a quarter-mile indoor race track equipped with 30 Electrocarts and other electronic entertainment devices.

For further information, contact Electronic Leisure Industries, Inc., phone (215) 735-8787.

ELECTROCART®

TITAN

MINUTE MISER

Photos courtesy of Cushman OMC

EXECUTIVE

Cushman—OMC

The Cushman Division of the Outboard Marine Corporation of Lincoln, Nebraska, U.S.A. produces three electric utility vehicles.

The electric 2-passenger "Minute Miser" is designed for in-plant commercial use. Top speed is 11 mph (18km/hr), range is 35 miles (56 km) per charge. The 24-volt system uses four deep-cycle 6-volt batteries and a 2.7 to 4.3 hp motor. Vehicle weight is 650 lbs (295 kg).

The "Executive" model has a 500-lb (227-kg) carrying capacity and an 11-mph (18-km/hr) top speed with optional motor. A 36-volt system uses a 5 hp maximum power DC series-wound motor. Thousands of these units are in service performing functions in security, VIP and plant

duties. An optional cab is available for outdoor use.

The "Titan" model features two versions, the "316" and the "318." The "316" has a 13 mph (21 km/hr) top speed, 35 mile range (56 km) and maximum 2,000 lb (907 kg) load capacity. The "318" model has a 48-volt battery supply, range of 28 miles per charge (45 km) and top speed of 20 mph (32 km/hr). This heavy-duty vehicle is also available in an enclosed cab version.

For more information, write: CUSHMAN-OMC, P.O. Box 82409, Lincoln, Nebraska, 68501, U.S.A.

BATRICADDY

BATRICAR
Photos courtesy Braune Batricar Ltd.

Braune Batricar

The Braune Batricar Limited of Stroud, England, manufactures a variety of small, electric-powered vehicles for utility, recreation, and handicapped persons.

The Batricar 4-wheeled electrically-driven invalid vehicle has a fiberglass body with pneumatic tires. The tiller steering control groups all controls together for one-hand driving. The infinitely-variable forward and reverse speed control system yields a top speed limit of 4 mph (6.4 km/hr) on level ground. The weight with one battery is 219 lbs (100 kg). The range is up to 6, 12, or 18 miles (9.6, 19, 29 km).

The new Batricar with bonnet has a top speed of 10 mph (16 km/hr). The Batricaddy is a golf cart designed to travel at 10 mph (16 km/hr) with a single seating capacity. A new version of the Batricaddy with a 40 mph (64 km/hr) maximum speed and 40 mile (64 km) range is due to be introduced presently. A 2 + 2 vehicle with the same performance will be introduced later.

Newton Elan and Queensway

One important function of the electric vehicle is to provide freedom and mobility to the handicapped. Although the speeds of electric wheelchairs and handicap vehicles is usually very low, in the 1.9 mph to 3.8 mph (3 to 6.1 km/hr) range, the use of electric power in this application gives a true sense of independence to a great number of handicapped people throughout the world.

The Newton Elan is a folding electric wheelchair-type vehicle with a two-speed gearbox, two 12-volt batteries, fingertip control, independent suspension, with an aluminum frame. The Newton Queensway has both two speeds and two levels of height control and is quite literally a motorized swivel chair. Powered by two 6-volt batteries, the 87 lb (39 kg) vehicle has two speeds: .3 mph (.48 km) and .6 mph (.96 km). The range is approximately 2.5 miles (4 km). The weight is about 116 lbs (52 kg).

NEWTON QUEENSWAY

Amigo

The Amigo is an electric vehicle designed for the elderly, handicapped, or for any application that would require a lightweight, highly maneuverable design. Powered by a 12-volt electric motor and battery, it is capable of continuous operation for three to four hours. The Amigo weighs 61 lbs (28 kg) less battery, and is available in four standard models including a mini-unit for children. It can be dismantled into four parts: seat, handle, battery, and base—for storage or transportation. The top speed is approximately 5 mph (8 km/hr) and is recommended for up to 150-lb (68 kg) riders. Heavier riders use a 3.5 mph (5.6-km/hr) version. The front-wheel-drive unit uses a 6-inch (150 mm) diameter front wheel.

For information write: Amigo Sales Inc., 6693 Dixie Highway, Bridgeport, Michigan 48722

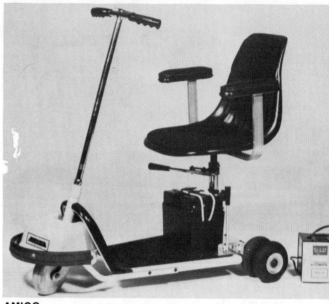

AMIGO

Amigo Boots

The AMIGO BOOTS is a supplementary carriage which converts the AMIGO into a maximum traction vehicle to allow travel over difficult surfaces and grades.

The AMIGO BOOTS uses dual 24-volt motors and two deep-cycle batteries. An electronic "joystick" provides control of steering, speed, and direction. Mechanical brakes lock the wheels of the BOOTS while the vehicle is being transported.

Another AMIGO innovation is the "AMIGO-AUTO." This four-door General Motors front-wheel-drive compact sedan is equipped with a power-lift carpeted platform which allows the operator an effortless means to transport the AMIGO.

AMIGO owners can order the AMIGO-AUTO through local GM dealers. Modifications are done at the Amigo Plant. For more information about the AMIGO BOOTS or AMIGO-AUTO, contact Amigo Sales, Inc., 6693 Dixie Highway, Bridgeport, MI 48722.

Photos courtesy Amigo Sales, Inc.

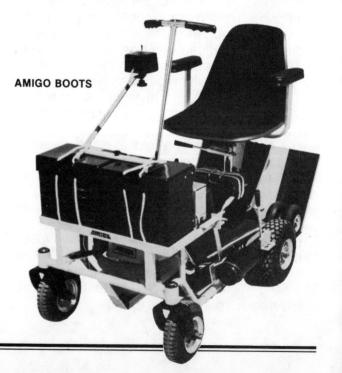

AMIGO BOOTS

Photos courtesy of Hyster Company Industrial Truck Operations

**WHITE
ELECTRIC FORKLIFT**
Photo courtesy of
White Motor Corp.

The Electric Forklift

A number of companies designed electric fork-lifts during the thirties. The early models used resistance controllers to vary speeds, which was inefficient. Today, modern forklifts use solid-state controllers—a major step enabling electrics to compete with their internal combustion counterparts handling loads of up to 10,000 lbs (4535 kg).

Certain jobs are ideally suited to electrics, which can quietly and safely operate indoors to perform both conventional forklift chores as well as highly specialized duty. The use of the electric industrial truck is now extensive throughout the world. The inherent design of the forklift, which is required to carry heavy ballast weight to balance loads, lends itself well to carrying batteries. This is one of the few examples of using battery weight as a design advantage.

As mentioned earlier, we have not endeavored to cover every electric vehicle manufactured worldwide. The inclusion of all commercial and industrial forklifts and burden carriers alone would require a massive volume to depict every model. The result would be an accurate but dull compendium. The author also suggests that readers peruse daily newspapers and magazines to keep abreast of timely additions to this growing field, many of which will be introduced after the publication of this edition.

Photo courtesy of Hyster Company Industrial Truck Operations

A NARROW AISLE HYSTER ELECTRIC REACH TRUCK

DEVELOPMENT IN AUSTRALIA

The "Electric Vehicle Project" is a research and development program of Flinders University of South Australia and is supported by both state and federal government funding. The vehicles designed under the Flinders University feature linear current, infinitely-variable controllers with regenerative braking. Motor power levels range from 5 to 40 kilowatts.

FLINDERS MK II INVESTIGATOR

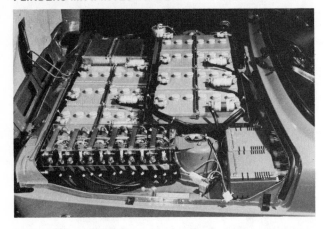

FLINDERS CF ELECTRIC VAN

Flinders CF Electric Van

The Flinder's delivery van incorporates the Bedford CF series body and has a maximum speed of 50 mph (80 km/hr) and a range of 50 miles (80 km) at a speed of 37 mph (59 km/hr). The 7165-lb (3249-kg) van carries 12 12-volt lead-acid batteries which supply energy to a 22-hp permanent magnet DC motor.

In the Flinders Project, vehicles are designed which serve as prototypes and are earmarked for limited production.

Flinders Electric Mk II Investigator

The four-passenger sedan shown uses a modified FIAT 127 body. Powered by a 10-kw motor, the vehicle has a cruising speed of 46 mph (74 km/hr) with a range of 45 miles (72 km).

Silent Power Electric Van

Australia's first production electric vehicle can be used as a commuter van or, with the rear seat removed, a commercial vehicle.

Built in Alexandria in Sydney, the van uses a Japanese-designed body and running gear and utilizes conventional battery technology.

Top speed is up to 50 mph (80 km/hr) with acceleration from zero to 31 mph (50 km/hr) in 10.4 seconds. Range is 31 to 44 mph (50 to 70 km/hr).

The four-passenger van has a 96-volt battery system and uses a four-speed manual transmission. Silent Power Company is reported to be in a joint venture agreement with Electric Passenger Cars and Vans, San Diego, California, U.S.A. For more information, contact Silent Power Company Pty., Limited, 290/294 Botany Road, (P.O. Box 197), Alexandria, NSW 2015, Australia.

SILENT POWER ELECTRIC VAN

DEVELOPMENT IN CANADA

MARATHON C-300 AND C-360 VAN

Marathon C-300

The Marathon C-300 is a 2-passenger production electric automobile with a fiberglass body and canvas top. The 2300 lb (1043 kg) vehicle has a 500 lb (227 kg) payload capacity. Operating range is 50 miles (80 km) with a cruising speed of 35 mph (56 km/hr). Twelve 6-volt deep-cycle heavy-duty batteries are stored behind the passenger compartment. The 72-volt 8-hp DC motor and variable-speed standard transmission are located under the front hood.

The Marathon is available in "high profile" and "low profile" models from Marathon Electric Cars, Ltd., 8305 Le Creusot, Ville De St. Leonard, Quebec HIP 2A2 Canada.

Marathon C-360 Electric Van

The Marathon C-360 is a 6-wheel utility van which has been engineered from the ground up as an electric vehicle. The C-360 and the C-300 (above) have been tested in the United States and Canada and have met all motor vehicle standards.

The C-360 has a tubular frame and all-aluminum body which provides a 500-lb (227-kg) payload for the 3080-lb (1397-kg) vehicle. A special, patented controller directs power from a 16 6-volt DC traction battery pack to an 8 hp DC motor through a 4-speed manual transmission. A top speed of 43 mph (69 km/hr), acceleration of zero to 30 mph (48 km/hr) in 15 seconds, and a cruising range of at least 35 miles per charge allow the C-360 to meet DOE performance standards.

The C-360 Van is available to the general public; contact Marathon Electric Vehicles Inc., 8305 Le Creusot, Ville de St. Leonard, Quebec, H1P2A2 Canada.

EVAC

Similar to the Electric Vehicle Council in purpose and scope, the Electric Vehicle Association of Canada (EVAC) sponsors many events, seminars, and conferences. Through keeping informed of developments and reporting relevant findings in a monthly newsletter, the EVAC hopes to achieve its purpose of reducing its nation's dependence on petroleum energy.

For information regarding EVAC, contact Electric Vehicle Association of Canada, 56 The Sparks Street Mall, Suite 100, Ottawa, Ontario, K1P 5A9.

DEVELOPMENT IN ENGLAND

LUCAS ELECTRIC LIMOUSINE

Photos courtesy of Lucas Electric Limousine

Lucas Batteries, Limited

One of the leading British electric vehicle manufacturers is Lucas Batteries, Ltd., of Birmingham, England. Efforts made by Lucas have created additional markets for their batteries and electric vehicle components.

The Lucas Electric Taxi is a result of strong product development in a vehicle designed for a specific purpose. The side-entry battery exchange system allows for rapid exchange. It has been designed to operate in a typical London cab working cycle.

The first Lucas Electric Taxi was demonstrated to the public at the London Motor Show in October, 1975. The result of additional studies led to the production of two prototype Mark III Electric Taxis. The controller used was a solid-state SCR type, incorporating regenerative braking. The projected range is 70 miles (112 km) to 140 miles (224 km) at a constant 30 mph (48 km/hr). The maximum speed of the vehicle is over 50 mph (80 km/hr) with acceleration of zero to 30 miles per hour (0 to 48 km/hr) in 14 seconds fully laden. Thirty-six lightweight 6-volt lead-acid traction batteries power a 216-volt DC, 37-kw (50 bhp) series-wound, 4,600 RPM motor.

The Lucas Electric Midi-Bus has a top speed of 50 miles per hour (80 km/hr) with a low speed range of about 112 miles (180 km) without passengers. The Midi-Bus has been in service between Birmingham and Manchester, England, a 40-mile (64-km) circuit, since early 1975.

The Lucas Electric Delivery Van/Personnel Carrier has demonstrated a variety of services

LUCAS ELECTRIC TAXI

LUCAS CF ELECTRIC VANS AND TRUCKS

All Photos courtesy of Special Projects Division, Lucas Batteries Ltd., Birmingham, England

for fleet operators, including the post office. It has a one-ton payload (907 kg) and can accommodate up to nine people plus the driver with space for luggage. The passenger-carrying version is called the Lucas Electric Pullman, designed for airport-to-hotel use; the non-passenger variety is called the Lucas Electric Delivery Van.

Two other variations of the delivery van are the Lucas Electric Limousine and the Lucas Electric Crew Bus, which are dome-roofed vehicles designed for passenger comfort and ease

of entry. Again, the battery pack has been designed for quick battery exchanges. The range for these models is 70 miles (113 km) per charge minimum and up to 140 miles (225 km) at 30 mph (48 km/hr) with a top speed of 50 mph (80 km/hr).

The Lucas Company believes this type of vehicle is ideal for use in areas where internal combustion vehicles are forbidden, such as inside food warehouses, supermarkets, postal sorting offices and hospitals.

The Enfield Electric

Historically, Great Britain's Enfield was one of the world's most successful electric cars. Produced in the late 60's and early 70's, the Enfield was widely publicized and available to the general public.

A four-passenger Enfield 465 was displayed at the First International Electric Vehicle Symposium, held in 1970 in Phoenix, Arizona.

This urban commuter coupe had a maximum top speed of 40 mph (64 km/hr), with acceleration from zero to 30 mph (48 km/hr) in ten seconds. Boasting an electrical efficiency of 83%, the vehicle could travel between 30 and 40 miles (48 and 64 km) per charge with a 208-lb (94-kg) battery pack. The Enfield weighed in at a trim 1450 lbs (657 kg), featuring a reinforced plastic body.

ENFIELD ELECTRIC COUPE

DEVELOPMENT IN ENGLAND (Ctd.)

LUCAS BATTERY-ASSISTED BICYCLE

Photo courtesy
Lucas Industries, Ltd.

Battery-assisted Bicycle

Lucas of England has developed a battery-assisted bicycle and conversion kit designed to minimize rigorous cycling. Lucas Industries Limited, a major manufacturer of electronic components and motors, does not intend to market the battery-assisted bicycle or kit. It built the prototype to evaluate its design feasibility and promote Lucas products for use by other electric bicycle manufacturers.

The conversion kit would have a .3 hp motor which would provide power, on demand, when the rider is pedaling. The motor is connected to the pedal chain via a small sprocket. This concept allows the use of the three-speed rear hub but also carries the restriction of having the pedals rotate every time the motor is engaged.

Two types of batteries may be used. A 16-amp-hour version provides a range of 4 miles (6.4 km) with constant power assistance and 10 miles (16 km) with intermittent use. An optional 30-amp-hour battery provides about twice the range. The 21 to 28 lb (9.5 to 12.7 kg) bicycle kit (depending on which battery is used) can, with minimum pedal assistance, achieve 8 mph (12.8 km/hr), 10.5 mph (16.8 km/hr), and 14 mph (22.5 km/hr) respectively in each of three speeds. These speeds are comparable to those achieved by pedalling.

For more information, contact Lucas Industries Limited, Great King Street, Birmingham B192XF, England.

Silent Karrier

The Silent-Karrier is a two-ton delivery van designed to handle a payload of 3,500 lbs (1587 kg). The vehicle is produced by the Chloride Group, Ltd., of London, England, and was developed jointly by Chloride, Chrysler of the United Kingdom, and The National Freight Corporation. The Silent Karrier has a range of 40 miles (64 km) per charge.

SILENT KARRIER

Photo courtesy of
Lead Industries
Association/Chloride

Photo courtesy of the Electric Vehicle News

The Milk Float

The United Kingdom has a population of over 56 million people. Each person drinks about five pints of milk per week.

This little tidbit of information may, at first glance, seem irrelevant, except that the United Kingdom operates a force of about 50,000 electric vehicles to deliver the milk to British inhabitants. The home delivery of milk and dairy products is unique to Great Britain, hence the existence of the "milk float."

The milk float averages abut 300 miles (483 km) per week of quiet, non-polluting duty. It makes one wonder why a similar application of multi-stop service has not been applied to a greater degree in other countries.

The British maintain that a reduction in pollution is merely a side effect or bonus derived from these vehicles, and that the major motivation is the economy and excellent service record which accompanies this type of delivery method. Economy allows this type of delivery service to exist in the first place, because if in-

ternal combustion vehicles at a higher price had to be used, the service would be endangered. Records of dependability from this form of mulit-stop-and-start transportation have been remarkable. And, although the initial cost of the electric milk float is high, the lower running costs easily outstrip the difference in purchase price.

With over fifteen million miles (24 million km) per year spent delivering over two hundred million tons (180 billion kg) of milk and dairy products, traveling more than forty miles (64 km) per day, while making up to 250 starts and stops daily, the British electric milk float is a credit to any commercial enterprise.

Residual benefits, such as quietness of operation, pollution-free service, and absolute dependability make one wonder why the use of electric vehicles for mail delivery and short-haul operations has not proliferated more rapidly in an energy-sensitive world.

TEILHOL 3-WHEEL COMMUTER CAR

TEILHOL CITICOME TRUCK

TEILHOL GOLF CART

Photos courtesy Teilhol Voiture Electrique

MIDINETTE DELIVERY VEHICLES

Photos courtesy CEDRE

DEVELOPMENT IN FRANCE

Teilhol Voitures Electriques

Teilhol of France produces electric vehicles for industrial, recreational, and commuter use. An additional model is a modified commuter version for use by a person confined to a wheel chair.

The "Citicome" trucks, K5 and K10, were developed as economical, "multi-stop," light-load delivery vehicles. The K5 is a flat-bed truck; the K10 is a step van with access through the rear doors. The Teilhol "Handicar," a mini-van modified for use by the handicapped, can be automatically tilted allowing the rear of the car to become flush with the pavement. The driver can wheel himself into the car and up to the steering wheel without leaving the wheelchair. A seat in the rear of the mini-van can be folded down to accommodate a second passenger.

All Teilhol models have front wheel drive and a 25 to 35 mile (40-60 km) range, using eight 12-volt batteries weighing 330 lbs (205 kg). Teilhol also produces golf cars and a bug-like three-wheeled commuter car. For further information, contact Teilhol Voitures Electriques, Zone Industrielle de la Masse, 63600 Ambert, France.

Midinette

The MIDINETTE, produced in France by CEDRE, is an ideal vehicle for small deliveries or use in airports and hospitals where maneuverability is an asset. With a power consumption of .1 kilowatt hour per km, the Midinette is an economical supplement to rapid transit and is already being marketed in Japan.

The Midinette has a 60-mile (96-km) range and can reach a top speed of 30 mph (48 km) in 10 seconds. Power is transferred from two series-wound DC motors through a dual transmission to the steerable front wheel. Two batteries are located between the rear wheels giving the Midinette a low center of gravity and good stability.

CEDRE produces two commuter models, the Midinette and the Soubrette, one children's car, the Formula 1, and a garden-size tractor, the Poly-Cultivator.

For more information contact CEDRE, 31310 Montesquiev-Volvestre, France.

DEVELOPMENT IN GERMANY

Electric vehicle development in Germany is a joint effort by automobile, battery, electrical, and heavy machine industries under the coordination of the GES (Gesell-Schaft Fur Electrischen Strassenzerkehr mbh, Dusseldorf), a subsidiary of RWE, the country's largest electric utility.

GES acts as a clearinghouse for development by component and vehicle manufacturers. Therefore, integration of mutually beneficial technology into all areas of the cooperative is realized.

A total of 20 MAN buses are experimentally servicing three public lines on a full schedule basis in Dusseldorf and nearby Monchenglad-bach. The MAN Electrobus Program is partially subsidized by the government. In October, 1974, in Monchengladbach, seven electric buses replaced diesels on a 25 mile (40 km) round trip with 88 stops between the city's center and a nearby town. A range of 50 miles (80 km) per battery charge was possible from each bus. Battery exchange takes only about five minutes, easily comparable to refueling a conventional diesel bus.

Mercedes-Benz hybrid electric buses will also be used in a similar program. Another GES test involved 20 Volkswagen and 30 Mercedes-Benz Electric Vans, with an additional 80 vehicles to be added at a later date.

MAN ELECTRIC BUS

MERCEDEZ BENZ HYBRID ELECTRIC BUS

MBB Electro-Transporter

An electric transport vehicle has been developed by MBB (Messerschmitt-Bolkow-Blohm) in Germany. MBB collaborated with Bosch for electric propulsion, Varta for batteries, and Bayer Chemicals for the self-supporting plastic chassis.

Gross vehicle weight is 7,275 lbs (3,300 kg); payload is 2,205 lbs (1,000 kg); battery weight is 1,918 lbs (870 kg).

Features include a 60 hp motor, a maximum vehicle speed of 50 mph (80 km/hr), and range of 37 to 65 miles (60 to 105 km).

The chassis can accommodate eight different body styles from a flatbed truck to a small bus. Plastic body construction allows current-carrying connections to be embedded in plastic.

Photo courtesy of Messerschmitt-Bolkow-Blohm

DEVELOPMENT IN GERMANY (Ctd.)

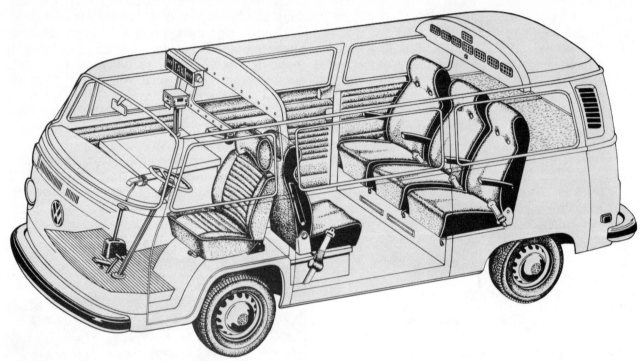

THE VOLKSWAGEN HYBRID-ELECTRIC CITY TAXI   Photo courtesy of Volkswagenwerk AG
Features include a bulletproof glass and steel wall which separates driver from passengers, and automatic electrically controlled right-side access door.

Volkswagen City Taxi

The Volkswagen Company, responding to the need for a city taxi, has produced a hybrid gasoline-electric model, based on the Microbus. This vehicle was specifically designed to be used as a taxi, including such considerations as special seats which carry up to four adults with room for luggage, a wheelchair, or baby carriage. Volkswagen considers this vehicle the taxi of the future.

The hybrid taxi uses a 50-DIN horsepower, 1600-CC gasoline engine and a Bosch DC shunt motor. In the electric mode, the vehicle achieves a maximum speed of 43.5 mph (70 km/hr). The hybrid mode produces a maximum speed of 64.6 mph (104 km/hr) and acceleration of zero to 62 mph (100 km/hr) in 31 seconds. The overall operating range is comparable to a conventional internal combustion engined vehicle; fuel consumption is 20 mpg (8.5 km/L).

In "hybrid" operation the vehicle's driving power comes from a combination of both the electric motor and gasoline engine. The vehicle starts out on electric power provided by eleven storage batteries, then switches to the gasoline engine at higher speeds. In cases where the gasoline engine cannot produce enough power to meet the vehicle's needs, the electric motor automatically resumes support, with both power systems used to propel the vehicle.

If the gasoline engine produces more power than needed at any time, the electric motor, acting as a generator, is used to recharge the batteries.

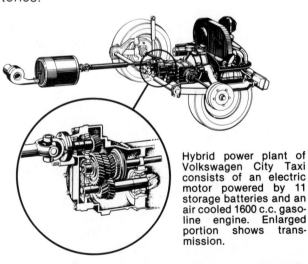

Hybrid power plant of Volkswagen City Taxi consists of an electric motor powered by 11 storage batteries and an air cooled 1600 c.c. gasoline engine. Enlarged portion shows transmission.

Photo courtesy of Volkswagenwerk AG

(LEFT) MERCEDES-BENZ ELECTRIC VAN (RIGHT) VOLKSWAGEN COMMERCIAL

Photo courtesy of Volkswagenwerk AG

A recent announcement from Volkswagenwerk AG indicated the production of an all-electric Volkswagen Commercial. The vehicle uses a 33-kw (44-bhp) motor with a continuous output of about 14 kw (22 bhp). Acceleration is zero to 31 mph (50 km/hr) in 12 seconds with a maximum speed of 44 mph (70 km/hr). A thyristor is used to control the energy from the 1896 lb (860 kg) battery pack, with a 144-volt, 180-amp-hour capacity. The Commercial has a range of 31 to 50 miles (50 to 80 km) on a single charge.

Actual development of the Volkswagen Electric Commercial started in 1969. Since 1972, experimental vehicles such as the Elektro Transporter have covered more than 310,000 miles (500,000 km) in service. The Volkswagen Electric Commercial will be assembled on the same production line as the gasoline version.

Prior to the announcement of Volkswagen production plans, tests were conducted by GES and Lufthansa German Airlines which aided in the accumulation of data on several GES-test bed vehicles, including a Mercedes-Benz Electric Van.

Volkswagen and GES mutually developed an electric passenger car using the chassis of an Audi 100. A new nickel-iron battery by Varta powered the experimental vehicle. Besides serving as a test bed for the new nickel-iron batteries, attention was also given to a new motor and a combination of hydraulic torque converter and electronic control system utilizing field weakening.

Germany considers the possibility of 20% electric vehicles by the year 2000. German designers say ten more years of research and development will be necessary to perfect a total electric infrastructure of vehicles, service, and electric power production.

Photo courtesy of Volkswagenwerk AG

The Elektro-Transporter or Volkswagen Commercial, showing side-loading battery access tray.

DEVELOPMENT IN GERMANY (Ctd.)

Mercedes-Benz Delivery Van, 307E

A new experimental van, the Mercedes-Benz 307E, deviates only slightly from its standard internal combustion powered counterpart. The manufacturer, Daimler-Benz, claims a lower cost of production and operation was the main objective in developing the vehicle. The van's range is 50 miles (80 km) and has a maximum speed of 43 mph (70 km/hr). Power is transmitted to a 20-kw DC motor through an automatic transmission and hydrodynamic torque converter.

DEVELOPMENT IN HOLLAND

The Witkar System

The Witkar "White Car" System, established in 1974, is an Amsterdam, Holland-based electric rental Cooperative Association with 3,000 members. Thirty five three-wheeled, 860 lb (390 kg) two-passenger 20-mph (32-km/hr) cars with polyester resin bodies are powered by nickel-cadmium batteries which recharge in minutes at five stations located throughout the central Amsterdam area.

A member inserts a magnetically-coded key into a station terminal, selects his destination and uses the first car in line. Members pay a one-time fee of 50 guilders ($20) for their card and a rental fee of one guilder (40 cents) for 10 minutes of use.

The Witkar System was conceived by Luud Schimmelpennink, now secretary of the Association, who plans to expand operations to 15 stations and 100 cars.

WITKAR CHARGING STATION

Photo courtesy of Lead Industries Association

Spykstaal

SPYKSTAAL MODEL 2000

For over twenty five years, Spykstaal has been one of Holland's leading manufacturers of electric-powered transportation. Numerous electrovan models serve industry as tractors, haulers, delivery vans, and trucks. Though these vehicles typically supply transportation in factories, airports, and shipyards, there are models specifically designed to function as library buses, portable flower stands, dental vehicles, and even motor homes.

Spykstaal meets the specific transportation needs of industry by offering a range of ten basic designs and over twenty-five models.

SPYKSTAAL MODEL 1500

SPYKSTAAL MODEL 4-110

SPYKSTAAL MODEL 200

SPYKSTAAL MODEL 412

SPYKSTAAL MODEL 3-110

DEVELOPMENT IN ITALY

HYBRID TAXI

AMBULANCE

Progetti Gestioni Ecologiche, an Italian firm, has designed a computerized rental system with recharging stations for city residents. This system was conceived to complement their production electric vehicle designs.

Their prototypes include a ten-passenger school bus, which weighs 2,734 lbs (1,240 kg) and can carry ten pupils plus a driver for a distance of 62 miles (100 km) urban and 87 miles (140 km) highway at 28 mph (45 km/hr). Top speed is 37 mph (60 km/hr).

The PGE ambulance is basically the same vehicle. This three-passenger automobile weighs 1,653 lbs (750 kg) and uses a 72-volt motor, producing a top speed of 37 mph (60 km/hr) and a range of 47 miles (75 km) urban and 68 miles (110 km) highway at 31 mph (50 km/hr).

The PGE Hybrid Taxi is basically the same external vehicle size as the ambulance and school bus, but weighs 3,197 lbs (1,450 kg) and is designed to carry a driver and four passengers with luggage. The 72-volt electric motor yields speeds of 37 mph (60 km/hr). The internal-combustion engine can yield 130 km/hr. Range is 62 miles (100 km) for urban and 87 miles (140 km) for highway driving at 28 mph (45 km/hr).

Other PGE vehicles include a hybrid van and six-passenger personnel carrier, plus a larger 3,638 lbs (1,650 kg) van which can carry 1,763 lbs (800 kg). Controls are solid state with thyristors and regenerative braking. Acceleration for the van is zero to 19 mph (30 km/hr) in six seconds.

Part of the PGE concept is a vehicle fleet hiring system to be used for town dwellers. This system is keyed into a credit card and computer. The renter picks up his vehicle at a charging station and returns it at another station, plugs in and leaves. PGE already has one prototype rental station located in Padua, Italy. Customers there are reported very satisfied with the computerized system.

The PGE M8 Electric Van

The PGE M8 is a production electric van featuring front-wheel drive and a streamlined aluminum body.

The 4200-lb (1904-kg) three-passenger van has a top speed of 40 mph (64 km/hr) and accelerates to 30 mph (48 km/hr) in 13 seconds. Range is 45 miles (72 km) per charge in average stop-and-start driving.

Power is regulated by a PGE solid-state controller to a 20-hp DC motor from a 2000-lb (907-kg) battery pack of 30 6-volt lead-acid batteries.

The M8 van has been used in a public awareness program by ENEL, the Italian national electricity agency.

For more information, contact Progetti Gestioni Ecologiche, Via Rosellini, 20124, Milan, Italy.

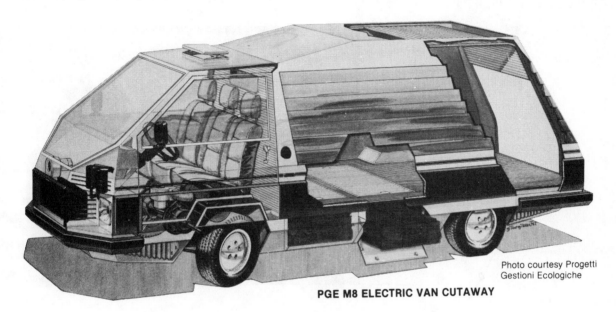

Photo courtesy Progetti Gestioni Ecologiche

PGE M8 ELECTRIC VAN CUTAWAY

ECOS

The Pininfarina Company, in conjunction with FIAT, has produced a prototype commuter automobile designed to carry four passengers.

The Ecos is a 2750-lb (1250-kg), front-wheel-drive, three-door sedan with a top speed of 50 mph (80 km/hr) and range of over 35 miles (60 km) per charge.

Power is supplied by a Magneti Marelli 16 lead-acid battery pack weighing 1060 lbs (481 kg), through a 96-volt DC 35-hp compound-wound motor via a solid state controller.

ECOS 3-DOOR SEDAN

Photo courtesy Carrozzeria Pininfarina-Torino

DEVELOPMENT IN ITALY (Ctd.)

Fiat XI/23 City Car

The Fiat XI/23 is a two-seat passenger car with a maximum speed of 47 mph (75 km/hr) and a range of 45 miles (70 km) at a constant 31 mph (50 km/hr).

This prototype city car features front-wheel drive, a 13.5 hp DC motor, with separate excitation, and a transistorized solid-state controller with regenerative braking.

The most significant advance is the use of Yardney nickel-zinc batteries which have a maximum capacity 1.75 times that of conventional lead-acid batteries.

Curb weight is 1810 lbs (820 kg), of which 370 lbs (166 kg) is batteries.

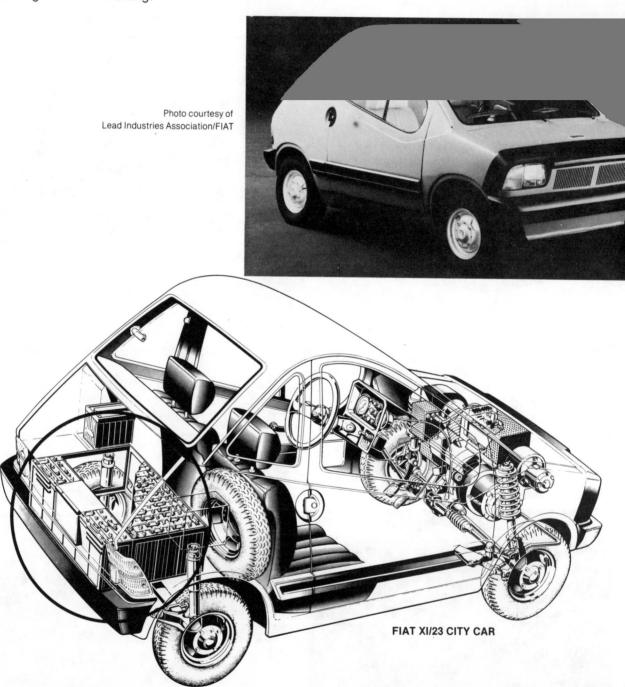

Photo courtesy of
Lead Industries Association/FIAT

FIAT XI/23 CITY CAR

ZELE MODEL '80

Zagato

The Zagato Zele 1000, Zele 2000, and the Nuova Zele are produced in Italy by Zagato, the famous coach builder. Zagato's newest model is the Nuova Zele '80, a four-passenger, 3-door commuter van. Powered by a 6-hp 60-volt DC motor and ten 6-volt traction batteries, the Nuova Zele can accelerate to 30 mph (50 km/hr) in 20 seconds. This practical commuter vehicle weighs 660 lb (300 kg) and has a 30 mile (50 km) range.

The 1000 and 2000 models are both two-door sport coupes with fiberglass bodies and weigh approximately 1100 lb (500 kg). The sport models have 6-hp DC motors and carry a 12-volt SLI battery which operates accessories. Top speed for the sport coupes is 40 mph (65 km/hr). Range per charge is 40 miles (65 km).

Zagato cars have been marketed in the U.S. under the name Elcar. Other Italian efforts have been centered around ENEL, the Italian electric utility. ENEL has sponsored an electric vehicle development program with Fiat since late 1973. Two Fiat 850-T models were used to demonstrate the difference between shunt and series DC motors.

Another Italian electric is a three-wheeled vehicle based on the Vespa car. Also, an electric car researched and developed by Gianni Roglianni and designed by Giovanni Michelotti was introduced in Turin in 1974. This small 1100-lb (500-kg) city car has a top speed of 37 mph (58 km/hr) and a range of 30 miles (48 km) per charge, using a 4-hp motor. Both the chassis and the body are primarily aluminum.

ZAGATO/ELCAR

Photo courtesy of Lead Industries Association/Zagato

DEVELOPMENT IN JAPAN

In the future, Japan may capture a large share of the American electric vehicle market. Reports indicate that current Japanese electric vehicle progress leads the efforts of all nations, including the U.S. Japan is a country where the small automobile is an accepted fact and pollution is at a dangerous level. The Japanese began funding their electric vehicle program in 1971.

Japan is the world's largest importer of oil, which further motivates them to accelerate development of electric vehicles. It is to their advantage to have worldwide oil consumption decreased. The electric vehicle is the cornerstone of that program.

A cooperative effort between the Japanese government and private companies contributes to the solution of technological problems. They have produced sophisticated prototypes which incorporate styling, sales appeal, and the latest technology. The Japan Electric Vehicle Association was established in 1976 with the guidance and cooperation of Japan's Ministry of International Trade and Industry. It is composed of manufacturers of vehicles and components and includes such companies as Toyota, Nissan, and Mitsubishi.

The development program includes electric passenger cars, trucks and buses. New batteries are being studied, along with components, electronic control devices, and motors. The result of this data has produced four types of lightweight and compact electric cars and trucks. In the first phase of this program, three vehicles were constructed with advanced lead-acid batteries. Seven types of lead-acid batteries, plus others using materials such as zinc, were also produced. In 1976, four second-phase experimental vehicles began demonstration tests in city and suburban operation. The vehicles ran a total distance of 1,864 miles (3000 km) averaging 50 to 62 miles (80 to 100 km) per day on flat and hilly terrain.

The Daihatsu, Mitsubishi, Toyota, and Toyo Kogyo Companies have been involved in developing ten different types of electric vans and trucks. In addition, ten types of electric vehicles have been fabricated since 1967 by Japanese electric utility companies for demonstration purposes. These have been basically gasoline vehicles converted to electric power. Demonstrations directed at newspaper delivery, milk delivery and service-oriented vehicles for power companies have been stressed. There are twelve electric buses in operation in large Japanese cities to date.

There are approximately 12,400 electric vehicles in practical use in Japan. Of these, 400 are in on-road use and 12,000 are used for service work such as ferry cars, golf carts, milk and newspaper delivery, etc. The Council on Electric Vehicles in the Ministry projects 200,000 electric vehicles for on-road use and 50,000 for service use in 1986.

Daihatsu Kogyo Co., Ltd., has developed the PREET system to introduce the public to electric vehicles. PREET is similar to the Witcar in Amsterdam (see Development in Holland). The PREET System is a rental car club which provides its members with the use of a small, two-passenger commuter vehicle on a "station to station" basis. Special service stations will be provided on roads, near hotels, department stores, and other dense traffic areas where the vehicles can be recharged and serviced. Renters can use the system by inserting their PREET membership card into the station computer to obtain a vehicle. The computer will calculate the length of time the car is used and deduct the charges from the member's bank account.

The electric vehicle industry in Japan has a major advantage in that Japan's auto industry is highly supportive of electromotive development, working closely with the government to co-ordinate research, development, and production of electric vehicles.

Eighteen Suzuki two-passenger prototype electric vans have been built since 1970, many under the auspices of the Japanese Electric Vehicle Association. The 2400-lb (1088-kg) four-door van carries eight 12-volt lead-acid batteries weighing 790 lb (358 kg), has an 8.2-hp series-wound DC motor, and features a rapid battery replacement system. The van has a maximum speed of 41 mph (66 km/hr) and a range of 56 miles (90 km) at 25 mph (40 km/hr) with acceleration from zero to 25 mph (40 km/hr) in 9 seconds.

For more information, contact Suzuki Motor, Hamamatsu-Nishi P.O. Box 1, 432-91 Hamamatsu, Japan.

Toyota EV-2

The EV-2 is a second-stage experimental electric automobile developed in cooperation with the Japanese government. The vehicle was designed for use in metropolitan areas similar to Japanese cities. These parameters include special attention to extended range and acceleration rather than high speed and the ability to climb grades. Speed limits in Japan are 25 mph (40 km/hr).

The four-passenger body is designed to be ultra-lightweight yet strong by incorporating curved surfaces and reinforced ribs for maximum strength. Total vehicle weight is 2,767 lbs (1255 kg). The 1169 lb (530 kg) hybrid battery pack consists of a high-energy-density zinc-air battery for range and an advanced lead-acid battery for power. A separately excited DC motor rated at 20-38 kilowatts powers the rear wheels through a two-speed automatic transmission and a solid-state controller.

TOYOTA EV-2   Photo courtesy of Lead Industries Association/Toyota

Maximum speed is 53 mph (85 km/hr); range is 283 miles (455 km) at a constant 25 mph (40 km/hr) and 155 miles (250 km) in a stop-and-go driving cycle. Acceleration is 0 to 25 mph (40 km/hr) in 6 seconds.

Nissan EV-4

Nissan Motor Company, manufacturer of Datsun motorcars, developed in cooperation with the Japanese government two experimental vehicles named EV-4.

The first vehicle, EV-4-P, is claimed to have the highest range of any electric vehicle powered by a lead-acid battery system. The range at 25 mph (40 km/hr) for the compact truck is 188 miles (302 km). Top speed is 54 mph (87 km/hr); acceleration is 0 to 25 mph (0 to 40 km/hr) in 6.9 seconds.

A 27-kw shunt-wound DC motor is controlled through an SCR chopper.

The second model, EV-4-H, is claimed to have the highest range of any electric vehicle. The compact truck uses a hybrid battery system of a zinc-air and lead-acid battery in com-

bination. Range at 25 mph (40 km/hr) is 308 miles (496 km). Top speed is 56 mph (90 km/hr) and acceleration is 0-25 mph (0-40 km/hr) in 4.9 seconds. The EV-4-H uses a 20-kw shunt-wound DC motor controlled through an SCR chopper with provision for regenerative braking. Total efficiency from battery to motor is 78%. The two-passenger truck construction relies heavily on fiber-reinforced plastic and aluminum. Vehicle weight is 5,490 lbs (2,490 kg). A special design consideration allows for easy battery exchange through a side-loading tray arrangement.

Photo courtesy of Nissan Motor Company

DEVELOPMENT IN JAPAN (Ctd.)

Photo courtesy Nissan Motor Company

Nissan Laurel

Two Japanese electric passenger cars were produced by Nissan in 1974. A Datsun 200L and a Nissan Laurel were developed to be used by VIPs at the International Oceanographic Exposition in Okinawa, 1975.

Designed for short trips, the five-passenger vehicles had a range of 40 miles (65 km). Top speed was 53 mph (85 km/hr). Features included air conditioning, power brakes, thyristor, and 2-speed automatic transmission. Total vehicle weight was 4,230 lbs (1919 kg.)

Photo courtesy of the Electric Vehicle News/Daihatsu

Daihatsu

This four passenger lightweight automobile prototype has a maximum speed of 55 mph (89 km/hr) and a range of 109 miles (175 km) per charge, at a constant 25 mph (40 km/hr). This vehicle can accelerate from 0 to 19 mph (30 km/hr) in 2.4 seconds. Gross vehicle weight is 2500 lbs. (1132 kg).

DAIHATSU J-S60 ELECTRIC VAN

Photos courtesy of
the Electric Vehicle
News/Daihatsu

**DAIHATSU J-S60
PICK-UP**

Daihatsu Motors

Daihatsu Motors of Japan produces the J-S60 Electric Van and the J-S60 Electric Pick-Up, which have 18-hp (14-kw) DC shunt motors and Daihatsu-designed 96-volt controllers. The J-S60's are powered by eight 12-volt lead batteries and have four-speed transmissions. The van can carry two passengers and a 330-lb (150-kg) payload, while the pick-up carries two passengers and a 550-lb (250-kg) payload. The J-S60's have a top speed of 46 mph (75 km/hr) and a cruising range of 44 miles (70 km) at 24 mph (40 km). For further information, contact Daihatsu Motors, 1-1, Daihatsu-Chu, Ikeda City, Osaka Prefecture, Japan.

Mazda Titan Hybrid Truck

This vehicle uses both diesel and electric power in combination. The DC electric motor uses series-parallel switching controls with four 12-v lead-acid batteries. The 2,977 cc diesel engine can power the 5,115 lb (2,320 kg) truck at speeds of up to 62 mph (100 km/hr) with a range of 6.2 miles (10 km). Batteries are automatically recharged while driven under diesel power.

MAZDA TITAN

Photo courtesy of Toyo
Kogyo Co., Ltd.

DEVELOPMENT IN JAPAN (Ctd.)

Toyo Kogyo

The Toyo Kogyo Company is one of Japan's largest vehicle manufacturers. Since 1966 several Mazda electric vehicles have been developed under an agency of the Ministry of International Trade and Industry (MITI).

One vehicle, the Ev3 Phase II, has a 127 mile (205 km) range at 25 mph (40 km/hr). This model, (not shown) is a lightweight flat bed truck weighing 1716 lbs (778 kg). Top speed is 45 mph (72 km/hr).

MAZDA BONGO VAN

Photo courtesy Toyo Kogyo Co., Ltd.

Mazda Bongo Van

This 5-seater minibus weighs 2,789 lbs. (1,265 kg). Top speed is 40 mph (65 km/hr); range is 37 miles (60 km) per charge. Vehicle weight is 2,789 lbs (1,265 kg). A 4-speed transmission is used. Eight 12-v lead-acid batteries supply power to the 19.2 kw DC motor.

Mazda Familia Passenger Car

The Familia is a four passenger automobile weighing 2424 lbs (1100 kg). Eight 12 v advanced lead-acid batteries provide power to the 11 kw DC motor via a Thyristor chopper. Top speed is more than 50 mph (80 km/hr). Range is more than 44 miles (70 km) per charge.

MAZDA FAMILIA PASSENGER CAR

Photo courtesy Toyo Kogyo Co., Ltd.

DEVELOPMENT IN INDIA

MINITRUCK

In collaboration with a Swedish manufacturer, Electromobile of Bangalore, India, has developed two electric vehicles. The Electrona-24 is an electric motorcycle and the Minitruck is an indoor freight carrier. Both are available for commercial distribution.

Early in 1979, the production prototype of the Electrona-24 had been completed and passed Indian government licensing requirements. The 230-lb (104-kg) two-wheeler is propelled by a 1-hp permanent magnet DC motor which receives power from two 12-volt lead-acid batteries. Maximum and cruising speed is 19 mph (31 km/hr) with a range of 31 miles (49 km). The controller is a series and parallel switching device with regenerative braking. Additional development is under way of a two-passenger version of the motorcycle using a 1.5-hp motor.

Electromobile's second vehicle, the Minitruck, features a variety of multi-purpose accessories designed for carrying light cargo. The 77-lb (35-kg) three-wheeler is operated by a series-wound motor powered by a 12-volt lead-acid battery. The vehicle's speed is approximately 3.7 mph to 7.4 mph (6 km/hr to 12 km/hr). It has a range of 25 to 30 miles (40 to 48 km).

ELECTRONA-24

DEVELOPMENT IN TAIWAN

In view of highly favorable conditions in Taiwan for the development of electric vehicles, the National Tsing Hua University has been conducting a research and development program. The project is designed to determine the technical and economic feasibility of manufacturing electric vehicles and marketing them in Taiwan and Southeast Asia.

Since 1973, the Tsing Hua Electric Vehicle Program (THEV) has developed four electric vehicle prototypes. The original design was a two-passenger, fiberglass-bodied vehicle which has a maximum speed of 56 mph (90 km) and a range of 99 miles (160 km) at 28 mph (45 km/hr). The subsequent three models are "mini-vans" designed for postal and telecommunication use.

Since 1978, the project has concentrated its efforts on research and development. A special plant of the Tang Eng Company has started production of ten vehicles per month to establish manufacturing and quality control systems while concurrently laying a firm foundation for future mass production.

TSING HUA MODEL 4

DEVELOPMENT IN NEW ZEALAND

KAWAKAWA CAR

Kawakawa Car

K. F. Edgecumbe, a member of New Zealand's Electric Vehicle Club, has built the Kawakawa car, a vehicle whose name is derived from the New Zealand town in which it was built. This remarkably light-weight, 900-lb (408-kg) mini-car has a unique and comprehensive safety system. The vehicle's design, battery pack location, and unusual emergency braking system work independently to protect passengers in a collision.

The batteries are housed in the front of the car, providing a crash barrier between the front of the car and its riders. The 600-lb (272-kg) battery pack is balanced over the front wheels to provide a solid block of weight which absorbs stress.

To guard against minor impacts, shock-absorbing foam fits tightly inside the nose of the car. Front suspension facilitates a "pendulum effect" which rocks or deflects passengers

away from the crash site on impact. This same safety feature helps the vehicle maintain an upright position even when turning corners at high speeds.

While most of the instruments can be found in their conventional dashboard positions, the most critical gauges are located on a flexible panel mounted in the center of the steering wheel. The steering wheel also serves as a hand brake, emergency power switch, and ignition kill-switch. In the event of a crash or emergency, a single push upward will immediately stop the vehicle.

The Kawakawa's two rewound motors originated from two Dodge starter generators. Each motor, mounted on a swing-arm, rear-suspension system, propels its own rear wheel.

For more information, contact New Zealand Electric Vehicle Club, 14 Hospital Road, Kawa, New Zealand.

DEVELOPMENT IN SPAIN

Electric Seat 127

The Electric Seat 127 is produced by Westinghouse S.A. of Madrid, Spain. The sporty, compact, two-passenger sedan uses the body and chassis components of the gasoline-powered Seat 127. The Seat 127 is a passenger car produced by the Seat Company, a FIAT licensee.

The Electric Seat 127 is a production model available to the public, with a cruising range of

40 miles (64 km) at 24 mph (38 km/hr), and a maximum speed of 45 mph (72 km/hr). The 2200-lb (997-kg) vehicle accelerates from zero to 30 mph (48 km/hr) in 11 seconds. Power from the 850-lb (385-kg) lead-acid battery pack is controlled by a Westinghouse S.A. solid state chopper to a 12.2 hp DC motor.

For more information, contact Westinghouse S.A., Avda Jose Antonio 10, Madrid 14, Spain.

DEVELOPMENT IN SWEDEN

Saab-Scandia of Sweden manufactures battery-powered motorized wheel chairs for the handicapped. One particularly advanced system, the Permobile, is available in versions which are designed to fit the specific needs of its user. All models can be used outdoors and can climb curbs and ramps.

SAAB-SCANDIA DELIVERY VAN

BATTERY-POWERED WHEEL CHAIRS

Saab-Scandia Electric Delivery Van

The Saab-Scandia van was designed in conjunction with a Swedish battery manufacturer, AB Tudor. The Swedish postal and telecommunication offices also assisted in the development of the prototype.

The 4,740-lb (2150-kg) vehicle is powered by a 12-hp shunt-wound DC motor. Power is supplied by a single unit, 144-volt lead-acid battery pack. The van has a cruising speed of 40 mph (64 km/hr) and a range of 62 miles (100 km) in city traffic.

DEVELOPMENT IN SWITZERLAND

Oehler Electro-Vehicles

George Fischer Brugg-Oehler Ltd., of Aarau, Switzerland, manufactures electric service vehicles, including an eight-passenger minibus, heavy duty tractors, small electric platform trucks for use in factories, and heavy-duty rider-seated platform trucks and dump trucks. These vehicles can handle extreme gradients and are available in many versions with a wide spectrum of load capacities. For further information, contact George Fischer Brugg-Oehler Ltd., Industriestrasse 44, CH-5001 Aarau, Switzerland.

OEHLER ELECTRIC TAXI

OEHLER PEDESTRIAN PLATFORM TRUCK

OEHLER RIDER SEATED PLATFORM TRUCK

DEVELOPMENT IN SWITZERLAND (Ctd.)

Pilcar

The Pilcar is the product of seven years of research by Pilcar of Switzerland. The four-seater is propelled by a 6-hp DC traction motor which receives power from an 84-volt lead-acid battery pack. The reinforced polyester hatchback can achieve a maximum speed of 55 mph (88 km/hr) and has a cruising range of 72 miles (116 km) at 40 mph (64 km/hr). Drive train features include automatic transmission and transistorized controls.

The manufacturer offers a three-year, unlimited mileage warranty to Pilcar owners. As of 1980, production of the vehicles was expected to expand to 400 or more units per year. The company was considering issuing licenses to manufacture the Pilcar in Belgium, France, Greece, Israel, and Canada. For more information, contact: Victor Perrenoud, General Manager, Rue Francois-Perreard 22, 1225 Chene-Bourg, Geneva, Switzerland.

PILCAR

ELECTRIC TAXI CABS

The next time you ride in a taxicab in a heavily-populated metropolitan area, notice two things: one, that the vehicle is moving very slowly and two, that the pollution level is usually quite high. You will observe long lines of taxi cabs waiting at taxi stands, idling their engines adding to the pollution level, and you'll see a great number of empty taxi cabs cruising for a fare. There is a need for a better system. In areas such as Chicago, for example, where the pollution concentrations are now higher than EPA standards, city governments should institute a plan which would incorporate electric taxicabs into their transportation grid.

The Lucas Electric Taxi, made in Britain, and the GES Hybrid Electric Volkswagen Microbus used as a taxi are two examples of the feasibility of electric vehicles using current state-of-the-art battery technology.

Surely, vehicles such as these could be assimilated into a large city's taxicab network. Perhaps the governing body of a metropolitan area should regulate the percentage of gasoline-powered taxicabs allowed within the highly congested areas. The balance of these vehicles could be electric-powered or electric hybrids. A map displayed on the taxi would tell the customer that the vehicle is electric and that trips would be limited to a five mile radius. Such a taxi would stay within the heavily-populated

PGE HYBRID TAXI

area, thereby reducing emissions in congested neighborhoods. The cab driver would benefit because short trips are profitable in tips; on short trip fares he receives more money per mile (km) and hour of driving. He could also be compensated with an incentive bonus for driving the electric. The money for this bonus could come out of the saving the taxi company would realize due to lower maintenance and replacement costs.

State-of-the-art batteries would start this program off, but as newer battery systems are developed and replace the old, the range and usable hours of operation could be increased.

The production of vehicles designed to be

LUCAS ELECTRIC TAXI

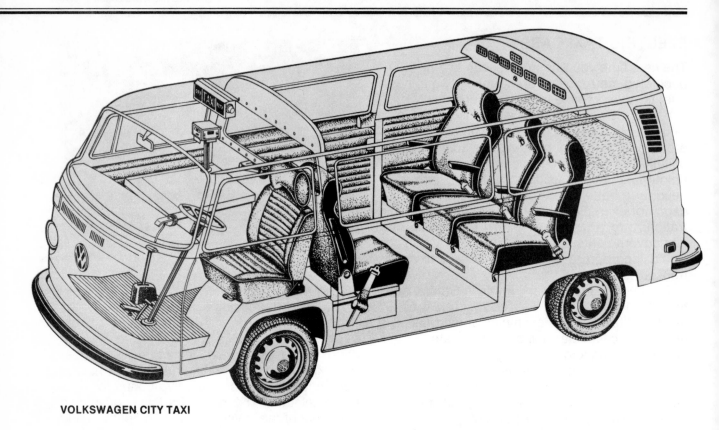

VOLKSWAGEN CITY TAXI

taxicabs will result in maximizing passenger and driver creature comforts. Provisions for carrying luggage would be needed because, although the electric taxi would not go to airports — bus, train terminals and hotels would be served. For city use, the electric taxi would never have to exceed 40 mph (64 km/hr) which is within today's technology. Materials could be plastic or rubber. After all, a rubber fender would never rust and could be bumped many times without ever leaving a dent. The use of hydrogen and oxygen fuel cells would be feasible because the number of cells that could be purchased for a fleet of taxicabs would rate a cost-saving quantity price. Then too, the heat required for winter operation could be converted directly from the hydrogen in a combustion-type catalytic heater.

An urban electric taxicab could be integrated into our system today. This is not beyond our technical capabilities. Hopefully, it is not beyond our political capabilities, because of the red tape necessary to implement such a system. Inhabitants and workers in congested areas must spend many hours a day in an atmosphere that is polluted beyond acceptable standards. An electric taxi would benefit these people in more ways than providing convenient clean transportation.

ELECTRIC MASS TRANSPORTATION

When the early railroad ran through an area, a city would sprout up as a natural consequence. The railroad industry was not merely a means of transportation, but literally an architect of the land.

Today, the relatively slow speeds of trains, due to equipment limitations and track deficiencies, seriously impair the value of the railroad as a passenger mode of transportation. The cost of maintaining a safe and clean right of way for a railroad is high, but insignificant compared with the cost of constructing a new rail system from scratch in today's economy. Also safety considerations must be made for passenger trains capable of traveling at speeds of 125 mph (200 km/hr) or more on existing tracks.

Today, there are many areas where high speed trains would not be feasible due to poor track conditions. A solution to the track problem must be reached or the railroad may be relegated to freight service.

Perhaps the railroads could benefit more from government participation. This is not to say that the government would own the railroads, but the road beds could be nationalized, thereby allowing them to be rebuilt and electrified. This process would convert the diesel-electric locomotives into pure electrics. As the electrification system progresses, the diesel-electric would run on total electric power more frequently.

This undertaking would be extremely expensive by any standard of economics. But, it would enable freight and passenger service to be powered electrically—from coal, nuclear, or other generation methods. This would allow the railroad industry to again become a valuable asset.

When one considers that it requires seven years from inception through research, development, and production to build an automobile from scratch, we can imagine how long it would take to modernize any significant portion of our rail system. Therefore this is a project that must be started immediately to bear fruit in 20 years.

For short-trip passenger use, perhaps new tracks can be installed in certain areas, but an entire revamping would be required to produce trains that can travel 500 mph, which is possible in the distant future. In the future transportation grid, more emphasis will be put on mass transportation because it can utilize electricity to its utmost potential. The concept of linear induction vehicles makes possible a mode of transportation that could certainly be called space age travel.

The idea for the linear induction device was suggested in 1895. The thought of transportation from one place to another without the use of wheels is certainly older than any other method of getting about. Remember that all animals, birds, fish, and insects do a pretty good job of getting from one place to another without wheels. Sail boats, surfboards, ice

MODERN RAPID TRANSIT
Photo courtesy of Boeing-Vertol Company
Boeing Rapid Transit cars service ground level, elevated and subway lines in Chicago, Illinois. Electric-train mass transportation has been in operation here since 1895.

skates, skis, and gliders are also examples of this method or transportation. The millipede is an insect that travels with the wave action of its legs, which is basically what happens in a linear induction device which travels on a wave of magnetic force. The linear induction motor has no moving parts. The vehicle is literally pushed along a monorail track or through a tunnel floating on magnetic cushions that provide frictionless travel. Prototype models have been developed by companies such as Messerschmitt-Bolkow-Blohm and Krauss-Maffei of Germany to prove that this type of vehicle is feasible.

Just when we will see linear induction vehicles on a wide scale will depend on many economic factors; however, when this mode becomes a reality, we will see less reliance upon air travel for short city-to-city commuter use.

Fastrans

The electric-powered Fastrans is a cantilevered monorail designed for urban transportation. The system uses vehicles designed to cruise at a speed of 75 mph (125 km/hr) along a 3-foot-wide (.91 m) monorail. The designer of the system, Ennis Sullivan, has emphasized in his plans minimum land usage. The guideway base requires only a 12-foot-wide (3.6 m) right of way.

The Fastrans vehicle is the same width as two city buses placed side by side; it provides seating for five passengers across. Each 15,532-lb (7043-kg) vehicle will transport 75

passengers. Vehicle operation is semi-automatic with an onboard operator and backup computer.

An advanced Fastrans model is planned which will achieve 125 mph (201 km/hr) and will have a 100-passenger capacity. This system will use the same guideway and mode of operation.

For more information, contact EWAY Engineering, 3947 Cedar Bayou, Dallas, TX 75234.

Transrapid—EMS

TRANSRAPID—EMS is a joint venture of two German companies, Messerschmitt-Bolkow—Blohm (MBB) and Krauss-Maffei. Their individual research and development since the late 1960's was combined in 1974 to produce high-speed ground transportation systems. The core of this technology is centered around magnetically-levitated, LIV's (Linear Induction Vehicles).

TRANSRAPID LIV BASIC VEHICLE

Photo courtesy of Transrapid—EMS (Krauss-Maffei & MBB)

Basic Vehicle

A basic test vehicle was demonstrated to the public in May, 1971, by MBB. This experiment proved the technical feasibility of a large-scale magnetically-elevated LIV. A speed of 56 mph (90 km/hr) was achieved on a 2,165-foot (660-m) straight test track by the 12,787 lb (5,800 kg) vehicle.

TRANSRAPID 02

Photo courtesy of Transrapid—EMS (Krauss-Maffei & MBB)

Transrapid 02

In October, 1971, Krauss-Maffei demonstrated to the public an 11-ton (11,300-kg) magnetically-elevated LIV with a maximum speed of 102 mph (164 km/hr).

Transrapid 03

Comparison trials between magnetically-levitated vehicles and air-cushion vehicles were made by using the TRANSRAPID 03, an air-cushion 87-mph (140-km/hr) LIV weighing 21,164 lbs (9,600 kg). Results of the tests proved the superiority of magnetic levitation, thereby halting air-cushion technology development.

Transrapid 04

TRANSRAPID 04 is the largest magnetically-levitated experimental passenger-carrying LIV in existence to date. A 7,874-ft (2,400-m) elevated test track is used to test components under realistic conditions and at higher speeds. The result of these tests is the basis for LIV research and development. The TRANSRAPID 04 has a weight of 40,786 lbs (18,500 kg) and a top speed of 155 mph (250 km/hr). Future vehicles with top speeds of up to 311 mph (500 km/hr) are anticipated.

TRANSRAPID 03   Photo courtesy of Transrapid—EMS
(Krauss-Maffei & MBB)

TRANSRAPID 04   Photo courtesy of Transrapid—EMS (Krauss-Maffei & MBB)

DEMAG & MBB Cabinlift

Two German companies, DEMAG and MBB, have developed a variety of systems incorporating the monorail concept. The Cabinlift is designed as a low-cost alternative to traffic tunnels linking office, industrial, hospital, and airport buildings.

The vehicles travel on rubber tires and use linear induction motors. Heated cabs vary in carrying capacity from 6 to 25 persons, and are totally automated.

Morgantown PRT System

Boeing Personal Rapid Transit (PRT) cars travel between two campuses of West Virginia University at Morgantown. The PRT system is a fleet of driverless rubber-tired vehicles which operate under fully automated computer control on 5.3 miles (8.5 km) of concrete guideway at a cruising speed of 30 mph (48.3 km/hr). Each vehicle uses a 70-hp compound-wound DC motor. The system was developed by Boeing Aerospace Company as a national demonstration project for the U.S. Department of Transportation's Urban Mass Transportation Administration. It is operated by West Virginia University with Boeing assistance. The Morgantown system is the only automated people mover currently in operation in an urban setting. It has carried four

DEMAG & MBB CABINLIFT Photo courtesy of Cabinlift DEMAG & MBB

million passengers since October, 1975. Forty five vehicles are presently employed; however, new plans include an expanded system with 28 additional cars.

MORGANTOWN PRT SYSTEM Photo courtesy of Boeing Aerospace Company

UTDC Light Rail Vehicle

The Urban Transportation Development Corporation, Ltd., (UTDC) of Toronto, Ontario, Canada, has produced a new light rail vehicle to be used on exclusive, semi-exclusive, or shared rights-of-way. The lower capital costs required for "light rail service" can allow construction of more transit route miles per dollar as compared with underground rapid transit. The vehicle can operate on streets or elevated platforms in a manner common to European cities.

In 1972, the city of Toronto decided to retain streetcar service in selected areas. The Toronto Transit Commission subsequently ordered 200 UTDC Light Rail Vehicles with deliveries scheduled for 1977.

The fully-loaded vehicle weighs 58,000 lbs (26,308 kg) and is scheduled to travel at 11 mph (18 km/hr). The use of solid-state controls with regenerative braking produces a 30% energy savings over conventional electric streetcars.

UTDC Advanced Technology Intermediate Capacity Transit System

A new system being developed by UTDC consists of small, quiet steel-wheeled trains for operation on street level, underground, or elevated rights-of-way. The lightweight trains will be about 120 feet (37 m) long and provide seating for 208 passengers. Propulsion and brakes will be executed by linear induction motors

UTDC LIGHT RAIL VEHICLE
Photo courtesy of
Urban Transportation
Development Corporation, Ltd.

mounted in the trucks. Disc and magnetic brakes will serve as emergency back-up.

An automated control system will allow for both driver and driverless operation of up to 20,000 passengers per hour.

UTDC ADVANCED TECHNOLOGY TRANSIT SYSTEM
Photo courtesy of Urban Transportation Development Corporation, Ltd.

Photo courtesy of Boeing Aerospace Company

Boeing PRT at the International Ocean Exposition, 1975

A system similar to the Boeing Morgantown PRT was used at the 1975 International Ocean Exposition in Okinawa, Japan. The system, produced by Boeing and Kobe Steel, Ltd., used sixteen computer-operated driverless cars over a 1.75 mile (2.8 km) stretch of two-way guideway. During the fair's six month run, the small rubber-tired electric cars carried four million riders.

Certain components of the system incorporated the StaRRcar concept originated by Alden Self-Transit Systems, Inc., of Natick, Maryland, U.S.A.

Photo courtesy of Ford Motor Company

Ford "ACT"

The ACT, "Automatically Controlled Transportation," was developed by the Ford Motor Company for the public. Two ACT systems are implemented, one at the hotel Hyatt Regency, Dearborn, Michigan, and the other installed at Bradley International Airport near Hartford, Conn.

The system is quite literally a "horizontal elevator" which is electrically powered and computer controlled.

At the Hyatt Regency Dearborn installation, the bi-directional vehicles glide quietly on foam-filled tires over 2,600 feet (793 m) of elevated guideway between the Fairlane shopping complex and the hotel.

Each vehicle will cruise at 25 mph (40 km/hr), and will accommodate 24 passengers (10 seated, 14 standing). The two-car system can transport up to 1,800 people per hour.

The "Electric Fireflies" of St. Louis

A shuttle system, affectionately named "The Electric Fireflies," was operated for 33 months by FTM (Future Transportation Models) of St. Louis, Missouri. The ten-passenger trams were used as a free shuttle in the city's Central West End. The Fireflies were supported by local merchants to provide transportation to their areas.

In this program, the Fireflies have carried over 100,000 passengers. The vehicles are now used for sight-seeing in the Missouri Botanical Gardens.

The ten-passenger battery-powered chassis were supplied by Centron Systems. The trams are manufactured by Pargo, Inc., of Charlotte, N.C.

Photo courtesy of Union Electric, St. Louis, Missouri

SOLAR-POWERED ELECTRIC AIRPLANES

A British developer and an American aeronautical engineer almost concurrently proved that solar-powered flight, if not feasible, is at least possible.

Several inventors, working independently of each other on two continents, have flown experimental manned electric aircraft, each of which was assembled at great personal expense.

The prospect of cross-continental passenger flight using the sun's energy as the sole means of power seems remote, even to the most exuberant scholar of aviation. Yet the feats of the two pioneers of sun-powered flight may have opened the doors to a new means of electric personal transportation of the future, lending new meaning to the familiar phrase, "things are looking up for electric vehicles."

The Solar Riser

A new milestone in aviation history was the first public manned flight of an aircraft powered exclusively by solar energy, on April 29, 1979 in California. Larry Mauro is inventor, designer, chief engineer, and pilot of the Solar Riser. The 125-lb (57-kg) ultra-light biplane was fitted with 504 solar cells, a small series-wound 3-hp electric motor, and a Hughes 500 23-lb (10-kg) helicopter nickel-cadmium battery. Flying weight with pilot was 290 lbs (131 kg). The Solar Riser was built to demonstrate the feasibility of flight using the direct power of sunlight for propulsion energy. Mauro's first flight produced a speed of 20-24 mph (32-39 km/hr) at an altitude of 30-40 feet (9-12 m) in 1.5 minutes for a distance of .5 mile (.8 km).

During test flights it was discovered that if the sun was covered by a cloud, solar electric energy dropped to nearly zero. Therefore, for reasons of safety, a battery was installed to store energy and offset the limited continuous output of the solar cell array.

According to Mauro, an alternate version of the plane using the same 30-foot (9-m) wingspan could accommodate twice as many solar cells as the original model. With a larger solar array and a lighter, more efficient battery, he predicts an improved craft could cruise continuously on solar power and use the excess solar energy to recharge the battery as it flies.

SOLAR RISER

The battery takes 45 minutes to 1.5 hours to recharge. To date his best flight was two miles (3 km) for six minutes at Oshkosh, Wisconsin, carrying a 130-lb (59-kg) pilot. Presently, the craft is on display in the Museum of Experimental Aircraft Association in Haines Corners, Wisconsin.

Mauro, an aeronautical engineer, is president of Ultralight Flying Machines which manufactures the Easy Riser, the conventional ultra-light biplane from which the Solar Riser was converted. The Easy Riser is available in kit form. The finished product, an ultra-light biplane, may be powered by a gasoline engine or used as a hang glider. For more information, contact Larry Mauro, 2960 Corvin Drive, Santa Clara, CA 95051.

The Solar One

Sustained solar-powered flight was also the goal of British inventor Fred To whose "Solar One" made its first nonpublic, documented solar-powered flight, a 60-foot (18-m) dash, achieving 48 mph (78 km/hr) near London on December 19, 1978. The Solar One uses 750 solar cells incorporated into its 69-foot (21-m) wingspan. While there is room for 230 square feet (21 square meters) of solar cells, economics would only allow the installation of cells on 38 square feet (3.5 square meters). The solar array provides energy for approximately eight minutes of climbing and a few minutes of cruising. It takes up to two hours to fully recharge the on-board 25 amp-hour nickel-cadmium battery pack. Four Bosch permanent magnet motors are connected by chain drive to a single propeller.

The 229-lb (104-kg) plane recorded a flight of .7 miles (1.1 km) at an altitude of 79 feet (24 m). The British team plans to add a lighter, more efficient DC motor in the hopes of accomplishing a Paris-to-London flight. The improved version has a projected cruising speed of 68 mph (110 km/hr) and a 298-mile (480-km) range.

The anticipation of less expensive solar cells and the application of projected improvements may help solar-powered aircraft become commercially successful. In the light of this prospect, the flight of these two solar powered experimental aircraft undoubtedly ranks with the first ventures of the Wright brothers.

Gossamer Penguin and Solar Challenger

In 1978, Paul Macready won over $300,000 in Kremer Prizes for man-powered flight with his Gossamer Condor and Gossamer Albatross.

A new model, the Gossamer Penguin, is designed to operate on solar power alone without carrying batteries. The craft has a 72-foot (22-m) wing span, weighs about 50 lbs (23 kg), and carries on its wing solar cells that supply energy to an electric motor which measures only 1.5 x 5″ (4 x 13.5 cm) and drives a rear-mounted propeller. With a flight speed of 15 mph (24 km/hr) and a maximum altitude of 10 feet (3 m), it has demonstrated that man can use solar energy exclusively for flight with no auxiliary battery pack.

A new project for Macready and his crew is the Solar Challenger, a solar plane that can negotiate long distances with a Paris-to-London flight being contemplated. The Challenger has a projected cruising speed of 30-40 mph (48-64 km/hr) at altitudes of 10,000 feet (3050 m) and a range of hundreds of miles. The plane will carry 47 lbs (21 kg) of solar cells on a 45-foot (14-m) wingspan. If the plane is able to perform to expectations, it will provide the first long distance solar-powered flight.

ELECTRIC POWERED BOATS

Vantage Electric Boats

The Vantage electric outboard motor system is a component package which is installed in a variety of boat models, primarily pontoon boats. Although the use of electric motors in boats for trolling is quite commonplace and the preferred method by many, there has been a trend to convert larger boats to electric power.

While the Vantage boat system is ideally suited to convert new or used houseboats, pontoon boats, deck boats, and other suitable hulls, the preferred method is to purchase a fully equipped boat with all electric equipment installed. A variety of horsepowers and battery packs are available to suit specific needs. Motor power ranges from 1 hp, 24 volts, for a small touring or park rental boat to 3 hp, 48 volts, for larger boats with heavy loads or long operating periods. The typical propulsion system consists of a DC electric motor mounted as an outboard motor with flexible coupler, rudder, and choice of propellers. Four to eight 6-volt, 185 to 225-amp, deep-cycling batteries supply power through a remote control for all-day use and equal battery drain. The batteries

VANTAGE 28′ SYLVAN HARDTOP   Photo courtesy of Vantage Boats

are charged by an automatic timer recharger.

An electrically-powered party or commercial tour boat can silently cruise the water at speeds of 4 to 8 mph (6 km/hr to 13 km/hr). Presenting no disturbance to wildlife or threat to the environment, the systems are ideal for nature programs in parks and areas which have restrictions against certain types or sizes of motors.

For information on conversion systems or fully equipped electric-powered boats, contact Vantage Boats, 6332 Lakeview Drive, Falls Church, VA 22041.

ALTERNATE FORMS OF TRANSPORTATION

Shell Kilometer Marathon Winner

With the increasing demand for more fuel-efficient automobiles, many people have wondered just how many miles per gallon (km/L) an internal combustion engined vehicle could achieve. A possible forerunner of cars to come was the winner of the Shell Kilometer Marathon, an 8.9-mile (14.3-km) race sponsored by Shell Oil and a German auto magazine. The winning vehicle was a diesel-powered three-wheeler that established an incredible new mileage record of 2281.8 mpg (970 km/L), breaking the month-old mileage record of 1722 mpg (735 km/L) held by a group of Dutch engineering students.

The futuristically designed record holder was built by a team of Mercedes-Benz apprentices from Stuttgart, and weighs 108 lb (48.9 kg). Power for the gas miser is supplied by a one-cylinder, ½-hp diesel engine.

While the two-foot (.6-m)-high vehicle, which averaged 12 mph (19.3 km/hr) during the race, may not win any prizes for passenger comfort, its body design significantly reduced aerodynamic drag and cut wind resistance to a minimum, both factors extremely important to fuel economy cars and electric vehicles.

While our future transportation mix may not include snail-speed vehicles such as the Shell Marathon winner, it will include higher mileage, conventional petroleum-powered automobiles. The new generation of efficient internal combustion vehicles will probably make the greatest impact on our energy scene in the next twenty years.

The Wood-burning ECAR

While the average electric car can travel 3.5 miles (6 km) on a single pound (.45 kg) of coal burned at the electric power utility, there is one vehicle that can travel a mile on a pound (.45 kg) of wood.

A record was set in the U.S. on December 11, 1979, when the ECAR travelled coast to coast, from Florida to California. The 2,700-mile (4344-km) trip was accomplished using a virtually unmodified 1978 Chevrolet station wagon pulling a special trailer. Fuel consumption for the entire trip was estimated at "one large Alabama tree." The ECAR was followed by a pickup truck which carried 3700 lbs (1678 kg) of wood scraps.

The one-wheeled trailer attachment or "boiler" reduced solid cellulose material into gaseous fuel. At periodic intervals, the trailer was loaded with about 100 pounds (45 kg) of wood chips which were ignited by a flare. Combustion in the reactor converted the solid material into gaseous fuel composed of carbon monoxide, hydrogen, and some methane.

Although this system produced 25 percent less power than gasoline, the ECAR could travel at normal highway speeds, with a maximum speed of 65 mph (88 km/hr). Approximately 25 lbs (11 kg) of wood yielded the equivalent energy of one gallon (4 L) of gasoline.

Econ, the firm that produced the experimental car, admits the ECAR used "low technology as an overall proof of concept" and the system will probably not be widely used for automobiles. However, it contends "wood burning is ideally suited for trucks, tractors, and stationary engines."

For more information, contact Econ, P.O. Box 821, Alexander City, AL 35010.

BIBERONNAGE

Historically, the relatively short range of electric vehicles has restricted their use to inner city driving. Early in this century, however, electric vehicle pioneers found a way to extend the limited range (some had only a 20-mile (32-km) range) by establishing a network of charging stations in metropolitan areas.

In 1901, six stations were installed in New Jersey to allow electric vehicle travel from New York City to Philadelphia. Within the next few years, large cities witnessed an expansion of the 24-hour-a-day charging station network. Boston had 32 boosting stations while New York had 41. In 1903, a long-distance record was set between the two cities. The course required five charges, with each stop taking two to three hours. As mentioned earlier in the history chapter, rural areas were generally off-limits to electric vehicles.

Today the concept of charging stations and boost charging is called "biberonnage." Taken literally, the French word BIBERONNAGE means "bottle feeding," but to the electric vehicle industry it means interim charging of electric and hybrid vehicles, to extend both the vehicle range and life of batteries.

For example, a car with a range of 50 miles (80 km) per charge can double that figure if the driver uses biberonnage. When he reaches his destination—say his place of work, a hypothetical 40 miles (64 km) away—and plugs in his car, he'll leave for home at the end of his work day with a fully charged vehicle.

Upon returning home, he will have completed 80 miles (129 km). A short recharge during the dinner and early evening hours will allow him to travel an additional 20 miles (32 km) in the late evening. Although the ability of a vehicle to travel 100 miles (161 km) per day is beyond the needs of most commuters, especially for second-car use, it is evident that biberonnage used with state-of-the-art electrics can help acquire public acceptance of even the most limited range vehicles.

This theory was examined by the German Group, GES in Essen. Preliminary tests revealed the practical benefits of biberonnage. Vehicles with 20-mile (32-km) ranges extended daily mileage to 60 (96 km).

If GES had filled its test vehicles to full battery weight, standard procedure for U.S. testing, the range would have been 45 miles (72 km). By reducing the battery weight and in-creasing the frequency of charging, the initial vehicle cost was lowered and electric consumption reduced (watts per mile/kilometer).

In some instances, the biberonnage process is like filling up a gas tank at the pump, and can take only a few minutes longer. Germany proved this point recently when it engineered a program to check biberonnage on electric buses. Operating continuously for up to 12 hours a day, the commuter bus is the perfect target for biberonnage testing. For test purposes, a charging station was constructed near the turn-around point of the daily bus route. The bus driver, upon completing his rounds, would stop at the charging station for quick mini-recharging before resuming passenger pick-up. With 10 minutes—the time required for the driver's rest break—the fully charged bus was on its way.

For cars, biberonnage requires no elaborate contraptions or schemes. In the city, electric power is readily available. In the less industrialized suburbs and rural areas, electricity is available in every building.

Daily use of biberonnage is not difficult because a significant portion of vehicle trips cover less than 15 miles (24 km). Vehicles can be charged at many destinations, even with today's rudimentary acceptance of electric-powered transportation. Because batteries are only partially discharged when a booster charge is made, rapid charging causes no harm to battery life. Early testing indicates that biberonnage, like regenerative braking, actually extends battery longevity.

Biberonnage helps facilitate the anticipated partial shift from gasoline-driven to electricity-powered vehicles by bridging the performance and efficiency gap between them. Today, with biberonnage, the electric vehicle industry no longer has to sit on its hands waiting for advanced, high technology batteries. By extending the range of present lead-acid batteries, biberonnage can increase the daily use of a vehicle to the range of a nickel-zinc system. When the nickel-zinc system is refined for public consumption, biberonnage can help the near-term batteries perform like "super-batteries." And, when the "super-battery" arrives, the range of an electric vehicle using biberonnage will rival the arch enemy of the electric car—the "gasoline buggy" of Henry Ford.

Home-Built Electric Vehicles

While the sophisticated laboratories of vehicle manufacturers in Japan, Germany, France, England, and the United States are developing prototype, test-bed, and pie-in-the-sky vehicles, the largest group of on-road electrics are developed in the basements and garages of thousands of do-it-yourself vehicle builders.

Many electric vehicle clubs and organizations have been formed to assist would-be inventors and fabricators. No one exactly knows when the phenomena began, but I suppose there were people installing motors into carriages and buckboards before Henry Ford's time. The notion of putting together a vehicle from scratch, or converting one thing into something else, can result in some extremely roadworthy vehicles.

As with many other hobbies, once a person is bitten by the bug, all financial rationale can go out the window. The pride in building something that is both practical and relatively exotic becomes the motivating force behind the majority of these projects. There is no feeling in the world like the one you get when a person comes up to you and says, "You mean you really built that yourself?"

Thomas Edison left a small seed of inspiration to all who have longed to build, design, and invent without worrying about large corporations dictating marketing strategies or pulling the strings. When you build your own electric, you can say to yourself, "Hey, I'm as good as General Motors, Ford, or Chrysler. I've put a working vehicle on the road."

As you will see in some of these examples in this chapter, the spirit of the home builder, inventor, and entrepreneur is certainly not dead in this country. In fact, it isn't even anywhere near dying. The clubs listed in this chapter may be contacted for further information.

PLEASE NOTE: Any build-it-yourself kits mentioned are sold directly through the kit manufacturers and have no relationship with the author or the publisher of this book.

Therefore, as with any purchase, the buyer must be aware of the potential problems that may arise. You would not attempt, for example, to build a complete electric car with fiberglass body if you did not have the knowledge of tools necessary to build a bookcase. Beginning any project such as this, one must understand the costs and possibility of undisclosed expenses. Remember, that after tallying up the prices for batteries, motors, controllers, frames, switches, wiring, and all the unseen expenses such as possible machining, welding, and fabricating, you may not be able to afford to build your own vehicle. In this case, it would, in my opinion, be unwise to start.

However, to those of you who do have the basic knowledge of tools and are familiar with other build-it-yourself projects, and are willing to tackle something as large as building an automobile, I can think of no better project to which you can dedicate your time. Sure, you can build a helicopter, plane, or boat. But none

of these have the ability to provoke public interest, awe, and envy as does driving your own electric vehicle down a main street on a summer day.

It would be impossible to describe all of the home-built electric vehicles in the United States, because of their vast numbers. Therefore, I have selected a few that are typical of this avocation.

Stockberger—Pinto

John Stockberger, a data specialist supervisor in Chicago, Illinois, has converted a 1971 Ford Pinto to electric power. The 2900 lb (1315 kg), 4-passenger automobile weighs only 500 lbs (227 kg) more than a standard Pinto.

Stockberger purchased a surplus U.S. aircraft generator through an advertisement in *Popular Mechanics* magazine for $100.

The motor was originally manufactured during World War II by the Jack & Heintz Company, and would cost over $1500 if produced today.

The Pinto had a burned-out engine when Stockberger found it in a wrecking yard. Its initial cost was $200. Therefore, the vehicle, complete with sixteen golf-cart batteries reflected an investment of $1200 total—plus a tremendous amount of spare-time work.

The batteries are carried in the trunk and partially up front with the motor. A standard transmission and clutch arrangement is used yielding 25 mph (40 km/hr) in first gear and 40 mph (64 km/hr) in second gear. (Third and fourth gears and the clutch are not used.)

Speed control is accomplished through voltage switching in four steps from 12 to 48 volts. The car is capable of speeds in excess of 40 mph (64 km/hr) and acceleration from zero to

STOCKBERGER PINTO

BATTERIES AND MOTOR OF STOCKBERGER PINTO

STOCKBERGER FIAT

30 mph (48 km/hr) in 15 seconds. The approximate maximum range is about 40 miles (64 km) per charge, although no test for exact range has been made. Recharging is achieved with an on-board charger using a standard 15-amp, 120-volt electrical outlet.

The automobile was completed in the winter of 1974. Since the summer of 1975, it has been in daily service commuting between the train station and John Stockberger's home in Batavia, Illinois—a round trip of 16 miles (26 km). Cost of operation, including electricity and battery replacement, is about 5 cents per mile (3¢

per km). Distilled water for the batteries is obtained by capturing the dehumidifier by-products from his home furnace/air conditioner.

Stockberger has also converted a 1974 Fiat 128 SL. The car is powered by a 400-amp Jack & Heintz 30-volt DC aircraft generator and 12 6-volt golf cart batteries in a 36-volt system. It has a range of about 50 miles (80 km) with a top speed of 45 mph (72 km/hr). Speed control is achieved using a DC transistor chopper.

Stockberger is a member and past president of the Fox Valley Electric Auto Association and has helped many people build their own electric vehicles. Many club members feel that the Fiat 128 is the ideal electric conversion vehicle.

WILLIAM H. SHAFER AND THE ELECTRIC DAF

William H. Shafer—DAF

In 1976, Bill Shafer, an engineer for Commonwealth Edison Company in Chicago, Illinois, converted a Dutch automobile, the DAF, to electric drive. Since then he has traveled 2218 miles (3570 km) and consumed 1108 kwh of electrical energy, or 0.5 kwh per mile (0.31 kwh per kilometer).

The vehicle carries four golf-cart batteries positioned over the rear axle and two golf-cart plus two SLI batteries in front.

A pump located in the rear trunk activates the Variomatic, continuously-variable ratio transmission. Speed is controlled by voltage switching 12, 24, and 36 volts to the motor armature. Top speed of the vehicle is 35 mph (56 km/hr); range is 21 miles (34 km); weight is 1800 lbs (816 kg), of which about 500 lbs (227 kg) is batteries.

Bill Shafer is a member of the Fox Valley Electric Auto Association of Illinois.

NSU CONVERTED BY KEN MYERS

Ken Myers—NSU

Ken Myers, another member of the Fox Valley Electric Auto Association, has converted a 1971 NSU 1200 to electric power. This vehicle carries only enough batteries to travel a 12-mile daily trip to work and back.

Eight six-volt golf-cart batteries power a 28-volt, 200-amp surplus shunt wound aircraft DC generator. Speed control is through battery switching in eight 6-volt steps and the transmission. First gear yields 21 mph (34 km/hr), and 42 mph (68 km/hr) is obtained in second gear. (Third and fourth gears are not used.)

One 12-volt accessory battery provides field current to the motor and power for accessories. The car weighs 1965 lbs (891 kg) which is only 100 lbs (45 kg) more than the conventional vehicle.

1955 Electric Metropolitan—
Keith E. Crock

The 1955 Metropolitan converted by Keith E. Crock of Sunnyvale, California, is far from a stripped-down version of a gasoline-powered car. The vehicle was converted with the objective of retaining all of the creature comforts inherent in the original version. His Metropolitan, which he converted to electric power in 1974, has won several awards, including best-looking auto and endurance awards. For three years, Mr. Crock has come in third place in distance runs, an excellent showing considering the automobile's curb weight of 3280 lb (1487.5 kg).

The electric Metropolitan has a top speed of 60 mph (96 km/hr) and a cruising speed of 26 mph (41 km/hr) with a maximum range of 51 miles (82 km). The 54-volt Jack & Heintz DC motor has regenerative braking through a diode switching controller.

Mr. Crock is currently the Educational Vice-President of the Santa Clara County EAA. He has built two electric vehicles since 1974.

He feels the electric Metropolitan is a product of his constant search for unique problem-solving techniques to provide dependable

1955 ELECTRIC METROPOLITAN

electric transportation. He experimented in many areas, continuously testing and researching various components to arrive at the most efficient combination. A tribute to the effectiveness of his efforts is evidenced by the fact that the original batteries are functioning after over five years of operation.

Jerry Mitchell—Amphicar

Jerry Mitchell, a Chicago television radio communicator and the Midwest's leading electric vehicle spokesman, built one of the most innovative and unique electric cars. Originally gasoline-powered, the Amphicar was appropriately named for its amphibious behavior.

Not only was the vehicle shaped like a boat, it could behave like one as well. Jerry Mitchell's electric Amphicar could reach a top speed of 70 mph (112 km) on the road and 5 mph (8 km) for 30 minutes in the water.

Water travel, made possible by twin propellers, was not recommended due to "top heavy" batteries, weight, and the high energy depletion caused by the drag coefficiency of water.

On land the Amphicar performed as an on-road electric car with acceleration from zero to 30 mph (0 to 48 km/hr) in 10 seconds. Range in "stop and start" traffic was 20 to 25 miles (32 km to 40 km). Highway driving range was 50 miles (80 km) at 35 mph (56 km/hr) or 35 miles (56 km) at 65 mph (104 km/hr).

Regenerative braking was provided by the motor using a series-parallel, stepped-contact controller. Jerry Mitchell's 2952-lb (1338-kg) electric Amphicar used three gears with a fourth added for open road driving.

AMPHICAR

**BILL PALMER AND THE
BATTERY PACK FOR THE
ELECTRIC VEGA**

Bill Palmer—Electric Vega

Bill Palmer, a member of the California-based Electric Auto Association, has converted a 1972 Chevy Vega to electric power. This home conversion, carrying 12 golf car batteries, has a range of 60 to 80 miles (97 to 129 km), depending upon speed and number of stops.

Of special interest is the Vega's speed controller which is equipped with regenerative braking. After spending several years of his spare time designing and building over 12 controller prototypes, Palmer finally developed a controller which could switch the batteries in six different combinations of series-parallel connections.

According to Palmer, the converted vehicle can easily exceed 55 mph (89 km/hr) and its operating cost is between one half and one third of the cost of a gasoline operated car.

BILL PALMER AND THE BATTERY PACK FOR THE ELECTRIC VEGA

Gildo L. Rozzi—Electric Renault Caravelle

Gildo Rozzi's 1960 Renault Caravelle conversion was completed in January, 1974. The sporty 2-door convertible weighs 2600 lbs (1180 kg) and carries 12 6-volt 215-amp-hour batteries.

Power is regulated by relays to provide series-parallel battery switching in four steps: 12, 24, 36 and 72 volts. The G.E. model 2 CM 77 aircraft starter-generator is rated at 30 volts DC, 400 amperes and 3,000-8,000 rpm. The drive train from the motor is through an electro-magnetic clutch and 4-speed manual transmission.

The vehicle has a top speed of 65 mph (104 km/hr) and has achieved a range of 60 miles (96 km) at approximately 25 mph (40 km/hr) at an Electric Automobile Association Annual Electric Car Rally. The average range under normal city driving conditions is about 40 miles (64 km) without discharging the batteries below a safe level.

Rozzi believes in recharging the batteries every evening after use and recharging at a low ampere rate to prolong their life.

GILDO ROZZI'S 1960 RENAULT CARAVELLE

AZTEC 7 XE

Clarence Ellers—Aztec 7 XE

According to its inventor, Clarence Ellers, the Aztec 7 XE is an electric sports car that can be converted from any standard transmission gasoline-powered car weighing approximately 2000 lb (907 kg). Ellers, who has toured the U.S. presenting workshops for Electric Automobile Association (EAA) members, has designed and built several electromotive vehicles. His electrically-converted Datsun pick-up truck weighs 3000 lb (1360 kg) and has a maximum range of 50 miles (80 km) per charge and a 28-mile (45-km) range carrying two people plus payload. The Aztec 7 XE is a sports car with an optimum range of 80 miles (128 km) and a cruis-ing speed of 35-45 mph (56-72 km/hr). The simplified two-step mechanical motor controller features regenerative braking.

Instructions for converting virtually any light-weight automobile are contained in his *Electric Car Conversion Manual.* The informative manual, with simplified wiring diagrams, also provides plans for a hybrid and a flywheel vehicle. A special section concerns incorporation of digital controls and instruments into the dashboard. For more information on how to obtain a copy of the *Electric Car Conversion Manual,* contact Clarence Ellers, P.O. Box 2781, Mission Station, Santa Clara, CA 95051.

**CLARENCE ELLERS
AND THE AZTEC 7 XE**

BILL WILLIAMS AND ELECTRIC DATSUN

Bill Williams—Electric Datsun

Bill Williams of Saratoga, California, motivated by the gasoline crunch of '73-74, converted his 1972 Datsun to electric power in 1976.

His electric Datsun has a cruising speed of 40 mph (64 km/hr) and a range of 40 miles (64 km) with a top speed of 58 mph (93 km/hr). The 2280-lb (1034-kg) vehicle uses a 30-hp DC aircraft starter/generator motor coupled to the standard Datsun four-speed manual transmission. Power is supplied by 12 6-volt batteries weighing 592 lb (268 kg) and is regulated by a transistorized controller equipped with regenerative braking.

After an investment of 1200 man-hours and $1570, a well-deserved "Most Beautiful Electric" award was given to Bill at the Electric Auto Association Rally in 1978. The car's license plate is, of course, "NO GAS."

Williams Enterprises is now offering an *Electric Auto Conversion Manual.* For further information, contact Williams Enterprises, P.O. Box 1548, Cupertino, CA 95014.

WILLIAMS' BATTERY PACK

WILLIAMS' CONTROL PACKAGE

JOHN BENSEN AND HIS
ELECTRIC VOLKSWAGEN BEETLE

John Bensen's VW Beetle

EAA member John Bensen has been driving his electric Volkswagen Beetle for over ten years. The electric Beetle carries ten 12-volt batteries which provide 120 volts to the 27-hp DC motor. An eleventh battery powers accessories. This system has enabled the vehicle to achieve a top speed of 65 mph (104 km/hr) and climb the steepest hills in San Francisco. Additional features include a motor circuit breaker, an on-off circuit breaker for the batteries, and regenerative braking.

Bensen reports that his vehicle's speed is controlled by resistors which, unfortunately, waste almost as much electricity as is used to power the automobile. He adds, however, that if equipped with more modern transistor controls, vehicle range would be increased two-fold.

The last three years before he retired, Bensen used the Beetle to commute to work. He calculates that it cost 20¢ for the energy used to make the 25-mile (40-km) round trip each day. (His area is very hilly and can run down batteries very fast.)

To govern motor speed, there are four stages of resistance on the foot throttle. Coupled with the 4-speed transmission, a total of 16 forward speeds are available, including four in reverse. The second gear is used in city driving.

Despite the limitations of a vehicle which Bensen has affectionately deemed "obsolete," it is obvious that this particular electric car has a few more good years. John Bensen, no doubt, would be quick to agree.

John Wasylina—Honda Civic

EAA member John Wasylina of Pleasanton, California, drives a 1974 Honda Civic that so closely resembles its gasoline powered counterpart that it's difficult to know his vehicle is powered electrically.

The 2180-lb (988-kg) two-door sedan has a top speed of 43 mph (69 km/hr) and a range of 60 miles (96 km) at 25 mph (40 km/hr).

Electromotive force is supplied by 12 Sears Die Hard RV/Marine 12-volt deep-cycle batteries to a Baldor 8-hp compound-wound motor. Power is regulated by a transistorized controller through a standard 4-speed transmission and clutch.

JOHN WASYLINA'S HONDA CIVIC

STERLING EV CONVERTED BY LEO SCHATZL

LEOPOLD SCHATZL AND HIS 1960 ELECTRO-PRINZ

Leopold Schatzl

Leopold Schatzl drove his electrically-converted NSU Prinz over 8,000 miles (12,875 km) between early 1973 to mid-1975. This was the first electric vehicle produced by the Ontario, California, electronics technician.

The Electro-Prinz is a 1960 NSU German subcompact which only weighed 1,200 lbs (545 kg) in its original form. The conversion was made possible with a surplus 10-hp aircraft starter-generator. Speeds of 25 mph (40 km/hr) and 40 mph (64 km/hr) with a range of 40 miles (64 km) per charge are achieved with the 36-volt, 220-amp-hour battery pack. The original six 175-amp-hour golf-cart batteries were exchanged for six 220-amp-hour units in 1975.

In 1975, Mr. Schatzl converted a 1965 Simca 1000, and presently is completing a Sterling, fiberglass-bodied sportscar.

Miny, the Electric Dune Buggy

Andy St. Amant has designed, constructed and redesigned his electric dune buggy since 1968. "Miny," the electric dune buggy, carries 20 6-volt 217-amp/hr batteries plus a 12-volt auxiliary. Total battery weight is 1350 lbs (612 kg).

The vehicle itself weighs 2530 lbs (1147 kg) without passengers and is powered by a modified Weco EF-40 series-wound DC motor with a EVC current limited transistorized controller. The motor is rated at 31 hp at 80% efficiency.

Top speed is over 70 mph (112 km/hr) without current limiting and 55 mph (88 km/hr) with transistorized controller. Maximum range is 150 miles (241 km) at 30 mph (48 km/hr). Acceleration from zero to 30 mph is 8 seconds and the average range at 45 to 50 mph (72 to 80 km/hr) is over 100 miles (161 km).

ST. AMANT'S DUNE BUGGY

An informative "how-to" book entitled "MINY, An Electric Dune Buggy" by Mr. St. Amant is available to home builders. Contact: Andrew St. Amant at 1325 Camino Verde, Walnut Creek, CA 94596.

Leonard Fisher's 1973 Subaru

With a little help from his friends and fellow members of the Fox Valley Electric Automobile Association in Batavia, Illinois, Leonard Fisher was able to convert his 1973 Subaru to electric power.

Fisher's Subaru is powered by a $69 surplus aircraft generator and can achieve a maximum speed of 42 mph (67 km/hr) with a cruising speed of 30 mph (48 km/hr). Range has been noted at approximately 50 miles (80 km) and acceleration from zero to 20 mph (0 to 32 km/hr) takes ten seconds.

The original four-speed transmission was left intact; however, the clutch assembly was removed with additional speed control accomplished through the use of a transistor chopper.

The total cost of converting the 1973 Subaru was $2300 including the $250 price of the original automobile which had a burned-out engine. The vehicle used 313 kilowatt hours of electricity during its first 1200 miles (1931 km) at an average cost of 1.84¢ per mile. The vehi-

FISHER'S SUBARU

cle is used about 65 miles (105 km) per week for work and errands.

Ken Myers, one of Fisher's co-builders, designed and constructed the automatic charger which simultaneously charges the 12 6-volt golf cart batteries and a 12-volt battery which is used to excite the motor's field and power accessories.

Paul Brasch—VW

Another Volkswagen conversion is this fiberglass sports car built by Paul Brasch of San Jose, California.

Power from the fourteen 12-volt batteries is supplied to a rewound Jack & Heintz motor. Top speed is 70 mph (112 km/hr).

Mr. Brasch is a member of the Electric Auto Association of California.

ELECTRIC POWERED VOLKSWAGEN CONVERTED BY PAUL BRASCH

VOLKSWAGEN CON-VERTED BY JOHN NEWELL

John Newell—VW

John Newell of Belmont, California, has constructed a fiberglass sportcar based on a VW chassis.

The most distinctive feature about this vehicle is that it carries 600 lbs (272 kg) of nickel-cadmium batteries. Power is applied to a Jack & Heintz 9-1/2-hp aircraft motor by battery- switching controls. The curb weight of the vehicle is 2,000 lbs (907 kg).

Mr. Newell is the chairman of the Electric Auto Association of California. The EAA currently mails over 500 copies of its newsletter throughout the U.S., Canada, Mexico, Australia, South America, and South Africa.

The EAA is a non-profit organization formed in 1967 by Walter Laski, now the editor of the newsletter and EAA president. For a sample of the newsletter, mail a self-addressed, stamped envelope to Walter V. Laski, 1674 Merrill Drive, Apt. 12, San Jose, California 95124, U.S.A.

The EAA has chapters in the many cities: (See page 191 for listings.)

For EAA membership information, send a self-addressed, stamped envelope to Mr. John Newell, 1249 Lane St., Belmont, California 94022, U.S.A.

A partial list of electric vehicles owned or built by EAA members:

TYPE	NUMBER
N.S.U. Prinz	5
Panhard Corvair	1
V.W. Bug	4
Opel	1
Renault Caravelle	3
Custom Built plywood body	1
Motorcycle	6
V.W. Dune Buggy	2
Pinto	1
V.W. Fiberglass body	2
Toyota	1
V.W.	11
Renault La Dauphine	3
Ottis	1
Lloyd	1
Subaru	1
Model "T" Ford	2
M.G.	2
3 wheel Aurenthetic	1
Bicycle	2
Renault Gordini	1
SAAB Station Wagon	1
Corvair	1
Fiat	2
Austin American	1
Sunbeam Imp.	1
Custom-built 1904 Olds	1
Custom dragster	1
GoGo Mobile	1
CitiCar	1
Kharman Ghia	11
Renault special customs	5
Custom designed & others	23

ELECTRIC AUTO ASSOCIATION EIGHTH ANNUAL RALLY

The Electric Auto Association has held eight annual rallies which provide their members a chance to compete and share their expertise. The most significant aspect of the rallies is that they increase consumer awareness of electric vehicle potential, stimulate public interest, and ultimately contribute to the general acceptance of electric vehicles for commuter transportation.

The September 20, 1980, rally was the largest ever, with 35 contestants competing in a 2.8 mile (4.5 km) course. Vehicles were judged in four categories: all electrics, hybrids, two and three wheelers, and commercial vehicles, with prizes awarded for endurance, efficiency, best looking and most practical.

One innovative feature of the EAA event is the way in which it encourages spectators to take an active part in the rally. The onlookers have an opportunity to board the autos and travel for one lap, with drivers changing passengers at each lap. Also, the awards for "Most Practical" and "Best Looking" are chosen by the onlookers, further involving them in the rally.

Bruce McCaskie's VW Dune Buggy won the prize for endurance for the fourth time with a 70 mile (112.6 km) run. Robert Kidder's VW Dune Buggy was second at 64.4 miles (103.6 km), and Gildo Rozzi (Renault), John Wasylina (Honda Civic) and Ray Bell (VW Aquilla) tied for third at 61.6 miles (99.1 km). Dave Hall's Jet Van won first prize in the commercial category, Clarence Eller's Datsun pick-up won in the hybrid class, and Charles Olson's Laverda won in the two and three wheeler class. In all categories, range and performance were significantly improved over the previous year. With attendance and EV performance continually increasing, future rallies promise to gain even more popularity and public appeal for EV's.

JOHN WASYLINA'S HONDA CIVIC

GUIDO ROZZI'S RENAULT CARAVELLE

RAY BELL'S VW AQUILLA

BRUCE McCASKIE'S DUNE BUGGY

**ROY KAYLOR
AND VW
CONVERSION**

Roy Kaylor, Jr.—VW

Roy Kaylor, Jr., a Menlo Park, California, electrical engineer, has been experimenting with electric vehicles since the early 1960's; he built his first in 1965. His hobby, which at first was the object of skepticism and ridicule, has now evolved into a lucrative business. One of Kaylor's more advanced designs is a two-passenger fiberglass prototype converted from a Volkswagen chassis.

The sleek sportscar has a curb weight of 1850 lb (839 kg). Range is 70 miles (113 km) at 50 mph (80 km/hr), and under optimum conditions, the vehicle can travel 120 miles (193 km) at 35 mph (56 km/hr). A 1976 freeway test over a 7200-foot (2200 m) pass yielded a 90 mile (145 km) range in a course from Nevada to California. Acceleration is from zero to 30 mph (48 km/hr) in a rapid 2.4 seconds.

A 30-hp compound-wound motor with a 100-hp peak is powered through a fully transistorized controller with regenerative braking, by 12 6-volt, 22-amp-hour batteries. The vehicle can be designed to carry from 6 to 16 batteries, depending upon desired operating characteris-

tics. Using a VW chassis, the Kaylor has four-wheel independent suspension and a four-speed transmission. Speed flexibility is achieved by retaining the VW transmission and clutch.

Conversion kits for VW models are available from Kaylor Energy Products. The motors in the Kaylor kit were originally used as generators on F-100 fighter planes (carefully inspected and refurbished, if necessary, before being sold).

A Kaylor Hybrid Module is available which is designed to fit in the space originally occupied by the VW gasoline engine, it produces an extended range of 400 miles (644 km). The 10-hp series-hybrid configuration can simplify conversion of VW-based cars.

Kaylor is working on still another project, an electric tricycle, which will also be offered in kit form.

For more information about these products and the Kaylor conversion manual, contact Kaylor Energy Products, 3162 Bay Road, Redwood City, CA 94063.

CONVERSION KITS

Frizzell's Electric Transportation Electric Volkswagen Conversion Kits

A Frizzell's electric Volkswagen conversion yields a dependable, quiet, simple commuter vehicle which is perfect for errands or just plain fun.

An electric VW uses only 0.6 kwh of electricity per mile and has a top speed of 50 mph (80 km/hr). The company claims that "anyone handy with tools can convert a VW bug by following our detailed instructions."

A Frizzell's conversion kit contains the following:

1. A CONTROL KIT which consists of a contactor panel, microswitch panel, resistance coils, and a safety switch.

   The microswitch panel contains 3 roller-type microswitches actuated by a sliding block. This block is connected directly to the accelerator cable. By depressing the accelerator pedal, the microswitches are activated in sequence from left to right, which in turn closes one of the contactors, allowing current to flow through the resistance coils to the motor. On full acceleration the current flows directly to the motor, bypassing the coils.

As a safety feature, a knife switch is provided, that will cut off all power from the batteries should the need arise.

2. A three-piece flexible motor coupling that connects the shaft of the motor to the transmission shaft.

3. One DC VOLTMETER with a 0-100 volt range.

4. One DC AMMETER with a 0-400 amp range. Both of these meters can be mounted in the dash.

5. A 400-amp SHUNT which is connected to the knife switch. The ammeter is connected to this shunt.

6. A BALDOR 72-VOLT 8-HP DC MOTOR and a custom-made mount that bolts directly to the transmission.

7. A 72-volt battery charger that can be ordered as either 220 volt or a combination 110/220 volt.

For more information, contact Frizzell's 'Electric Transportation, P.O. Box 59, Maynard, MA 01754.

Lyman Electric Products—VW and Pinto Conversion

For those desiring to build their own electric vehicles, Lyman Electric Products offers electric motors for VW's and Pinto's. The company stocks assembled cars ready for delivery, plus complete conversion kits and a variety of electric vehicle components.

The maximum speed of one of their models is 60 mph (97 km/hr) with a range of 25 to 60 miles (40 km to 97 km), depending on number of batteries, speed, terrain, and driving conditions. The motor is 72-volt DC series wound with a series/parallel controller.

For further information, contact Lyman Electric Products, 15 Meadow Street, Norwalk, CT 06856.

LYMAN PRODUCTS ELECTRIC MOTOR

CONVERTED ELECTRIC BUG

Vantage Electric Conversion Kits

A Vantage "Electric Bug Kit" will convert a standard Volkswagen into an electric car which can pay for itself. All of the necessary components to convert any rear-engined Volkswagen car or bus are included in the following kits:

1. *STANDARD KIT* for Bug, Squareback and Fastback, contains one 18-hp DC electric motor operated at 72 volts from 12 225-amp-hour, lead-acid batteries charged by a 72-volt battery charger using 110 or 220 AC current.

2. *VW BUS KIT* contains one 18-hp DC electric motor operated at 96 volts from 16 225-amp-hour batteries charged by two 48-volt battery chargers using 110-volt AC current.

3. *BUG (MINIMUM KIT)* contains one 18-hp DC electric motor operated at 60 volts from 10 225-amp-hour batteries charged by a 60-volt battery charger, using 220-volt AC current. Vehicle top speed is limited to 40 mph (64 km/hr). •

Options include: 1) dual voltage battery chargers which can charge the main power pack and the auxiliary 12-volt accessory battery at the same time; 2) improved lead-acid batteries which provide 27% more running time for about 10% increase in kit cost and additional weight of 3 pounds (1.36 kg) per battery; 3) complete installation in the customer's VW chassis. The car to be converted must have mechanically sound clutch, transmission, brakes, and shocks.

Other Makes of Cars

Electric car conversion kits can be installed in lightweight, standard-shift cars such as Honda, Vega, Chevette, Datsun, Toyota, and Pinto with the design and construction of a mounting adaptor plate to couple motor to transmission.

Performance for a standard, converted VW is 45 to 55 mph (72 to 88 km/hr) for 30 to 40 miles (48 to 64 km). Range and speed is slightly less for a van or station wagon. Speed is controlled by contact or switching the motor and using the four speeds of the transmission through the conventional clutch.

For Volkswagen conversions, the electric motor replaces the gasoline engine and the rear seat converts to a battery box. The net weight increase over the original vehicle is 500 lbs (227 kg). The converted chassis can also serve as the bed for a body conversion such as the Bradley GT. Instructions can also be provided to retain the seating for 4 passengers.

For complete information on price and component availability, contact Vantage Electric Car Kits, 6332 Lakeview Drive, Falls Church, VA 22041.

MECHANIX ILLUSTRATED HOMEBUILTS

Since 1975, starting with the Urbacar, construction plans for homebuilt vehicles have been offered by the publishers of Mechanix Illustrated Magazine (USA). The current offering of electric vehicles is the Urba Electric (introduced in 1977), the Urba Trike, the Urba Sport Trimuter, and Hybrid-Electric which were conceived and developed by Quincy-Lynn Enterprises. Prototypes of each model have been built by Robert Q. Riley, who described specifications and construction procedures in articles published in Mechanix Illustrated beginning in April 1975.

URBA ELECTRIC

The Urba Electric

Urba Electric's styling compares favorably with gas-powered sports cars. Innovative features of this homebuilt include a variable speed transmission and regenerative braking. Unlike most electric cars, the Urbacar's propulsion motor runs at a constant, energy-efficient rpm with vehicle speed electronically controlled by the continuously-variable transmission.

The 1400-lb (634-kg) vehicle is powered by eight 6-volt deep-discharge traction batteries and can achieve a maximum speed of 55 mph (88 km/hr) with a range of 65 miles (105 km).

According to Riley, his prototype was an easy, straight-forward construction project. Although he does suggest the need for familiarity with craft work, the process of building an Urba Electric requires only time and effort. Engineers from Delco-Remy, a division of General Motors, "unofficially" sent off for the plans and built an Urba Electric in approximately three months.

Urba Trike

A cross between a sports car and a motorcyle, the Urba Trike carries eight 6-volt golf cart batteries which deliver power to an 8-hp surplus aircraft generator. The 950-lb (431-kg) three-wheeler can achieve a maximum speed of 55 mph (88 km/hr), accelerate from zero to 35 mph (56 km/hr) in 9.5 seconds and has a range of 60 miles (97 km) at 25 mph (40 km/hr). The Urba Trike features a 4 voltage step controller with regenerative braking. Handling of the fiberglass-and-urethane-bodied vehicle is similar to that of a motorcycle.

Like other homebuilt plans produced by Mechanix Illustrated, the instructions for the Urba Trike include plans for an alternate model. The modified version has an increased battery power of 72 volts and a new 8-hp motor (instead of a surplus model) which boosts the vehicle's maximum speed to 65 mph (105 km/hr) with a range of over 100 miles (161 km) at 25 mph (40 km/hr). An Urba Trike may be assembled with any of three motors using a salvaged motorcycle frame and the axle assembly from any subcompact car.

URBA TRIKE

Urba Sport Trimuter

The latest addition to the Urba family, the three-wheeled Urba Sport Trimuter, can be built with either gasoline or electric drive. Compared with four-wheelers, the wedge-shaped vehicle has excellent handling. The majority of the vehicle's 1400 lbs (634 kg)—for the eight battery version—is carried by the two rear wheels giving the Trimuter less rolling resistance and increased cornering capacity. Plans for this vehicle offer a choice of two electric propulsion motors. The prototype built by Riley and David L. Carey is propelled by a surplus aircraft generator and powered by ten deep-discharge golf cart batteries. The weight of the ten-battery version is 1550 lb.(702 kg). The vehicle has a range of 60 miles (97 km) and a maximum speed of 60 mph (97 km) and a maximum speed of 60 mph (97 km/hr). One important option is a Baldor 8-hp motor which, although more expensive, provides better performance and greater range.

Riley and Carey report that the Urba Trimuter is easier to build than the Urba Electric or the Urba Trike because the entire suspension system and steering assembly parts for the Trimuter can be purchased from wrecking yards.

The fiberglass-and-urethane-bodied vehicle is classified by the federal government as a

URBA TRIMUTER

motorcycle and not a car. Registration and licensing requirements for a motorcycle are not as rigid as a homebuilt car.

The final cost of any Quincy-Lynn vehicle, as well as performance details, depend upon the preferences of the buyer. The choice of motor and other components allow the owner's finished product to be tailor-made. The project promises to be a rewarding experience which will produce a highly personalized, low-cost vehicle.

Complete plans are available from Mechanix Illustrated. The package includes a booklet of detailed instructions and parts sources as well as work sheets of plans. For information, contact Mechanix Illustrated Plans Service, P.O. Box 8162, Greenwich, CT 06836.

Quincy-Lynn Hybrid Electric

The hybrid/electric is built on a VW beetle chassis and features a machined adapter plate which mates a 72-volt 8-hp electric motor directly to the VW transaxle.

The 72-volt battery pack consists of 12 6-volt lead-acid batteries. Vehicle speed is controlled by a transistorized chopper with the elimination of the clutch. Functioning as a series-hybrid, the onboard generating system is comprised of a gasoline-engine-powered generator which can be operated while driving or when parked.

At 35 mph (56 km/hr), the 33-amp output of the generating system provides about 40% of the current required to run the vehicle, extending range to about 125 miles (201 km). At 35 mph (56 km/hr), fuel consumption is 80 mpg (34 km/L). Fuel consumption varies with vehicle speed; therefore, a 30-mph (48-km/hr) speed increases range to 227 miles (365 km) at 68 mpg (30 km/L). At 50 mph (80 km/hr) range drops to

QUINCY LYNN ELECTRIC HYBRID

65 miles (104 km) while fuel consumption becomes 115 mpg (49 km/L). Vehicle top speed is 55 mph (88 km/hr).

As with other Quincy-Lynn vehicles, the futuristic four passenger hybrid/electric is offered as a build-it-yourself project. Plans may be ordered from Mechanix Illustrated magazine or directly from Quincy-Lynn Enterprises, P.O. Box 26081, Phoenix, AZ 85020.

King Engineering Conversion Kits

King Engineering of East Syracuse, New York, produces electric conversion kits for Volkswagen Bugs, squarebacks, fastbacks, and vans. The basic kit contains all components necessary for the conversion. You supply 12 golf cart batteries and material to fabricate battery-mounting components.

A DC motor is connected directly to the VW transaxle. In addition to the motor, the kit includes a solid-state control system with regenerative braking adaptor plate, battery charger, motor cooling blower, and cables.

The vehicle pictured is the prize-winning sports model which won performance awards for two consecutive years at the annual Mt. Washington Alternative Regatta. The prizes were top honors in 1977 and the highest efficiency prize in 1978. The vehicle, using a Bradley body on a Volkswagen chassis, successfully climbed Mt. Washington with three passengers aboard.

The sports model has a top speed of 55 mph (88 km/hr) and a range of 60 to 70 miles (97 to 113 km) at a constant 40 mph (64 km/hr).

The most time consuming part of the conversion is the design, construction, and mounting of battery boxes and supports. With a squareback, hatchback, or van, the job can be done in a weekend. The Karmann Ghia or Beetle re-

KING CONVERSION KIT   Photos courtesy King Electric Vehicles

quires just 30 to 60 hours. Installation of the King drive components will take about 10 to 20 hours.

King recommends using a 1969 or newer Volkswagen body and chassis.

For more information regarding conversion kits, and component parts and motors for electric vehicles, send $2.00 for basic information and price list, or $9.00 for a detailed information kit with photos to King Electric Vehicles, Inc., P.O. Box 514, East Syracuse, NY 13057.

KING ELECTRIC GT

Heald Kits

The Heald Company manufactures gasoline and electric vehicle kits for home, farm, and industrial use. Although the majority of the assembled items include a variety of haulers and bikes, the company has recently released a new electric utility vehicle. The "Heald Hauler," is powered through a torque converter by a 36-volt permanent-magnet motor. Energy is supplied by deep discharge batteries.

Top speed is 10 mph (16 km/hr) with a hand-operated speed control. According to the manufacturer this vehicle can be built in 6 to 12 hours following step-by-step instruction.

For more information contact Heald Inc., P.O. Box 1148, Benton Harbor, MI 49022.

HEALD HAULER

ELECTRIC TOURING BIKE BUILT BY SHELDON SHACKET

Sheldon Shacket—Electric Touring Bike

Sheldon Shacket, the author of this book, has built over 15 two and three-wheeled electric vehicle prototypes.

The Model Three is a lightweight electric bicycle built on a Raleigh three-speed frame. Power from the type 27 marine battery, rated at 95 amp hours, is directed through a single-speed on/off switch. The motor is a 1/2 hp, permanent-magnet type with vee-belt drive to the rear wheel. Range is 20 miles (32 km) at 16 mph (26 km). Top speed is 18 mph (29 km).

Other vehicles built include a 2-wheeled vehicle with a top speed of over 50 mph (81 km) and another long-range bicycle with a 35 to 50 mile (56-81 km) range at 16 mph (26 km) using 2 golf-cart batteries.

Electric Mini-Bike Plans

Sheldon Shacket also offers instruction plans to convert a conventional gasoline-powered mini-bike to electric power. A converted mini-bike is a family project designed to produce a dependable recreational vehicle which can last for many years.

Using a 1-hp starter motor and chain drive, the electric mini-bike can carry two people at speeds up to 25 mph (48 km/hr). The instruction plans are simplified and written for youngsters or adults. To obtain a set of plans, send $3.60 to S. Shacket, 875 N. Michigan Ave., Suite 1557, Chicago, IL 60611.

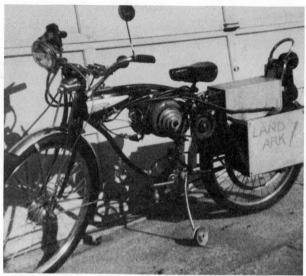

TWO BICYCLES BUILT BY RICHARD NESS

Richard Ness—Electric Bicycle

Richard Ness is a Chicago, Illinois, machinist who has built two electric bicycles.

His first model, the "land-ark", uses a one-horsepower DC traction motor and belt drive to the rear wheel. A reinforced frame and rear wheel help carry the two 12-volt SLI batteries, rated at 80-amp-hours each.

The vehicle has two forward speeds, 15 mph (24 km/hr) and 30 mph (48 km/hr). Range at 15 mph (24 km/hr) is 30 miles (48 km) and 15 miles (24 km) at 30 mph (48 km/hr). This electric bike has been in service for three years.

Mr. Ness recently completed building a lighter weight electric bike with belt drive and a higher speed motor.

Tony Lamb—Solar Powered Bicycle

Tony Lamb's solar-powered bicycle has demonstrated such promise for the elderly and handicapped that the U.S. federal government has appropriated a quarter-million-dollar grant to produce the four wheeler for citizens in Ventura County, California. The vehicle owes its conception to Lamb's solution for making a three mile trip to the market.

Powered by energy converted into electricity through a solar collector to a 12-volt standard car battery, the bicycle has a range of 20 miles (32 km) and a maximum speed of 8 mph (13 km/hr). Recharging simply involves leaving the 200-lb (91-kg) four wheeler in the sun for six hours. Lamb reports that up to 50% extension in range can be achieved by pedalling part of the time.

According to Lamb, a future production model will be equipped to carry four batteries which would provide a range of 80 miles (50 km) and a speed of up to 40 mph (25 km/hr). This economical vehicle costs a mere $\frac{1}{10}$¢ per mile to operate.

LAMB'S SOLAR POWERED BICYCLE

Electric Bicycle Pusher

On a given day, frustrated drivers stuck in rush hour traffic may look out their windows and see Dave Ferre' pass them at a steady clip of 15 mph (24 km/hr). He will not be in a car, however. He will be riding his electric bicycle propelled by an Electric Bicycle Pusher (EBP), his own invention.

The EBP uses a 12-volt motor from a 1962 Ford V8 and a standard golf cart six-volt battery. The combination of a 12-volt motor running at half voltage provides reduced power and cool running. Ferre''s bicycle can travel 25 to 30 miles (40 to 48 km) per charge. Original construction costs were estimated at $150 with a penny-a-day operating expense.

The motor and battery fit neatly into a 2-wheel trailer which attaches to the base of the seat by a ''pusher bar.'' For stable operation, the push action is at the center of gravity. A switch is mounted on the top of the handlebars to start and stop the unit. The EBP can start from a dead stop; however, greater efficiency is achieved by pedalling a few feet before engaging the power switch.

Ferre''s EBP has an important advantage. The bicycle itself is not modified in any way; therefore, the unit can be quickly and easily removed for conventional riding.

For more information, write David A. Ferre', Box 10090, Rochester, NY 14610.

Evi Gemini

The Gemini by Electric Vehicle Engineering, Inc., of Lawrence, Massachusetts, is a ''ground up'' vehicle designed for industrial or commuter use. It can be purchased as a production model or in kit form for the home-builder. The tubular steel frame chassis is covered with zinc primer and epoxy paint to resist possible corrosion from the batteries. The chassis, which has an integral roll bar, may be fitted with three body styles: roadster, pick-up, or station wagon.

The 2500-lb (1134-kg) Gemini, with three passengers aboard, has a 50-mile (80-km) range and a cruising speed of 35-40 mph (56-64 km/hr). Acceleration is zero to 30 mph (48 km/hr) in 12 seconds. Twelve Exide batteries weighing 720 lbs (327 kg) supply power to a DC motor through an electronic speed controller to a direct drive differential.

Electric Vehicle Engineering has also compiled a comprehensive report reviewing the advantages of the electric vehicle. Numerous

EVI GEMINI   Photo courtesy Electric Vehicle Industries, Inc.

tables, graphs, and factual data illustrate the economic, ecological, and energy conservation benefits inherent in electric vehicles.

For more information regarding the Gemini contact Electric Vehicle Industries, Inc., 21 West Street, Lawrence, MA 01841.

PUBLICATIONS

Flight Systems Electric Vehicle Components Catalog

FLIGHT SYSTEMS is a corporation with 14 years experience in solid state electronics. During the past ten years, the firm has concentrated on developing solid state controls for industrial electric vehicles. Late in 1979, FLIGHT SYSTEMS expanded into the on-the-road electric vehicle market with an Electric Vehicle Components Catalog. The catalog is designed to make the firm's Electric Vehicle Components Division a single mail order distribution point for electric vehicle parts and information. Using its experience with electric vehicles and contacts with dealers/manufacturers, the Division has been able to locate and buy parts that are normally unavailable to the single-item purchaser.

Two editions of the Electric Vehicle Components Catalog have now been published. The broad scope of the catalog provides coverage of batteries, motors, motor adaptors, control systems, meters, gauges, accessories, technical articles on motor selection and speed control, and reviews of user experiences. The first edition contained an initial selection of all the parts necessary to build or maintain an electric vehicle, with emphasis on the VW Beetle. The second edition has been expanded to include the hard-to-find parts for many of the popular conversion plans on the market today. In addition, the firm has completed its own conversion of a Chevrolet Chevette called the "Chelectric." The catalog includes custom designed and fabricated parts for this conversion.

The current edition of the catalog is available for $2.00 ($3.00 first class and Canada; $4.00 overseas) from FLIGHT SYSTEMS, Department QEV, P.O. Box 25, Mechanicsburg, PA 17055.

CHELECTRIC

The Electric Vehicle News

Electric Vehicle News is one of the electric vehicle industry's most popular trade journals. Published quarterly by Porter Corporation, *Electric Vehicle News* is the oldest and most reliable of all electric vehicle publications. It supplies in-depth, up-to-date, comprehensive articles on all aspects of electric vehicle development.

A typical issue contains regular columns titled "EV World," "New Products," "Tidbits," and feature-length articles focusing on recent developments.

Advertisers in *Electric Vehicle News* are among some of the most influential corporations currently contributing to the field of electromotive propulsion.

Once a year a special directory is published in the *Electric Vehicle News* listing all companies involved in every facet of the industry.

For subscription information, contact Electric Vehicle News, P.O. Box 533, Westport, CT 06880.

Battery Vehicle Society

The Battery Vehicle Society is an all-volunteer organization in England established in 1973 to keep electric vehicle enthusiasts informed of technical and historically significant developments in the electric vehicle industry. Members are kept abreast of the latest in equipment and developmental programs through a quarterly journal, *Battery Vehicle Review*, which contains specialist articles, news items from around the world, personal glimpses of their members' electric vehicle projects, book reviews, and a calendar of electric vehicle events.

The Society has no commercial ties but it is affiliated with the Transport Trust of Great Britain. For membership information, contact: Mr. R. A. Pryor, Battery Vehicle Society, 8A Queens Park West Drive, Bournemouth, Dorset BH8 9BY, England.

EVO News

The EVO newsletter provides a comprehensive look at electric vehicles from a variety of aspects and related areas of interest. Virtually every facet of the electric vehicle industry is examined by this informative periodical. Each issue explains new innovations in electric vehicles, separates fact from fiction about product feasibility, provides vehicle specifications, and examines pending government legislation.

Further, EVO News keeps readers up-to-date by describing the latest breakthroughs in electric vehicle design and reprinting newspaper articles as they occur on the subject. EVO News also supplies the addresses of companies to contact regarding published articles. For more information, contact EVO News, 4900 Blank Road, Sebastopol, CA 95472.

The Do-It-Yourself Hybrid Manual

The "Do-it-Yourself Hybrid Manual" serves as a newsletter, providing the most up-to-date information regarding gasoline-electric hybrid vehicles. The informative booklet, replete with diagrams and photographs of the latest hybrid technology, explains how hybrids run and relates their advantages. It also lists current conversion components available for purchase.

The manual discusses and diagrams some of the more successful hybrid conversions and touches on the history of electric vehicles, specifically hybrids.

For more information, contact Ideal World Publishing Company, P.O. Box 1237-EG, Melbourne, FL 32935.

Electric Auto Association Chapters

Ampex
Paul Mauch
1815 Walnut Drive
Mt. View, CA 94040

Baltimore
S. J. Michalski
8013 Gough Street
Baltimore, MD 21224

Burbank
I. L. Weiss
512 N. Mariposa-#C
Burbank, CA 91506

Bakersfield
Hal Neufeld
140 E. Norris Road
Oildale, CA 93308

Contra Costa
M. Rosenstein
514 Odin Drive
Pleasant Hill, CA 94523

East Bay
J. D. Fahey
1460 Summit Road
Berkeley, CA 94708

Eugene
Otto Barlow
88 Lincoln Avenue-#B8
Eugene, OR 97401

Eugene-Spr.
Russ Idler
3656 Village Avenue-#2
Eugene, OR 97402

EVA/DC
David Goldstein
9140 Centerway Road
Gaithersburg, MD 20760

Fox Valley
Len Fisher
2161 Sandburg
Aurora, IL 60506

Grand Forks
Leroy Sletten
RR1
Larimore, ND 58251

Hew-Packard
Fred Meyers
14690 Sal Tmontes Way
Los Altos, CA 94022

Little Rock
Clay Jones
605 West Scenic Drive-#E25
North Little Rock, AR 72118

Minneapolis
Richard Landry
1006 13th Avenue
Minneapolis, MN 55414

Milwaukee
David Parez
32515 South Illinois Avenue
Milwaukee, WI 53207

Marshalltown
Mike Yantis
1606 West Church Street
Marshalltown, IA 50158

Moorestown
Sid Kreitzberg
379 Boxwood Lane
Cinnimison, NJ 08077

North Bay
Jim Bottorff
P. O. Box 4047
San Rafael, CA 94903

Peninsula
Jean C. Bardon
540 Moana Way
Pacifica, CA 94044

Portland
Larry Wilkinson
Route 3, Box 107X
Hillsboro, OR 97123

Redding
James Briody
1886 Kern Drive
Redding, CA 96001

Rogue Valley
George Holbrook
2755 Elliott Avenue
Medford, OR 97501

Sacramento
M. Fostar
376 Spreading Oak Lane
Rancho Cordova, CA 95670

San Francisco
Jesse D. Wall
225 Edna Street
San Francisco, CA 94112

San Jose
Paul Brasch
1040 Delna Manor Lane
San Jose, CA 95122

Santa Clara
W. W. Palmer
44 Dior Terrace
Los Altos, CA 94022

SEVA
J. Allen Smith
4th & Pike Building-#610
Seattle, WA 98101

Springfield
John D. Elliot
1856 Cheviot Hills
Springfield, OH 45505

St. Louis
Bob Buchholz
1636 Country Hill Lane
Manchester, MO 63011

Tulsa
J. Haraughty
5941 East 25th Place
Tulsa, OK 74114

Tucson
Howard Shapiro
2000 East Roger Road-#G59
Tucson, AZ 85719

Waco
B. V. Miller
402 North 39th Street
Waco, TX 76710

Willamette
Randy Morgan
1134 Moneda Street N.
Salem, OR 97303

Eastern
Guy Davis
3135 Shirlene Road
Norristown, PA 19403

Red Bank
Robert G. Baxter
88 McLean Street
Red Bank, NJ 07701

Houston
Robert Nixon
4224 Albans
Houston, TX 77005

Columbus
Michael S. Beebe
2321 Duncan Drive-#4
Fairborn, OH 45324

National (All other areas)
Walter Laski
1674 Merrill Drive-#12
San Jose, CA 95124

ETV-1

Contemporary Legislation

We have discussed the participation of the German and Japanese governments regarding legislative impetus applied to electric vehicle development. Other activity is underway in Sweden, France, Italy, England, USSR, The Republic of China, and Taiwan. In each case, government and business efforts are tied together for mutual achievement.

The United States has one ongoing government program which was passed into law on September 17, 1976, after a Congressional override of a presidential veto. Public Law 94-413 is The Electric and Hybrid Vehicle Research and Demonstration Act of 1976. The Act is designed to promote electric and hybrid vehicle research and development and to provide up to 7,500 demonstration vehicles within 72 months of the enactment of the law.

The entire program is under the jurisdiction of the Energy Research and Development Administration (ERDA), now a part of the Department of Energy (DOE).

Presently, the electric auto industry in the U.S. is a composite of equipment and component manufacturers. These entrepreneurs assemble electric cars in small numbers. The largest manufacturer to date is the Sebring

Vanguard company which has produced a total of only 2,000 cars in the last few years.

Public Law 94-413 is designed to stimulate small businesses to develop electric vehicle technology.

The first phase of the Act called for a study of current "state-of-the-art" electric vehicles. The next stage will define performance standards and contract the purchase of 2,500 demonstration vehicles. The final phase calls for the delivery of 5,000 demonstration vehicles with higher performance standards. On February 25, 1978, several amendments to the E/HV Act of 1976 were signed into law by President Carter after passing both houses of Congress. One provision of the amendments allows for an extended period of demonstrations through 1986, and for the acquisition of a total of 10,000 vehicles, compared with the 7,500 indicated in the original Public Law 94-413.

Other provisions for near-term electric vehicle demonstrations called for four small manufacturers to produce two vehicles each. This contract awarded each manufacturer $100,000 to cover the cost of both vehicles.

U.S. Government Department of Energy goals for the future include stimulating the use of electric vehicle through the mid-1980's, and encouraging mass production of suitable electric vehicles by 1986 and hybrids by 1988.

Furthermore, as "full performance" electric hybrids undergo development, they will be ready for commercialization by 1995.

The ultimate goal is to reduce oil imports and increase employment by helping industry develop an integrated electric vehicle market. Prospects of replacing a good proportion of the U.S. "second" and "third" cars with electric vehicles could account for up to 16 million electric automobiles by the year 2000. This is a potential savings of about 500,000 barrels of oil per day.

The infusion of government money, up to $160 million in a five year period, will stimulate industry to develop the subsystems and infrastructure necessary to allow the electric automobile and truck to be mass produced in the United States.

General Electric/Department of Energy Demonstration Vehicle (ETV-1)

The U.S. Department of Energy has awarded a $6 million two-year contract to the Research and Development Center of General Electric for development and construction of two four-passenger experimental electric automobiles. The sub-compact electrics are powered by lead-acid battery systems and based on a design developed jointly by General Electric and Chrysler Corporation. These integrated test vehicles can achieve a maximum range of over 100 miles (161 km) per charge and an urban driving cycle of 75 miles (121 km) per charge and an urban driving cycle of 75 miles (121 km) per charge with a top speed of 65 mph (105 km/hr) and cruising speed of 55 mph (89 km/hr). Each vehicle carries 18 Globe-Union batteries and incorporates regenerative braking.

The DOE has instructed the developers to design the electrics with special consideration given to mass production techniques that will make possible a purchase price and operating costs competitive with conventional cars. The sporty two-door hatchback coupes feature sleek styling for low aerodynamic drag, independent front and rear suspension, low rolling resistance, radial tires, computerized electronic controls with push button convenience, an onboard charger, and regenerative braking.

Garrett DOE Vehicle (ETV-2)

The Garrett AiResearch Company of California has produced two near-term electric test vehicles for the U.S. Department of Energy contract under Public Law 94-413.

The ETV-2 vehicle design features a regenerative flywheel/electric motor design configuration. The unusual power train consists basically of two identical motors, a flywheel with special gearing and microprocessor controls.

The main drive motor is a 31-hp separately excited DC unit with a speed range from zero to 11650 rpm and is connected directly to the rear wheels through gears and a silent chain.

The second motor is connected to a high-speed (25000 rpm) flywheel which allows the battery to store kinetic flywheel energy at low cruise level energy consumption. The laminar composite flywheel is composed of rings of epoxy Kelvar and epoxy/fiberglass, and housed in a low pressure aluminum chamber.

A differential planetary gear set functions as a fully automatic, infinitely variable electromechanical transmission.

The key feature is a solid state digital microprocessor which controls power train operation, including flywheel speed control and regenerative braking. By insuring a lower battery discharge rate during acceleration, the flywheel/motor arrangement can extend the cycle life of the battery pack.

The ability of the microprocessor to distinguish the needs of the motor, battery,

DOE/GARRETT ETV-2

generator, and flywheel provides additional power for high-power modes such as acceleration and hill climbing, and regenerative braking which converts vehicle kinetic energy into retrievable flywheel energy.

The low-profile, four-passenger coupe weighs 3237 lbs (1468 kg) including 1056 lbs (479 kg) of Eagle-Picher lead-acid batteries.

Maximum range is 107 miles (171 km) with an urban driving cycle range of 74 miles (118 km). Top speed is 60 mph (96 km/hr) for passing with a cruising speed of 55 mph (88 km/hr).

The Garrett Company has extensive flywheel experience and is one of the Signal Companies. Subcontractors for this project include The Brubaker Group for body design and All American Racers for suspension design.

"2 x 4" PROGRAM

In June 1978, the U.S. Department of Energy Nevada Operations Office awarded contracts to four U.S. small businesses to improve two vehicles each, using existing off-the-shelf technology and components. The project has been dubbed the "2 x 4" program because it procured two vehicles each from four separate manufacturers.

The vehicles have greater reliability than present state of the art technology and can carry at least 2 persons plus cargo.

Performance goals are a range of 30 to 45 miles (48 to 72 km) in stop and go driving, a passing speed of 48 to 58 mph (77 to 93 km/hr), ability to climb 30 percent grades, and acceleration from zero to 30 mph (48 km/hr) in 11 seconds.

Other considerations are vehicle safety in operational and nonoperational modes, maintainability, and battery life.

The four companies selected were Battronic Truck Corporation of Boyertown, Pennsylvania; Electric Vehicle Associates of Cleveland, Ohio; Jet Industries, Inc., of Austin, Texas; and South Coast Technology, Inc., of Santa Barbara, California. The four contractors will incorporate improvements into their production vehicles.

The vehicles were delivered to the Mobility Equipment Research and Development Command of the U.S. Army (MERADCOM) for further DOE testing in March, 1979.

South Coast Technology Corp. (2 × 4)

The South Coast Technology converted VW Rabbit carries two passengers a projected 70 miles (113 km) in stop and go driving. Acceleration is zero to 30 mph (48 km/hr) in 10 seconds with a top speed of 59 mph (95 km/hr). The front-wheel-drive sedan uses a separately excited shunt motor and a solid state controller providing regenerative braking.

The Volkswagen Corporation of the United States is highly interested in the potential success of this contract.

SCT CONVERTED VW RABBIT

Jet Industries (2 × 4)

The Jet Industries Electra Van 500 is an electric van with over seven years of research and development. The Model 600 is a multi-purpose design with improvements such as a more powerful motor, solid state controller with regenerative braking.

Top speed for the four-passenger van is 52 mph (84 km/hr) with a range in stop-and-go driving of 43 miles (70 km). Acceleration is zero to 30 mph (48 km/hr) in 11 seconds.

JET INDUSTRIES ELECTRA VAN 500

Electric Vehicle Associates (2 × 4)

The contract assignment to improve the EVA "Change-of-Pace" Electric AMC Pacer station wagon includes a modified motor, improved controller with regenerative braking, and a more efficient torque converter and differential.

The "2 x 4" contract vehicle is the fourth improved generation of the four-passenger station wagon design. The strong chassis and body design of this vehicle has a proven crash-tested record for safety. Projected performance includes a top speed of 56 mph (90 km/hr) with acceleration from zero to 30 mph (48 km/hr) in 11 seconds. Range is 40 miles (64 km) of stop-and-go driving.

EVA ELECTRIC PACER STATION WAGON

Battronic Truck Corporation (2 × 4)

The Battronic pick-up truck is an improvement of the famous Battronic Mini-Van which has been used in the Lead Industries Association GoLIAth program and the Electric Vehicle Council programs.

The basic Mini-Van frame was the starting point for the electric 2-passenger pickup truck design. Performance goals are acceleration of zero to 30 mph (48 km/hr) in 11 seconds, a range of 41 miles (66 km) in stop-and-go travel, and top speed of 50 mph (80 km/hr).

BATTRONIC PICK-UP TRUCK

U.S. GOVERNMENT HYBRID PROGRAM

Hybrid vehicle development in the United States has been given a significant boost by a federally funded program. The U.S. Department of Energy (DOE) has contracted for the development of hybrid vehicles under another provision in Public Law 94-413, The Electric Vehicle and Hybrid Research Development and Demonstration Act of 1976. Hybrid vehicles first came under consideration about ten years ago as a means of reducing pollution, but now, with the increasing scarcity of petroleum reserves, hybrid vehicle development is an integral part of the U.S. Department of Energy.

There are two basic programs administered by the DOE focusing on research and development of hybrids: the Electric Hybrid (EHV) program and the Near-Term Hybrid Vehicle (NTHV) program, which concentrates on developing experimental test vehicles from the ground up. Both of these programs are managed by the Jet Propulsion Laboratory (JPL) in Pasadena, Calif., which has issued a state-of-the-art report on hybrids and their potential.

In the JPL study, a total of only 81 hybrids was identified worldwide. All of them are essentially proof-of-concept vehicles and none as yet are in production. But despite the present lack of availability of hybrids, the JPL report concluded that hybrids have enormous marketing potential because they can significantly reduce petroleum use while offering the performance and range comparable to conventional automobiles. This latter point is highly significant because one of the major drawbacks of electric cars to the American public is the loss of mobility and flexibility associated with state-of-the-art electric vehicles.

The parallel hybrid vehicle gas/electric system is designed to propel the vehicle in three separate modes. At low speeds, in stop-and-go traffic, vehicle propulsion relies almost totally on electric power, with an electric range varying from about 15.5 miles (25 km) to 62 miles (100 km) depending on hybrid model and battery capacity. When more energy is required, as in passing, the system draws power from both electricity and gasoline with each energy source complementing the other. At freeway speeds, the vehicles use gasoline power predominantly and perform like conventional internal combustion engine cars. If the gasoline engine power output is greater than the vehicle's need at the time, the excess power is used to charge batteries. Thus, the system operates at a constant speed and load for maximum fuel economy. Obviously, low speed urban driving in the all-electric power mode saves the greatest amount of gasoline.

The first phase of the NTHV program consisted of the preliminary studies necessary to develop an experimental hybrid passenger automobile. There were four contractors competing for the contract for final design and fabrication of test vehicles. General Electric was awarded the 8 million dollar, 30-month contract by DOE through JPL.

In devising specifications for the test hybrid, each contractor had to characterize an automobile that typified the driving needs of the average family. In all cases, the model chosen was a five-passenger small mid-size car. A 1985 version of the selected reference vehicle, incorporating the expected weight reduction and efficiency improvements likely to be mandated by the government, was projected by each contractor in order to provide a realistic basis for comparison with the NTHV design which is scheduled for production in the mid-1980's.

The performance specifications developed by the contractors generally exceeded the minimum of those required by the JPL, with one exception; no contractor was able to exceed the acceleration time requirement (50 mph in 12 sec. or 0-50 km/hr in 6 sec). It was then pointed out that some contemporary internal combustion passenger cars are unable to achieve the required acceleration. However, the rest of the JPL minimum requirements were found to be compatible to projected 1985 vehicle capabilities.

Once usage and performance standards were established, the contractors had to develop a hybrid system that would meet the requirements. The hybrid system design selected for maximum performance and energy conservation was the parallel propulsion system configuration (where both engine and electric motor are directly connected to the drive train), preferably with a flywheel secondary storage unit. The series configuration (where the electric motor drives the vehicle and the gasoline engine recharges the batteries) was not selected because the parallel system was more efficient with higher performance. However the system still needed some means of co-ordinating the three separate power modes to optimize

Photos courtesy General Electric Research and Development Center

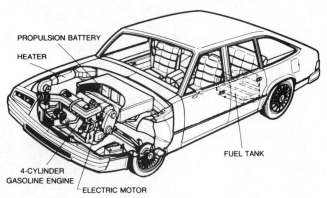

"HYBRID" AUTOMOBILE

PROPULSION BATTERY

HEATER

FUEL TANK

4-CYLINDER
GASOLINE ENGINE

ELECTRIC MOTOR

This is a design model of an experimental "hybrid" automobile—with both a gasoline engine and an electric motor under the hood—that the General Electric Research and Development Center, Schenectady, N.Y., will develop for the U.S. Department of Energy.

propulsive energy. A microcomputer incorporated into the system will ensure that stored electric energy is used as much as possible to maximize fuel conservation, and automatically distribute the load to the electric motor and/or gas engine when both are being used simultaneously. The computer will control the overall operation of the vehicle to ensure the electromotive power is exploited to its fullest. The combustion engine and electric motor will work together in synergism thereby reducing gasoline or synthetic fuel consumption while maintaining vehicle performance.

With preliminary design studies completed, GE has the basic plan for its hybrid. The proposed experimental model will have an 80-hp gas engine and a 40-hp electric motor, with advanced lead-acid batteries developed by Globe-Union, Inc., and a microcomputer to determine load split. The mid-size, five-passenger four-door sedan will weigh about 3950 lb (1791 kg) and have front-wheel drive with parallel propulsion. The hybrid's 10-battery pack weighs 770 lb (349 kg) and will be recharged by plugging into a wall socket, regenerative braking, or by the gasoline engine when in use. Chrysler has been awarded the contract to supply body design.

At the present time, there are still many difficulties that have to be worked out in hybrid design. Obviously, one of the biggest problems is development of a low cost, long-lived battery.

With the current level of technology, the advanced lead-acid battery seems slightly more cost competitive than nickel-zinc or other near-term batteries. More economical controllers will also be helpful in system design. Improvements in aerodynamics, use of lighter materials, suspension modifications to accommodate the hybrid power train, and tires that reduce rolling resistance will have to be incorporated into the structure and design of hybrid vehicles. Most of these problems are likely to yield to improved technology. However, a much more serious drawback to mass marketing of hybrids is their high initial cost, anywhere from 1.2 to two times the purchase price of an internal combustion automobile. The present hardware for hybrids may be adequate in terms of performance, but considerable cost reductions are required.

The DOE projects savings of 40-70% over fuel consumption of internal combustion vehicles. The hybrid makes least energy demands precisely in the area where most energy in the U.S. is consumed today, while still providing the mobility and independence of movement that Americans cherish. The electric hybrid could do much to clean up the atmosphere of congested cities and, if the cost of a hybrid becomes competitive, could well become the most popular electric vehicle in production.

DOE/GE/TRIAD

Photo courtesy of General Electric Company

DOE/GE/TRIAD Electric Vehicle

An experimental vehicle design was funded by the DOE under a $265,000 contract in 1976. The co-developers are the General Electric Company, Chrysler Corporation, Triad Services, Inc. (a design firm), and ESB, Inc.

The DOE contract calls for an experimental short trip vehicle with a 55 mph (88 km/hr) top speed and acceleration of 0 to 30 mph (48 km/hr) in ten seconds. Range for stop and go cycle is 75 miles (120 km) per charge. Other goals are: A $5,000 (1975 U.S. Dollars) mass produced price, with a minimum life of 100,000 miles (160,000 km).

The vehicle is designed to use advanced lead-acid batteries, regenerative braking, and microprocessor electronic controls. The 2,942 lb (1350 kg) vehicle will carry 1182 lbs (536 kg) of batteries.

TAX CREDITS FOR ELECTRIC VEHICLES

On June 12, 1978, Senator James A. McClure introduced a bill (S.1320) to amend the Internal Revenue Code of 1954 to "allow a credit for the purchase of an electric vehicle or for converting a vehicle powered by an internal combustion engine to electric power."

This bill allowed a 10% credit to the taxpayer for the taxable year against the cost of purchasing or converting to electric power, not to exceed $1,000. A similar bill was introduced in the House of Representatives by Charles E. Grassley of Iowa, who was a co-sponsor with Congressman Mike McCormack (the primary sponsor) of Public Law 94-413, The Electric Vehicle Research Development and Demonstration Act of 1976.

As of this writing, S.1320 is still pending and, if it is not made into law, Senator McClure has indicated that he will reintroduce it in the 97th Congress.

ELECTRIC VEHICLE CAFE RATINGS

Recent U.S. governmental electric vehicle activity includes a bill introduced in the House of Representatives by Congressman Tom Corcoran of Illinois. "The Electric Vehicle Act of 1979" would allow electric vehicles to be included in the Corporate Average Fuel Economy (CAFE) rating for automobile manufacturers.

A specific miles-per-gallon rating would be assigned to electric vehicles based on several factors including the national average of electricity production using petroleum. The CAFE rating for electric vehicles could range from 70 to 185 miles per gallon, depending upon vehicle efficiency and other factors. The actual figure will be established by the Secretary of Energy, using a special equation based on "harmonic" average of equivalent petroleum-based energy. (This figure is not available at this writing).

A companion bill (S.624) was introduced on March 24, 1979 in the Senate by Senator James A. McClure of Idaho and co-sponsored by Senators Matsunaga, Schmitt, Johnston, Domenici, and Levin. Finally, on January 7, 1980, President Carter signed the Chrysler Guarantee Act of 1979 (P.L. 96-185) which in Section 18 amended Public Law 94-413 (the E/HV Act). This amendment directed the Secretary of Energy, in consultation with the Secretary of Transportation and administrator of the EPA, to conduct a seven-year CAFE evaluation program for electric vehicles with a final report to be provided to Congress in 1987.

The inclusion of electric vehicles in the CAFE ratings can take place in the 1983 model year and will hopefully provide an incentive for the large auto manufacturers to produce significant quantities of electrics. Previously, the CAFE ratings applied only to gasoline and diesel-fueled passenger automobiles and light duty trucks whose primary use is on public roads, streets, and highways.

The mandatory fuel economy legislation of 1975 requires all vehicle manufacturers to attain a fleet average fuel economy of 27.5 miles per gallon (9.75 km/l) by 1985. This law forces the manufacturers to improve consumption by using 40% less fuel in 1985 than 1975.

The automobile manufacturers would be able to reduce governmental pressure to achieve 27.5 miles per gallon (9.75 km/l) with the inclusion of electrics in their vehicle fleet. This would allow them to continue production of high profit luxury automobiles which may not be capable of achieving the mandated mileage requirements.

Meeting Our Future Energy Needs

HOW WE WILL MEET OUR FUTURE ENERGY NEEDS

If we are to have electric vehicles in the future, we must have the capacity to generate electric power. Power to run our cities, power for our farms, our cars and airplanes. Without energy, our cities would freeze, transportation would grind to a halt, we would be unable to feed our people—our world would be virtually uninhabitable. The power must come from somewhere, and it must be plentiful. Where will this power come from?

We can no longer depend upon our free fossil-fuel reserves. Free, because we do not pay for their production or replacement costs. Since you cannot produce oil, you are merely charged for the privilege of pumping it out of the ground. Oil is nature's gift. Some day the free ride will be over. Today, power-generating stations cannot supply electric home heating that can compete with oil heat. Oil is so artificially inexpensive, we can't afford to use anything else economically. In the future, when we will be crying out for oil to use for lubrication, personal transportation, aircraft, and the specialized applications for which oil has no substitute, we will wish that today's oil had been more expensive.

Only the cost of extraction and refining, not the "dearness" value is included in the market price of today's oil. In these terms oil is practically free. We don't produce oil; it is the result of a multi-million-year process. You won't find it on the moon or any other planet because it is a product of life.

Therefore, we need to seek out more plentiful sources which will provide us with unlimited power. We must then connect the power to our homes, factories, vehicles, and cities. One solution is to establish a society whose energy is based on electricity and hydrogen. There is a possibility that together, they can provide for all of our needs.

New methods for electricity production will be developed and old methods refined. Hydrogen can help supplement natural gas and other fossil-fuels. Hydrogen can also be used to "store" energy, to increase power plant efficiencies. The concept of an economy based on hydrogen is one outlook for the future.

The idea of a totally electric "hydrogen economy" is not new; its potential application to our society has been extolled by some scientists for many years. It may or may not make sense to you, but it does offer a method to acquire the electric power necessary to achieve the goals of future transportation.

HYDROGEN

In "The Mysterious Island" written by Jules Verne in 1874, a reference was made to hydrogen power. One character responded to a question about what would happen if we ran out of coal and other fuels. He said, "Yes, my friends, I believe that water will one day be employed as fuel, that hydrogen and oxygen which constitute it, used singly or together, will furnish an inexhaustible source of heat and light . . ."

The sources of energy with hydrogen as a backbone could lead to the construction of a worldwide network of inexhaustible, clean power that will be both compatible with nature and with the desire for man to rise above his present state of development.

Hydrogen may be an alternative to natural gas. If natural gas is the first fossil fuel source to be depleted, hydrogen could be used as a substitute in our pipelines. Perhaps at first the hydrogen will be mixed with natural gas products, and then with synthetic gas derived from coal gasification.

Compared with natural gas, hydrogen cannot produce the heat value volume for volume, and the cost of hydrogen is far greater than natural gas. However, the impetus of higher gas prices could eventually close the price gap.

How powerful is hydrogen as a fuel? Liquid hydrogen has been powering rocket vehicles from the very beginning of our space program. The first practical hydrogen and oxygen fuel cells were used to supply electric power to virtually all U.S. spacecraft. So we can see that hydrogen is a valuable power source.

Hydrogen-powered automobiles have been built. After studying their advantages, perhaps solutions to storage and safety problems will make hydrogen transportation an integral part of a 21st Century society.

Vehicle demonstrations have shown that hydrogen: (1) burns more efficiently in a lean air mixture than does gasoline, (2) burns cooler than gasoline with a non-luminous flame, (3) allows the use of ultra-high compression ratios, thereby increasing the horsepower of the engine, and (4) is virtually non-polluting.

Because any heat engine can basically be converted to use hydrogen, some scientists see the hydrogen-oxygen engine as the successor to the fossil fuel internal-combustion engine.

Hydrogen was proposed as a fuel for engines in the early 1800's. (Hydrogen itself was discovered in 1766 by Cavendish.) Efforts were made in 1923 by the British engineer, Sir Harry Ricardo, to convert an internal-combustion engine to hydrogen.

There are three basic combinations that use hydrogen for fuel in an internal combustion engine: hydrogen-air, hydrogen-gasoline, and hydrogen-oxygen. A number of hydrogen-air vehicles were entered by several universities as student projects in the Urban Vehicle Design Competition of 1972. Later a group of U.C.L.A. engineering students continued to work on their hydrogen-converted 1972 Gremlin, using a specially-modified Ford V8 engine. The hydrogen was stored as a gas in two commercial cylinders mounted behind the front seats. The two cylinders weighed 300 pounds (136 kg) each, carried six pounds (2.7 kg) of hydrogen stored at 6,000 psi (422 kg/cm²), allowing for a total range of about 60 miles (96 km). A top speed of over 90 mph (145 km/hr) was recorded.

One driving report indicated that smooth and detonation-free acceleration could be achieved when the vehicle was full-throttled at ten mph (16 km/hr) in high gear. In an emission test conducted in 1973, the U.C.L.A. Gremlin registered zero hydrocarbon and carbon monoxide emissions. Later, students at Brigham Young University employed water injection techniques to lower combustion temperatures and increase power.

Another U.C.L.A. experiment used a four-cylinder Datsun engine designed to burn liquid hydrogen, stored at − 423°F (− 253C), which is only 37° (21C) above absolute zero. Special cryogenic storage tanks with a capacity of 50 gallons, were used. Each thermos-bottle type container weighed 50 pounds (23 kg) and carried 30 pounds (14 kg) of fuel which gave the Datsun pickup a range of 600 miles (965 km).

A more recent U.C.L.A. project included a design for a hydrogen-powered U.S. Postal Service delivery truck which carried liquid hydrogen in a cryogenic storage tank with water injection to reduce emissions and backfiring. A regular gasoline tank was used to store the water required. The range for the vehicle was 450 miles (724 km) at normal driving speeds, consuming 30 pounds (14 kg) of hydrogen. Since trucks, buses, ships, and trains could, with some modification, run on liquid hydrogen, these modes of transportation could endure virtually in their present form if fossil-fuels become rare. The range of a jet could be doubled by conversion to liquid hydrogen.

Hydrogen becomes a liquid when compressed and cooled to − 423°F (− 253C). Of course, this cryogenic form of storage requires a subsystem capable of maintaining this low temperature. The available energy in liquid hydrogen approaches 2½ times the power of gasoline per unit weight. Hydrogen produces more energy per pound than any other fuel.

Another method, hydride storage, releases hydrogen when heated. This system is attractive because of its more normal, ambient storage temperatures. When a hydride storage system is used, storage takes up 50% more space than current gas tanks. There is also a 300-pound (136 kg) weight penalty, but this is offset by the normal storage temperatures. Hydride systems work when certain metals such as magnesium and titanium are fused with hydrogen. The hydride thus formed is then heated to release the hydrogen at a later time. Heat could be supplied partially by the engine exhaust to liberate the hydrogen. New hydride research is being conducted to help solve storage problems.

The most efficient use of hydrogen in an automobile would be the hydrogen-oxygen mixture which uses pure oxygen instead of air. Of course, an additional tank would have to be carried. This has always been a problem with hydrogen cars in general. The problem of storage is a fact that we must live with if we will ever see hydrogen cars as a reality in the future.

Because of the expense involved with hydrogen production, we may not see hydrogen automobiles in general use until the 21st Century. Progress in hydrogen-powered vehicles will be an interesting subject to follow in the years to come.

The main argument against the proliferation of hydrogen as a fuel is the fact that it becomes very expensive to produce. If electrolysis is used to electrically split water into hydrogen and oxygen, the application of large amounts of power is required. Producing hydrogen with the electrolysis process is an expensive method, therefore cheap, abundant electricity is needed. If the price of the electricity can be reduced or more efficient means of power perfected, hydrogen production on a large scale will be more feasible.

"On site" production of hydrogen from a power station could be accomplished with off-peak energy salvaging. Also, the construction of nuclear power plants in safe, remote areas such as deserts could produce fresh water and pure oxygen as by-products, while supplying hydrogen to our electric system.

It is possible that even with the energy conversion costs at both ends, a hydrogen pipeline may be cheaper to operate than conventional electric transmission lines.

Studies indicate that because hydrogen can store energy, it has a built-in advantage over power lines.

In 1970, eight million tons of hydrogen, or about three trillion standard cubic feet, were produced. The hydrogen produced is being used for ammonia production (42%), and petroleum refining (38%) plus uses for metallurgy and food processing.

Some people associate hydrogen with danger. Perhaps the most memorable event which precipitated this wary regard of hydrogen was the accident of the Zeppelin Hindenburg, which went up in flames in Lakehurst, New Jersey, in 1937. The Hindenburg used hydrogen to fill its gas bags for buoyancy.

Because hydrogen is the lightest element, risks of ignition can be less than gasoline because leaks will diffuse quickly in any ventilated area, reducing the potential of flame travel. If hydrogen is handled intelligently and care is taken to provide proper ventilation, and prevent causes of accidental ignition, then hydrogen is as safe as any other fuel we are presently using.

The Los Alamos Federal Test Facility conducted a test with a 500-gallon (1893 l) liquid hydrogen spill. It was observed that once in the gaseous state, hydrogen disperses into the atmosphere quickly and becomes harmless within 60 seconds. This is contrary to gasoline which, when spilled, collects in pools around an accident site, remaining a hazard for a long time. Even when completely mixed with air, hydrogen will not detonate unless it is compressed or ignited by a strong spark.

The basic building block of the hydrogen society in the immediate future will be the implementation of several existing concepts of energy production. These technologies all have one thing in common—they must face and conquer technical obstacles before they will be acceptable. All of us must cooperate to allow the breakthroughs of science and the participation of many nations to overcome technical barriers.

One company has been in the vanguard of hydrogen research. The Billings Energy Corporation of Independence, Missouri, under the guidance of Roger E. Billings (who has been an active innovator in the field since 1965) has produced many hydrogen-powered vehicles. In addition, their research has resulted in patents issued for hydride technology. Billings also in-

BILLINGS HYDROGEN HOMESTEAD

dicates that ''hydrogen can be produced from low grade U.S. coal at a cost which is equivalent to the cost now paid to import foreign oil.'' He also adds that ''this is already being done on a commercial scale all over the world.'' Using this technology, hydrogen could come on stream when utilization equipment and a distribution network is established.

One French auto manufacturer, Peugeot, has contracted for the Billings conversion of one of its vehicles to hydrogen power. The French interest in hydrogen is understandable in light of its dependence on expensive foreign oil. Proposed nuclear energy electricity production in France could use hydrogen for off-peak energy storage.

Billings has established a hydrogen homestead for several years in Provo, Utah, which includes a 25-room home using hydrogen for cooking, heating, and hot water. Part of the homestead includes a Cadillac Seville which runs on either gasoline or hydrogen and a tractor powered by hydrogen. Electricity is used to convert water into hydrogen by electrolysis and storage is in metal hydrides. Future plans for the homestead include on-site solar and/or hydroelectric-generated electricity for hydrogen generation.

Additional plans include the construction of a pilot hydrogen utilization community in Independence, Missouri, which will include 25 residences and 100 vehicles.

Another project includes a coal gasification plant to produce hydrogen to run an entire city. The Forest City plan will replace kerosene with hydrogen as a fuel for electricity production. Surplus hydrogen will be used for industry, public and private vehicles, and farm equipment.

Plans for the longer term include the construction of ten full-scale coal gasification plants each producing 300 billion BTU's per day.

Today the Billings Energy Corporation manufactures products which relate to hydrogen generation and hydride storage.

For more information, contact Billings Energy Corporation, 18600 East 37th Terrace South, Independence, MO 64057.

ALTERNATE SOURCES

A key factor in alternate energy development is how much attention world governments will devote to the subject. There are ''ongoing'' projects today, some of which are not fully functioning, economical or even well designed. Some are struggling first and second generation systems, that will provide valuable information for scientists, engineers, and designers to help third, fourth and fifth generation systems which may give us hard facts and solutions to major problems.

The aviation industry did not move from the Wright Brothers' airplane to the SST in one step; there were evolutionary processes that followed before a level of sophistication could be achieved. The opponents of alternate energy sources may ridicule their inefficiency or relatively low power output. But, in the future, when we must extract from this earth the power which we cannot obtain through fossil-fuels, their opinion will undoubtedly change.

Nuclear Fission

Today nuclear power generates about 3% of our electricity. By the year 2000 this may be increased to 50%. The thermal efficiency of nuclear reactors is about 33% for light water reactors and 40% for the experimental breeder reactors which actually produce more fuel than they consume.

The advantages of nuclear power are many. It is clean, has low pollution, is relatively safe, inexpensive, and quiet.

The disadvantages are centered around the potential hazards regarding the disposal of radioactive waste materials which remain deadly for as long as 250,000 years.

Coal

Coal-fired power generating plants now supply about 47% of our electricity. Modern coal-fired boilers are about 40% efficient. This compares quite favorably to the average automobile which has a 16% efficiency.

The advantages of coal are that there are several hundred years of reserves which will provide power for electricity *and* supply hydrocarbon derivatives which can replace oil and gas in the future.

Coal's disadvantages include the increasing costs of mining, problems with restoring mined areas, health hazards and costly ''laundering'' of high sulfur coals. (See also Coal Liquefaction, page 205).

Coal Liquefaction (Synfuel)

During the final three years of World War II, Hitler's army and air force ran on synthetic fuel made from coal. Many believe that without liquefied coal, Hitler could never have started the war. As Allied armies overran Germany in 1945, thousands of documents were captured that described the coal liquefaction process, which involves changing the molecular structure of coal by increasing the hydrogen-to-carbon ratio and converting it into liquid fuel.

These documents were kept in various repositories in the U.S. and Great Britain, untouched and untranslated, until 1975. In that year, Texas A & M University started the German Document Retrieval Project; so far about 10% of the 500,000 captured German pages have been studied.

It was Friedrich Bergius who first developed the coal liquefaction process in 1912, which earned him the 1931 Nobel Prize in chemistry. The Bergius process begins by grinding coal and mixing it with natural or synthetic oil to form a slurry. The synthetic oil can be made as a byproduct of the liquefaction process. The slurry is then put into reactors. Using molybdenum and tungsten sulfide as catalysts, and adding hydrogen, the slurry is heated to 752° F (400° C) and 6000-7000 lbs (2721-3174 kg)/sq. in. (2.5 cm) of pressure is applied. This causes the coal to break down into liquid, a synthetic crude oil that can then be refined like natural crude oil.

A variation on this method, the Fischer-Tropsch process, forces mixtures of carbon monoxide and hydrogen to react in the presence of metal catalysts. This procedure is used to liquefy coal that is low in hydrogen, such as South Africa's, which has filled much of its liquid fuel needs since the 1950's using this coal process. U.S. coal, however, is high in hydrogen and the Bergius process is the preferred method.

Estimates of U.S. coal reserves range anywhere from 100-1600 years of supply, and as the cost of coal liquefaction is comparable to natural oil on the world market, it would seem that there would be no hesitation in massive production of synfuel. But critics of coal liquefaction feel that a fuel program based on coal will not produce a stable or environmentally safe energy situation. For one thing, most coal cannot be recovered cheaply or easily, and like oil, coal is a nonrenewable resource. The coal-based technologies in existence are highly polluting, requiring large amounts of water, which become contaminated, and producing significant amounts of carcinogenic materials. Production of synfuel at this time does require a trade-off in environmental and health considerations.

Gasohol

The use of alcohol as a motor fuel is not a new concept. In fact, it was the recommended fuel in 1895 of Nikolaus Otto, the father of the internal combustion engine. After World War I, France temporarily used a 50/50 mixture of gasoline and alcohol in all government automobiles. During the Depression, many U.S. farmers used home-made alcohol to power their tractors. An alcohol fuel plant was built in Atchison, Kansas, but had to shut down in 1939 because it couldn't compete with cheap oil.

At the present time there are two main alcohol fuels proposed as an alternative to gasoline: methanol (methyl alcohol) and ethanol (ethyl alcohol), both of which can be produced from grain products, starches, or wood. Although they have a higher octane rating and can operate over a wider range of air/fuel ratios than regular gasoline, they cannot match gasoline in pure energy density. A gallon (3.8 liters) of methanol produces 56,560 btu; ethanol 75,760 btu; and gasoline 115,400 btu. As a result, mileage is considerably reduced with alcohol fuels.

While hydrocarbon emissions are lower with methanol and ethanol, there is an increased amount of aldehyde emissions (an air pollutant), although some believe that a catalytic converter could eliminate aldehyde emissions. Because alcohol is more corrosive than gasoline, engine fuel systems would have to be modified. In addition, because alcohol does not vaporize as easily as gasoline, starting an engine in cold weather with pure alcohol can range from difficult to impossible. But if a gasoline/alcohol blend is used, a new problem presents itself. If a small amount of water accumulates in the gas tank, the alcohol will separate from the gasoline, a phenomenon known as phase separation; this will cause the engine to stop.

There are ways to combat these problems. A dual fuel system, using gasoline to start the car and methanol to keep the engine running, can overcome the problem of cold weather starts.

An ether injection system, which injects ether directly into the intake manifold during cold weather, allows the car to start even in below freezing temperatures. An ethanol/gasoline blend is much less prone to phase separation than a methanol blend.

Many companies and many countries are conducting serious experiments with alcohol fuels. Volkswagen has invested massively for research into an 85/15 blend of gasoline and methanol. Methanol was chosen because it can be produced from a variety of sources, such as coal, wood, grain, and garbage. According to Volkswagen spokesmen, fuel consumption has been reduced because the gasoline/methanol blend burns more efficiently than straight gasoline. The problems of phase separation and cold weather starts have reportedly been solved by the addition of some isopropanol to the gas/methanol mixture.

The Brazilian government hopes to replace all conventional automobiles with ethanol-powered cars. Ford, GM, Fiat and VW are heavily involved in supplying Brazil with ethanol-burning cars. Although these vehicles use more fuel per mile (km), the engine has more power because of the higher octane rating of ethanol. Originally, Brazil added ethanol (made from sugar cane) to gasoline to provide a larger market for its sugar industry, but with its increasing dependence on foreign oil, Brazil has decided to increase its ethanol-producing capacity to alleviate that dependence.

In 1979, the U.S. Congress created the National Alcohol Fuels Commission, which will fund research. But many critics of gasohol feel that it takes more BTU's of energy to produce a gallon of alcohol in terms of extraction, distilling, and refining than that gallon can produce. Presently, ethanol is more expensive to produce than gasoline although, given the rising tide of oil prices, this situation will not remain that way for long. The advantage of using ethanol, aside from the higher octane rating, is that it can be made from cellulose, a renewable source and a material found abundantly in garbage. With government subsidies of ethanol production, and more energy-efficient distilling plants scheduled for construction, many large oil companies are investing in ethanol production.

Gasohol is not the ultimate panacea for the energy crisis. But, like all the other fuel alternatives, it can play a significant role in reducing fossil fuel consumption, especially for the hybrid electric vehicles of the future.

Solar Power

While the power derived from the sun is our most renewable form of energy, significant advancements in technology are required before solar energy can seriously affect the use of fossil fuels.

Solar technology was once almost exclusively the province of small, pioneering firms. Now big industry is getting involved, and the result of this competition is increasing more efficient and less expensive solar systems.

The primary weakness of solar energy is its reliance on direct sunlight. For this reason, heating a home with solar power alone is still unfeasible. Excellent results, however, are obtained by using solar energy to heat hot water which can result in a fuel savings of 50-70%. Japan has solar water heaters in two million homes. In contrast, the U.S. has about 35,000 homes which use sunlight to produce hot water.

One way to solve the problem of having a continuous energy supply when there is no sunlight is to use a hybrid system that combines solar equipment with conventional heating systems as a back-up. Hybrids are on the market that can be combined with gas, oil, or electric furnaces, and can also provide air conditioning and hot water.

The cost to install solar devices should be balanced against projected fuel savings. However, there are other economic advantages to solar power. The resale value of any building with solar heating devices is likely to be much higher and many states are providing financial incentives with savings on income, sales, and property taxes.

Government and private industry are conducting research into many different types of solar systems. For example, the Jet Propulsion Laboratory (Pasadena, Calif.) and Lewis Research Center (Cleveland, Ohio) are doing research on solar power systems comprised of a parabolic array of small mirrors that concentrate the sun's heat directly into a small turbine engine/generator unit. These systems can be sold to small communities, farms, industries, and even individual homes to provide supplemental electric power and for special uses such as recharging electric car batteries. Work is also being conducted on much larger versions of this system.

One of the great paradoxes of solar energy is that, of all the energy alternatives to fossil fuels, it has the greatest potential and one of the

HELICAL WIND TURBINE

least advanced technologies. While the use of solar power is increasingly more efficient and economical, existing solar systems, which can offer the solution to our long-term energy problems, are still in the developmental stage.

Wind Power

The energy extracted from wind is associated with solar energy because the wind blows as a result of the sun's effect upon air masses. Overall potential for wind power on a large scale remains quite low. However, this source of energy can be successfully adapted to private homes, small industries, and localities with favorable conditions.

HELICAL WIND TURBINES

While it would be impossible to cover wind-power in any depth in this publication, one unique invention deserves mentioning.

William Allison, an automotive engineer from Detroit, Michigan, has developed an eight-blade windmill with an outward appearance which represents a departure from conventional twin-blade windmills. Referred to as the "wind engine" by the inventor, the unusual design features four pairs of blades positioned along a horizontal axis. The blades, which are arranged in a helical manner and positioned at strategic angles and intervals, lack the traditional air-foil shape. (See illustration.)

According to Allison, the wind engine will out-perform other wind machines and achieve higher power-extraction efficiencies than other propeller designs. The wind engine's turbine can operate at a speed of 200 rpm which drives a Borg-Warner gear box in a 1-to-17 ratio, resulting in 3400 rpm at the shunt-wound General Electric DC variable-output generator. This combination produces electricity at wind velocities ranging from 4 to 50 mph (6 to 80 km/hr). Allison's designs when tested have illustrated that four or more pairs of blades generate the best efficiencies. More than 56 percent of the energy produced by the wind can be extracted when wind velocities are only 8 to 12 mph (13 to 19 km/hr). Fifty nine percent is the theoretical maximum for energy produced by a wind turbine. Allison's helical propeller designs have been successfully tested at the University of Massachusetts and the University of Michigan.

Environmental Energies, Inc. of Michigan, one of the several licensees of Allison's patents, tested a 20-foot (6-m) version. Results confirmed predicted efficiencies. The company now markets the wind engine ranging in tower heights from 40 to 100 feet (12 to 30 m) and is geared to low-cost mass production. Allison is licensing several companies to produce his designs. A range of windmill sizes is available, up to 80 feet (24 m) in diameter.

The helical wind turbine's high efficiency has prompted the Michigan Department of Transportation to award a contract to Environmental Energies to provide a 24-foot (7-m) version of the windmill for a roadside information center.

For more information regarding the licensees of the Helical Wind Turbine, contact William D. Allison, 39 Radnor Circle, Grosse Pointe Farms, MI 48236.

Geothermal

Goethermal energy is power from the earth's molten core. Steam-powered generators convert the heat into electricity at about 20% efficiency. This method is used in several areas of the world. Unfortunately the areas where this energy may be extracted are limited. Also, possible dangers exist from potential earthquakes and land cave-ins.

Waste or Garbage Recycling

Because it is free, garbage is a cheap fuel. The use of waste to produce electricity provides power while disposing of an unwanted commodity. Benefits of waste recycling include the potential to produce synthetic oil and methane gas. Also, there is significant revenue acquired from recycling metals from garbage.
(See also Methane gas, page 210).

Flywheels and Other Storage Systems

The key to higher efficiencies from nuclear and hydroelectric power plants is "energy storage"—storing energy during periods of low demand, to be used at peak demand periods.

Because alternating current cannot be stored efficiently, it must be generated as it is used. Use of power is heavily concentrated during daytime business hours and thus power plants are idle at night. Storage of power generated at night would allow use during the day, minimizing requirements to build power plants and allow them to operate in a more efficient mode. The flywheel is one of man's oldest inventions and can provide an efficient method to store energy. Flywheels have a higher storage capacity than do batteries. A 200-ton flywheel designed for a power plant could achieve storage efficiencies of up to 95%.

Other storage systems include batteries of advanced design. Also, alternate methods use large reservoirs above a river or stream into which water is pumped during off hours to be extracted later when the demand is higher, to spin turbines and generate power.

Magnetohydrodynamics

Magnetohydrodynamics, or MHD, is a recent invention which is an alternative to conventional power station generators. In this system, a rocket exhaust containing conductive particles passes through a magnetic field, producing electricity with an efficiency potential of 60%. The fuel used can be oil, coal dust, or gas. The prime advantage of the system is that it has no moving parts. Development may provide MHD power plants capable of supplying electric power to the United States in the next decade.

The high efficiency of MHD power and other advantages over nuclear power, such as safety and less waste heat add to its attractiveness.

Tar Sands

The world's largest petroleum deposit is not in the Middle East or Alaska but in Alberta, Canada. The Athabasca Tar Sands contain nearly a trillion barrels of oil. Canada has the largest tar sand formations, but smaller deposits are also found in the U.S. in Utah, Oklahoma, and Kentucky.

The process required to obtain petroleum from tar sands is expensive and difficult. Bitumen, a natural asphalt, is separated from the sand with a hot water method. After numerous stages of refining, one barrel of crude oil is obtained from about 2½ tons (2266 kg) of tar sand, at a cost of about $20/barrel as opposed to 40¢ per barrel for the Saudis to refine oil. Mining tar sands poses problems, too. Strip mining is the least expensive but most environmentally damaging process. Improvements in tar sand refining and mining will be necessary before plants become economically feasible and make significant fuel supply contributions.

Gopher Plants

Gopher plants (*Euphorbia lathyris*) are inedible desert plants that produce a resin which can be refined into petroleum products. The cost of refining is said to be competitive with today's oil prices.

Hydrogen Fusion

Hydrogen fusion is the light at the end of the alternate energy tunnel. It is the source of power which causes the sun to radiate energy over the earth, and it is a major building block of the future.

Nuclear fusion is the result of fusing or combining the nuclei of atoms together—the opposite of nuclear fission which splits atoms apart to create energy.

The principal fuel for thermonuclear fusion is deuterium, a naturally occurring material found in sea water. There is enough deuterium in the oceans to supply energy for several million years, and it is infinitely more economical than uranium.

Thermonuclear fusion produces little or no radioactive wastes unlike fission which produces plutonium—a waste product that remains deadly for 250,000 years. Unfortunately, fusion must reach the break-even point before it can be used to generate power. Break-even is the point where the reactor can manufacture more power than it consumes.

Gravity, magnetism and inertia are the three forces capable of generating the enormous heat and pressure required to produce a fusion reaction. The sun provides an example of gravitational fusion in which molecules are forced together due to the gravitational pull of the solar mass.

Magnetic fusion is being studied in Japan, the Soviet Union and in the United States. Scientists at the Lawrence Livermore Laboratories in the U.S. have been working on fusion projects for over 25 years. Their effort includes the use of a magnetic mirror confinement which holds hot "plasma" (an ionized gas of separated negative electrons and positively charged nuclei) in a magnetic "bottle."

The goal of this system requires the deuterium fuel pellet to be raised to 100 million degrees and held at that temperature for up to 1 second. The plasma must then be held in the magnetic bottle and compressed at a 10,000 to one ratio to produce "ignition," the point at which fusion occurs.

Inertia-induced fusion can occur when tremendous force is applied to a fuel pellet. The hydrogen bomb is one application of inertial fusion.

A LASER (Light Amplification by Stimulated Emissions of Radiation) fusion project is underway at Los Alamos Scientific Laboratories in the U.S. In this system, laser beams are focused simultaneously on a deuterium-filled fuel pellet. The duration of their first fusion demonstration in 1977 was 20 to 30 trillionths of a second.

The Hearthfire system at the Argonne National Laboratories in the U.S. uses an ion-beam accelerator to produce a 50,000 watt beam for inertial fusion experiments. A billion times this power is within the reach of technology.

During inertial fusion, the energy from a laser or ion beam generator vaporizes the fuel pellet's outer layer with more than 10 trillion watts of electricity producing an inward explosion or implosion which can meld two nuclei into one.

Safety considerations for fusion are substantially less than nuclear fission. A fusion reactor cannot "run away" because the extremely difficult conditions necessary to create a reaction must be precisely maintained or ignition ceases.

The experimental fusion device which can achieve the break-even point may not be in operation until the 1980's. Because of the long time span necessary to develop a commercial power plant after the first fusion break even demonstration, we will probably not see fusion in commercial use until the 21st Century. This parallels the development of nuclear fission reactors which were demonstrated in 1942, yet did not become a practical reality until 1967.

There is no doubt that the aggregate total of man's technology will be required to effectively produce a successful hydrogen fusion reactor. Some sources indicate that it may be up to fifty years before we see one actually in use, producing electricity to be applied to our energy system. The time table will be contingent upon breakthroughs in development, technological advances and perhaps luck. One thing remains clear, however, that when and *if* hydrogen fusion becomes a reality, we will see an abundance of energy on earth.

HEARTHFIRE

Methane Gas

The most abundant source of natural gas is derived from underground wells. Like oil, it is one of those irreplaceable fossil fuels destined for extinction. But unlike oil, it can be derived from other sources, most notably garbage and manure. At the present time, the world seems assured of a steady supply of the latter two items.

Since 1969, Dual Fuel Systems, Inc., of Montebello, California, has been promoting compressed natural gas, or methane, installed in conventional vehicles to allow the use of either gasoline or methane. The conversion system is quite simple and has few components. To modify any vehicle to methane merely requires the installation of two to four storage cylinders with a capacity of 3½ gallons, a pressure regulator, a gas/air mixture attached to the carburetor and a dash-mounted fuel selector control and fuel gauge.

So far, dual fuel systems have been installed in fleets all over the world. In New Zealand, the Auckland and Wellington Gas Companies are working to convert 150,000 public and private vehicles to methane. The Alaska Gas and Service Company, Southern California Gas Company and Pacific Northwest Bell have all converted their service vehicles to methane gas.

In addition to vehicle conversion, Dual Fuel Systems manufactures methane artificially from sewage, animal waste, agricultural waste, and landfill material. Sewage treatment produces methane as a byproduct, usually mixed with hydrogen sulfide, a noxious gas that can be easily and economically removed. The Binax System, operated by Central Plants, Inc., an affiliate of Dual Fuel Systems, has been installed at the water treatment plant in Modesto, California, providing enough natural gas to operate all of the city's cars and trucks.

Compressed natural gas, or methane, has a number of advantages over refined petroleum products. On a cost-per-mile basis, methane is more economical and costs less to produce, at the present time, than diesel oil. It is also a more reliable source of fuel because it can be manufactured artificially. Using methane also reduces engine wear. The engine starting procedure is easier with natural gas because there is no choke, no raw gas to wash down cylinder wall lubrications, and no crankcase oil dilution. In cold or hot weather, engines start faster because the fuel is already in a gaseous state.

Additional benefits include fewer oil changes and prolonged spark plug and muffler life. Pollution is reduced by using natural gas in automobiles because methane gas is cleaner burning. This is especially important for vehicles used in confined areas such as mines or factories where emissions could be fatal.

Use of compressed natural gas in automobiles, however, does have some drawbacks. Cars do not perform quite as well on methane because of its lower BTU capacity. Also, the dual fuel system installation of about $1200 must be amortized into fuel costs. But the biggest problem with methane gas conversion in cars is the necessity for a central fueling site. The dual fuel system is most practical for fleet vehicles, either public or commercial, where vehicles return to a central fueling point each day. For this reason, cities and government agencies are ideally suited to use methane for: public transportation, emergency and service vehicles, heating and cooling of public buildings and emergency standby use in schools and hospitals.

Shale Oil

Shale oil is a fine-grained rock that contains a material called kerogen, which, when heated to 900° F (464° C), produces synthetic oil and gas. It is estimated that, in the U.S., three Western states have shale deposits with 1.8 trillion barrels of oil, of which 600-800 billion barrels may be recoverable. As in the case of tar sands, the main problems are mining and refining.

Thermal Conversion of Waste

Biomass refers to anything that can be naturally grown and then converted into fuel. It includes burning logs in a fireplace and converting sewage, garbage, and waste to produce electricity and natural gas. The extraction of natural gas from garbage has already been discussed, but a much more direct method of obtaining power from garbage is simply to burn it.

There are several processes for converting waste to usable fuel: 1) One method is to convert the garbage to a solid fuel pellet, after a refining process that removes all the recyclable materials, and then sell the solid fuel blocks as a charcoal substitute. 2) Perhaps the easiest way of reducing garbage to energy is to burn all of the non-recyclable material and use its heat to produce steam, which can then be sold to industries. 3) A more experimental method is the use of certain garbage-eating bacteria that produce a combustible gas as a product of their digestion.

Converting waste to energy is still relatively new and there are some problems associated with this industry. Various materials found in landfills can cause explosions when burned, and many plants for processing garbage have inefficient exhaust systems, creating pollution and noxious fumes. However, cities where landfill sites are scarce or which object to unsightly garbage dumps can benefit from eliminating refuse by burning it for energy.

THE PLACE OF THE ELECTRIC VEHICLE IN THE FUTURE

No one can paint with any accuracy an energy picture of the world in the year 2000. Trends indicate that the fossil fueled private and commercial vehicles may become rare or extinct in the 21st Century. The priority of petroleum products will be directed to more essential uses, such as the production of plastics and fertilizers.

The development of a totally electric, hydrogen economy seems attractive when considering the alternatives. In such a society, electric vehicles will contribute to conservation of fossil fuels. But, individual habits regarding energy waste must change before we can face some of the problems of the distant future.

The concept of vehicle rentals may take an unusual twist in the future. The average urban dweller could have one or two electric vehicles and rent a gasoline or hydrogen powered road vehicle for vacationing. The rented pleasure vehicle could be more luxurious than one could imagine, with onboard computer, entertainment, and recreational facililties. The cost of such a vehicle would be beyond the reach of the average person to own, but not to rent for a week.

The rental concept may be taken to another extreme to include rental of both commuter vehicle and "battery time" used. Plastic, rubber and non-corroding metals could lead to rental vehicles which are exceptionally strong and long lived, to maximize investments.

Now that we have observed the vast potential for alternate power, it is easier to understand how electric vehicles enter into the overall picture of the future. Although the new uses of hydrogen as a combustible gasoline substitute will make possible the existence of such familiar modes of transportation as airplanes, trains, cross-country trucks, and oceangoing vessels, personal transportation will probably be dominated by electric vehicles.

Electric vehicles complement the hydrogen society in that they will act as storage reservoirs for off-peak nuclear power station production.

MASS TRANSPORTATION OF THE FUTURE

There are some people who take a dim view of mass transportation in general. They feel the majority of cities, such as Los Angeles, are not suitable for mass transportation to begin with. In some regards, their arguments sound valid; the majority of people would prefer to own their own automobiles over other methods of transportation. The autonomy and freedom a private vehicle offers cannot be matched by even the most sophisticated mass transportation system.

Our modern highway systems, which are a means of transporting millions of human beings from one place to another, can also be thought of as mass transportation. The automobile, considered part of that system, after all, does serve the masses.

It may also be true that even if the electric trains, monorails, buses, or subways were subsidized by the government to the point that they were absolutely free to all users, it is doubtful the conventional automobile would be endangered. The freedom of mobility that Americans have enjoyed is one which will not be relinquished easily. To be able to come and go as one pleases is in many instances a justification for the private vehicle that even a price of $2.00 per U.S. gallon would fail to deter.

Therefore, we must consider the small electric urban automobile integrated into a partially automated highway system, as a real life example of mass transportation.

Today, we see progress being made in giant steps in subminiature electronics, micro-processers and technology of a truly advanced society.

Eventually, a micro computer will control all aspects of engine control, accessories, instrumentation, time keeping and entertainment.

We may speculate on various topics such as:

totally automated vehicles which can be programmed to drive passengers to specific destinations, park themselves, recharge and return upon command.

Investment will have to be made in urban and highway systems to meet the needs of electric vehicles. Highways will have to provide a special lane or "power strips" to allow high speed electric vehicle use which would effectively increase range and performance. City streets will have to be constructed in a similar manner and vehicle owners charged for energy consumed. Charging stations will begin as an adjunct to regular service stations. Battery packs will be exchanged and owned by manufacturers. When the battery system has reached the end of its useful life, the manufacturer will recycle the components, minimizing the power required to build new batteries.

No one can say if we will see underground highways, double, triple and quadruple decked highways—or any highways at all. Perhaps a reconstruction of urban housing will attract suburban dwellers back to the inner-city. They can be remodeled, refurbished, and even made attractive by rent subsidies.

Some considerations for the mass transportation of the future include moving sidewalks, or people-moving devices, or totally automated minibuses that could be programmed to stop at certain points by the passengers. These suggestions are directed to the task of moving people from one place to another. There may be a trend to move places from person to person.

It is absurd to see a woman use a 4,000 pound car to go three miles to purchase a bag of groceries. Perhaps we should eliminate the necessity for this trip altogether. An in-home minicomputer could be connected to the neighborhood supermarket. The woman could code in the required groceries, to be dispatched to her by electric delivery van. The purchase would be billed directly to her bank account. The use of large, centralized supermarket warehouses could even eliminate the need for a neighborhood supermarket altogether.

When one stops to consider the total fuel use related to driving to and from work, non-essential shopping, and frivolous waste, it is easy to see where we can reduce our overall oil consumption by a significant amount without endangering the quality of life to which we are accustomed.

The use of moving lunch wagons could service large office buildings in downtown areas. Car pools for large companies could get groups of people to work in one vehicle.

By bringing the services to the home we can eliminate fuel used for transportation. The trend toward the static rather than the mobile form of communication may enable us to even further compartmentalize ourselves in our daily life.

It is conceivable that a person's occupation could be conducted in the comfort of his own home. If micro-processers that could interconnect both home and office are employed, there would be little need to deliver the employee twenty miles or so to work, when work could be merely an extension of his own home environment. If a salesman desired to call upon a client, the sale could be negotiated as easily via a videophone or holographic (three-dimensional illusion) image that would enable him to call upon many prospects in a day.

The necessity to travel great distances, and consume large quantities of fuel in the process, to visit one's relatives across the country, may also be eliminated by holographic conference rooms, situated in large metropolitan communication centers. Real-life illusions of a family meeting with people present from various cities at one time in one room with cross conversations and absolute realism, may negate the need for unnecessary travel.

Let us be concerned with the end product before we devote our energies to an antiquated concept. Surely, the steam driven train of the turn of the century was considered a technical marvel, one which the average layman would be hard pressed to improve. Yet the airplane and trucking industry have devastated the railroads.

Future generations may view the antiquated gesticulation of the internal combustion engine as a humorous side-note to a misguided era of man's development which relied upon primitive fuels, producing outrageous energy consumption, pollution, and wastefulness.

In the future, every factory or office building roof will be equipped with solar cells for collectors to accumulate energy. In heavy metropolitan areas, the surface area of a roof approaches or approximates the ground area. This space is totally ignored. We must trim down the waste, so that we may enjoy our lives in a cleaner and more efficient manner—not to make us automatons—but to allow us to live clean, healthy and productive lives in a streamlined, wasteless society.

THE BAY AREA RAPID TRANSIT (BART)

Photo courtesy of Bay Area Rapid Transit District

The Bay Area Rapid Transit connects Oakland to San Francisco, California through a 75 mile
(120 km) highly automated system.

Some day the outmoded concept of getting from one place to another could quite possibly be replaced by "traveling" via holographic image, at the speed of light, 186,000 miles per second (299,000 km/sec). Is this the ultimate interpretation of transportation in the future?

INVENTIONS TO SAVE THE WORLD

Every once in a while a magazine or newspaper features a story about an "uneducated tinkerer" who stumbles upon "the secret of perpetual motion." And of course, every legitimate scientific source proceeds to tear the new invention to shreds. But this does not deter the stalwart followers of a new concept—even if its merits have not really been proved. Remember, they do sell millions of astrology books each year.

Still, the public in its great optimism will believe almost anything; I, being a member of the public at large, have been known to swallow a few farfetched ideas myself. My position is that of an interested skeptic. I am receptive to new ideas, reserving the right to review the evidence for myself. I will accept any promising new concept until such time as it is proved unequivocally fallacious. And will defend to the death the right of any entrepreneur, inventor, or tinkerer to offer an idea to the public. The idea

may or may not be a fraud, but I believe the public has a right to know and to judge for itself.

In the light of the above, I present a few of the innumerable inventions which have received some notoriety in the past few years. I do this with the caveat that, while I personally may not believe all that you are about to read, much of it has not been *disproved* to my satisfaction. Remember, in the past, a host of inventors have been condemned for presenting "impossible" ideas. And, by the same token, many of them deserved the condemnation. You be the judge.

The Magnatron Motor

In April, 1979, material was issued to the press involving a "fusion" motor called the MAGNATRON. The motor, according to its Elgin, Illinois, inventor, Rory Johnson, was capable of powering an automobile for 100,000 miles (161,000 km) without refueling. The readily available fuel would cost $400.00 for a refill, weighing 1.07 lb (.486 kg), equivalent to 5,000 gallons (18,900 l) of gasoline.

The Magnatron was designed to produce electricity by the nuclear fusion of reprocessed deuterium oxide and galium, using a laser. The process was not thermonuclear fusion such as the hydrogen bomb, but a recombinant process, much like combining hydrogen and oxygen to produce water.

The motor, requiring a mounting space of only 30″ (76 cm) in diameter and 19¼″ (49 cm) deep, would be retrofitted into any existing automobile. Potential models were being developed in 310 hp @ 1000 rpm, 470 hp @ 2000 rpm and 525 hp @ 4000 rpm versions.

Typical projected performance in an automobile was calculated at a range of 110,000 miles (161,000 km) per charge (refueling) with acceleration using a 1974 Buick Electra as an example, of zero to 60 mph (96 km/hr) in 7.2 seconds and zero to 123.3 mph (198 km/hr) in 14.3 seconds. The approximate cost for a Magnatron with fuel was calculated at $4,000. The 475-lb (215-kg) engine could be used for automobiles, tractors, stationary power plants, and farm related jobs.

The inventor is an electrical engineer with a doctorate in physics and holder of 161 patents.

Mota Fuel

From as early as 1914, reports have emerged of men demonstrating a pill or powder which, added to either tap or distilled water, magically converts it into "high octane" motor fuel.

The Mota fuel (atom spelled backwards) has received the overwhelming support of everyone who has witnessed a demonstration. Recently in Illinois, one such promoter was found guilty—although the fuel itself was never proved fraudulent—of selling more than 100% of his invention, thereby bilking his investors out of thousands of dollars. In fact, the majority of his investors, some of them educated people with positions in energy-oriented companies, would have gladly donated *more* money to the cause, even after finding out the gentleman had sold more of his invention than he owned.

The "demonstration" sometimes involved the investor supplying the automobile with an empty tank or a brand new lawnmower engine, the water and the container. In some cases, the investor actually poured the powder into water. The green liquid performed better than high test gasoline and upon testing had the octane rating and characteristics of aviation fuel. Whether this was indeed a parlor trick or a real product has never really been determined.

Even after being found guilty, the man was released on probation because of his age. You see, he'd been selling shares in his product for over 40 years!

The Static Electric Motor

In the spring of 1973, Edwin V. Gray, a self-educated inventor, introduced a super-efficient motor which used the principles of static electricity.

Gray's EMS motor was based on a secret method to generate and mix static electricity with direct current. Demonstration reports indicated the motor ran "cold" without the excessive heat build-up usually associated with electric motors. The lack of heat was the demonstrable evidence that extremely high efficiencies were being achieved.

The motor's operational torque occurred when energy was pulsed by capacitors for a fraction of a millisecond. This current was a combination of static electricity mixed with direct current. The motor allegedly could return unused electricity back to the battery pack. Theoretically, the motor could return more energy than it consumed because it captured static electricity from the atmosphere as it ran.

From 1957 on, literally hundreds of people have invested in the project. The eventual demise of EV Gray Enterprises began in July, 1974, when Gray's plant was raided by the Los Angeles County District Attorney's office. Many charges were issued against Gray and subsequently dropped. The litigation eventually resulted in the payment of a minor fine for violating Securities and Exchange Commission regulations regarding the unauthorized sale of stock. During this period, the working model of the motor had been confiscated by the authorities. The court action slowed the progress of the EMS motor to a virtual standstill but did not diminish the optimism of Gray and his investors. Gray has repeatedly refrained from making claims about his motor, in particular from any reference to perpetual motion. It is also to be noted that Gray's work was not totally without the approval of the scientific community. Reports indicated the endorsement of highly respected scientists.

Perhaps we may hear more about Gray's cool-running static electric motor. If it really does work and contributes to transportation of the future, it may provide a super-efficient power plant for electric cars. If it really can pull static electricity out of thin air to make wheels go around, more power to Edwin Gray. The market is waiting and there are plenty of people out there with money to invest. The key question remains: does it really work?

ELECTRIC VEHICLE COUNCIL

The Electric Vehicle Council (EVC) is a voluntary, non-profit association of organizations involved in electric vehicle development. Founded in 1967, the Washington-based council is a leading international source of electric vehicle information. Member organizations include electric vehicle clubs, research and development groups, trade associations, power utilities, corporations, technical libraries, consultants, universities, and government organizations.

One of the EVC's most important contributions to the industry is the Electric Vehicle Exposition and Conference. Since 1978, the EVC has sponsored this annual three-day conference, allowing interested individuals the chance to attend lectures, view displays, and witness an electric vehicle parade. A typical cavalcade involves over 65 electric vehicles. Each conference and exposition hosts more than 5,000 representatives from industry, federal, state and local governments who view the conference as an expansive information exchange.

In an effort to review and update the progress of electric vehicle technology, the "EV EXPO" features exhibits of the latest products and developments in on-road and off-road battery-powered and hybrid vehicles as well as components such as batteries, motors, controllers, and chargers. To provide food for thought about relevant issues and barriers facing the electric vehicle industry, specialists provide technical papers at their lectures.

Together, the displays, speeches, and technical papers lend credence to a fledgling industry and familiarize interested individuals with new developments and problems in the growing field of electric vehicles.

EV EXPOS have been held in Chicago, Ill. (April, 1977); Philadelphia, PA. (October, 1978); and St. Louis, Mo. (May, 1980). The host city in October, 1981, is Baltimore, Maryland.

For more information contact:
The Electric Vehicle Council
1111 19th Street, N.W.,
Washington, D.C. 20036

EV "EXPO"

Directory of Select Electric Vehicle Associations and Clubs

American Public Power Association
2600 Virginia Avenue, N.W.
Washington, D.C. 20037
USA

Australian Lead Development Association
95 Collins Street
Melbourne, Victoria 3000
AUSTRALIA

Battery Council International
111 East Wacker Drive
Chicago, Illinois 60601
USA

Canadian Electric Vehicle Association
P.O. Box 4044, Station E
Ottawa, Ontario, K1S 5B1
CANADA

Copper Development Association, Inc.
405 Lexington Avenue
New York, New York 10017
USA

Denver Electric Vehicle Council
P.O. Box 7326
Colorado Springs, Colorado 80907
USA

Electric Auto Association
1674 Merrill Drive No. 12
San Jose, California 95124
USA

Electric Vehicle Association of Great Britain, Ltd.
30 Millbank
London SW1P 4RD
ENGLAND

Electric Vehicle Council
1111 19th Street, N.W.
Washington, D.C. 20036
USA

Electric Vehicle News
P.O. Box 350
Westport, Connecticut 06881
USA

European Electric Road Vehicle Association
Place du Trone 1
B-1000 Brussels
BELGIUM

Independent Battery Manufacturers Association, Inc.
100 Larchwood Drive
Largo, Florida 33540
USA

Institute of Electrical & Electronics Engineers
345 East 47th Street
New York, New York 10017
USA

International Lead Zinc Research Organization, Inc.
292 Madison Avenue
New York, New York 10017
USA

Japan Electric Vehicle Association
2-5-5 Toranomon, Minato-ku
Tokyo, 105
JAPAN

Lead Industries Association, Inc.
292 Madison Avenue
New York, New York 10017
USA

Motor Vehicle Manufacturers Association of U.S.
320 New Center Building
Detroit, Michigan 48202
USA

New Zealand Battery Electric Vehicle Club
14 Hospital Road
Kawakawa
NEW ZEALAND

Scandinavian Lead Zinc Association
22 Sturegatan
Stockholm
SWEDEN

Society of Automotive Engineers, Inc.
400 Commonwealth Drive
Warrendale, Pennsylvania 15096
USA

U.S. Department of Energy
Electric and Hybrid Vehicle Systems
Transportation Energy Conservation
Washington, D.C. 20585
USA

Unipede
39 Avenue de Friedland
75008 Paris
FRANCE

Manufacturers of Electric Vehicle Related Products

AM General Corporation
14250 Plymouth Road
Detroit, Michigan 48232
USA

Ahlstedt Manufacturing Company
Montague, Michigan 49437
USA

Allis-Chalmers Corporation
Industrial Truck Division
Milwaukee, Wisconsin 53201
USA

Ambac Industries Incorporated
American Bosch Electrical Products Div.
P.O. Box 2228
Columbus, Mississippi 39701
USA

American-Lincoln, Div. of Scott & Fetzer Co.
1100 Haskins Road
Bowling Green, Ohio 43402
USA

American Micro-Car
115 Florida Street
Farmingdale, New York 11735
USA

AMIGO Inc.
6693 Dixie Highway
Bridgeport, Michigan 48722
USA

Asser Transportmiddelen Fabriek B.V.
Dr. A. F. Phillpsweg 13
Assen
NETHERLANDS

Autolift Division
Plymouth Locomotive Works, Inc.
607 Bell Street
Plymouth, Ohio 44865
USA

B & Z Electric Car
3346 Olive Avenue
Signal Hill, California 90807
USA

BMS Manufacturing
81-900 Industrial Place
Indio, California 92201
USA

Baker Material Handling Corporation
5000 Tiedeman Road
Cleveland, Ohio 44144
USA

Baldor Electric Company
Fort Smith, Arkansas 72902
USA

Banner Industries, Inc.
Bell Street
Plymouth, Ohio 44805
USA

Barrett Battery, Inc.
3317 Lagrange Street
Toledo, Ohio 43608
USA

Barrett Electric Service, Inc.
P.O. Box 4037, Heritage Station
Schenectady, New York 12304
USA

Barrett Electronics Corp.
630 Dundee Road
Northbrook, Illinois 60062
USA

Battronic Truck Corp.
Third & Walnut Streets
Boyertown, Pennsylvania 19512
USA

Bendix Corporation
401 Bendix Drive
South Bend, Indiana 46624
USA

Berix Electric AB
Box 3015
462 03 Vanersborg
SWEDEN

Big Joe Manufacturing Company
7225 N. Koster Avenue
Chicago, Illinois 60646
USA

Blue Giant Equipment Corp.
310 Creekside Drive
Tonawanda, New York 14150
USA

The Boeing Company · Vertol Division
P.O. Box 16858
Philadelphia, Pennsylvania 19142
USA

Borg-Warner Corporation
700 South 25th Avenue
Bellwood, Illinois 60104
USA

Robert Bosch Corporation
2800 South 25th Avenue
Broadview, Illinois 60153
USA

Bradley Automotive
14414 · 21st Avenue North
Plymouth, Minnesota 55441
USA

Braune Batricar Ltd.
Griffin Mill
Thrupp
Stroud, Glos. GL5 2AZ
ENGLAND

Briggs & Stratton
3300 North 124 Street
Milwaukee, Wisconsin 53222
USA

Brubaker Group
10315 W. Pico Boulevard
Los Angeles, California 90064
USA

C & D Batteries
Division of Eltra Corporation
3043 Walton Road
Plymouth Meeting, Pennsylvania 19462
USA

C.E.D.R.E
31 310 Montesquieu-Volvestre
FRANCE

Cableform, Inc.
Zion Cross Roads
Troy, Virginia 22974
USA

Cableform Limited
Green Lane, Romiley
Stockport, Cheshire SK6 3JQ
ENGLAND

Canada Battery
4 Commerce Crescent
Acton, Ontario
CANADA

Canada Power Skoot Ltd.
115 Torbay Road
Markham, Ontario L3R 2M9
CANADA

Centron Systems, Inc.
567 North & South Road, Ste. #7
St. Louis, Missouri 63130
USA

Chloride Group Limited
52 Grosvenor Gardens
London SW1W OAU
ENGLAND

Chloride Industrial Batteries
3001 Fairfax Trafficway
Kansas City, Kansas 66115
USA

Chloride Industrial Batteries Ltd.
P.O. Box 5, Clifton Junction
Swinton, Manchester M27 2LR
ENGLAND

Chloride Technical
Wynne Avenue
Swinton, Manchester M27 2HB
ENGLAND

Clark Equipment Company
Industrial Truck Division
24th & Lafayette Streets
Battle Creek, Michigan 49016
USA

Club Car, Inc.
P.O. Box 4658
Augusta, Georgia 30907
USA

Commuter Vehicles Inc.
Division of General Engines Co., Inc.
P.O. Box 1479
Sebring Air Terminal
Sebring, Florida 33870
USA

Coventry Climax Ltd.
Fork Lift Truck Division
Sandy Lane
Coventry CV1 3DX
ENGLAND

Creative Automotive Research
8136 Byron Road
Whittier, California 90606
USA

Crescent Battery & Light Co., Inc.
818 Camp Street
New Orleans, Louisiana 70180
USA

Crompton Batteries Ltd.
Stephenson Street, Newport
Monmouthshire NPT OXJ
ENGLAND

Crompton Electricars Ltd.
Crown Avenue, Dukestown
Tredegar, Gwent NP2 4EF
ENGLAND

Cushman-Outboard Marine Corp.
P.O. Box 82409
Lincoln, Nebraska 68501
USA

Daihatsu Motor Co., Ltd.
1-1 Daihatsu-cho
Ikeda-city, Osaka 563
JAPAN

Daimler-Benz AG
Postfach 202
7 Stuttgart 60
WEST GERMANY

Dana Corporation
Spicer Clutch Division
P.O. Box 191
Auburn, Indiana 46706
USA

Dayton Electricar Corp.
7523 Brandt Pike
Dayton, Ohio 45424
USA

John Deere Company
Moline, Illinois 61265
USA

Delco Products Division
General Motors Corporation
P.O. Box 1042
Dayton, Ohio 45401
USA

Delco-Remy Division
General Motors Corporation
2401 Columbus Avenue
Anderson, Indiana 46011
USA

Die Mesh Corporation
629 Fifth Avenue
Pelham, New York 10803
USA

EHV Systems, Inc.
1699A Roosevelt Avenue
Bohemia, New York 11716
USA

Eagle-Picher Industries, Inc.
P.O. Box 47
Joplin, Missouri 64801
USA

Eagle Vehicles Inc.
8181 Hoyle Avenue
Dallas, Texas 75227
USA

Eaton Corporation
11000 Roosevelt Boulevard
Philadelphia, Pennsylvania 19115
USA

El Bilar AB
Skolsparet 31
Gothenburg S 42431
SWEDEN

Electric Auto Corporation
2237 Elliot Avenue
Troy, Michigan 48084
USA

Electric Carrier Corporation
8603 Crown Hill Drive
San Antonio, Texas 78209
USA

Electric Engineering
East Kalamazoo Street
East Lansing, Michigan 48823
USA

**Electric Passenger Cars
and Vans, Inc.**
5127 Galt Way
San Diego, California 92117
USA

Electric Vehicle Associates, Inc.
9100 Bank Street
Cleveland, Ohio 44125
USA

Electric Vehicles, Inc.
2736 Winfield Drive
Mountain View, California 94040
USA

Electric Vehicle Industries
9 Yard Road
Bedford, Massachusetts 01730
USA

Electrodrive Pty. Ltd.
72-90 Cambridge Street
Collingwood, Victoria 3066
AUSTRALIA

Electromobiles (India) Limited
Webb's Complex
26, M. G. Road
Bangalore 560 001
INDIA

Electrona S.A.
Rue du Pre-Landry 20
CH-2017 Boudry/Ne
SWITZERLAND

Elroy Engineering Pty. Ltd.
20 Lutanda Close
Pennant Hills 2120, N.S.W.
AUSTRALIA

Eltra Corporation
P.O. Box 931
Toledo, Ohio 43694
USA

Energy Development Associates
1100 W. Whitcomb Avenue
Madison Heights, Michigan 48071
USA

Energy Research Corp.
3 Great Pasture Road
Danbury, Connecticut 06810
USA

Engler Instrument Company
250 Culver Avenue
Jersey City, New Jersey 07305
USA

Evelec S.A.
Rue de la Pepiniere 41
Bruxelles 1000
BELGIUM

Exide Corporation
101 Gibralter Road
Horsham, Pennsylvania 19044
USA

Exxon Chemical Co. U.S.A.
780 Lee Street
Des Plaines, Illinois 60016
USA

FMC Corporation
Power Control Division
120 N. Broadway
Milwaukee, Wisconsin 53202
USA

Fabbrica Accumulatori Uriano SpA
Corso Milano 88
37100 Verona
ITALY

Fabbrica Italiana Magneti Marelli SpA
20099 Setso S. Giovanni
Milano
ITALY

FIAT
Strada del Drosso 145
10135 Torino
ITALY

Flight Systems, Inc.
P.O. Box 25
Mechanicsburg, Pennsylvania 17055
USA

Fox Products Company
4720 N. 18th Street
Philadelphia, Pennsylvania 19141
USA

Frizzel's Electric Transportation
47 Great Road
P.O. Box 118
Maynard, Massachusetts 01754
USA

Fulmen (UK) Ltd.
Blackwater Way, Aldershot
Hampshire GU12 4DR
ENGLAND

Furukawa Battery Co., Ltd.
No. 256, 2-Chome, Hoshikawa-Cho
Hodogaya-Ku, Yokohama
JAPAN

GEWA Rehabteknik AB
Box 3059
161 03 Bromma
SWEDEN

The Garrett Corporation
9851 Sepulveda Boulevard
Los Angeles, California 90009
USA

General Battery Corporation
P.O. Box 1262
Reading, Pennsylvania 19603
USA

General Electric Company
685 West Rio Road
P.O. Box 8106
Charlottesville, Virginia 22906
USA

General Motors Corporation
Chevrolet Division
3044 West Grand Boulevard
Detroit, Michigan 48202
USA

General Motors Corporation
Truck and Coach Division
660 South Boulevard, East
Pontiac, Michigan 48053
USA

Gould, Inc.
30 Gould Center
Rolling Meadows, Illinois 60008
USA

Grumman Allied Industries, Inc.
445 Broad Hollow Road
Melville, New York 11747
USA

Gulf & Western Industries, Inc.
1 Gulf & Western Plaza
New York, New York 10023
USA

**Gurgel Industria e Commercio
de Vehiculos Ltda.**
KM 171, Rodovia Washington Luiz
Rio Claro
Sao Paulo, S.P.
BRAZIL

HB Electrical Mfg. Co., Inc.
P.O. Box 1466
Mansfield, Ohio 44901
USA

H-M-Vehicles, Inc.
1116 East Highway 13
Burnsville, Minnesota 55337
USA

Harbilt Electric Vehicles Ltd.
Rockingham Road
Market Harborough
Leicestershire LE16 7PU
ENGLAND

Heald Inc.
P.O. Box 1148
Benton Harbor, Michigan 49022
USA

Hobart Brothers Company
Power Systems Division
1177 Trade Road East
Troy, Ohio 45373
USA

Honeywell Motor Products
4301 Kishwaukee
Rockford, Illinois 61109
USA

Hybricon, Inc.
11489 Chandler Boulevard
North Hollywood, California 91601
USA

Hydrel Power Co.
P.O. Box 992
Springfield, Massachusetts 01101
USA

Hyster Company
P.O. Box 2902
Portland, Oregon 97208
USA

International Harvester
401 North Michigan Avenue
Chicago, Illinois 60611
USA

JMJ Electronics Corp.
P.O. Box 25971
Oklahoma City, Oklahoma 73125
USA

Japan Storage Battery Co. Ltd.
Kisshoin, Minami-ku
Kyoto
JAPAN

Jet Industries, Inc.
P.O. Box 17184
Austin, Texas 78760
USA

Kalamazoo Manufacturing Co.
1827 Reed Street
Kalamazoo, Michigan 49001
USA

King Electric Vehicles, Inc.
P.O. Box 514
East Syracuse, New York 13057
USA

Tony Lamb Electric Vehicles
P.O. Box 532
Newbury Park, California 91320
USA

Lear Siegler, Inc.
280 East Riley Street
Zeeland, Michigan 49464
USA

Lektro, Inc.
Route 1, Box 925
Warrenton, Oregon 97146
USA

Lucas Electric Vehicle Systems
Evelyn Road
Birmingham B11 3JR
ENGLAND

Lyman Electric Products
15 Meadow
So. Norwalk, Connecticut 06856
USA

McGraw-Edison Company
Edison Battery Division
P.O. Box 28
Bloomfield, New Jersey 07003
USA

McKee Engineering Corporation
411 West Colfax Street
Palatine, Illinois 60067
USA

Marathon Electric Vehicles Inc.
8305 Le Creusot Street
Montreal, Quebec, H1P 2A2
CANADA

Mawdsley's Ltd.
Dursley
Gloucestershire GL11 5AE
ENGLAND

Melex U.S.A., Inc.
1201 Front Street, Suite 210
Raleigh, North Carolina 27609
USA

Mercury Clutch Division of ASPRO, Inc.
1201 Camden Avenue, SW
Canton, Ohio 44706
USA

Mule Battery Mfg. Co.
600 Park Avenue
Cranston, Rhode Island 02910
USA

Newton Aids Ltd.
2-A Conway Street
London WIP 5HE
ENGLAND

Nippon Yusoki Co., Ltd.
1-1,2-Chome, Higashikotari
Nagaokakyo-Shi
Kyoto
JAPAN

Nissan Motor Company Ltd.
1, Natsushima-Cho
Yokosuka
JAPAN

Nordco Electric Vehicle
Division of Nordco Products
26701 Redlands Boulevard
Redlands, California 92373
USA

Oldham Batteries Limited
Hyde Road
Denton, Manchester M34 3AT
ENGLAND

Onan
1400 73rd Avenue NE
Minneapolis, Minnesota 55432
USA

PMI Motors
Division of Kollmorgen Corp.
5 Aerial Way
Syosset, New York 11791
USA

Palmer Industries
P.O. Box 707, Union Station
Endicott, New York 13760
USA

Palmer Sales & Service, Inc.
3043 West Colter Street
Phoenix, Arizona 85017
USA

Pedalpower
Division of General Engines, Inc.
591 Mantua Boulevard
Sewell, New Jersey 08080
USA

Permobil Foundation
P.O. Box 90
86100 Timra
SWEDEN

Pilcar
1225 Chene-Bourg
Geneve
SWITZERLAND

Polaris E-Z-GO
Division of Textron Inc.
P.O. Box 388
Augusta, Georgia 30913
USA

Porter Industries, Inc.
Box 380
Allen, Kentucky 41601
USA

Prestolite
Division of Eltra Corporation
P.O. Box 931
Toledo, Ohio 43694
USA

Progetti Gestioni Ecologiche
Via Rosellini 1
20124 Milano
ITALY

Propel, Inc.
210 New Market Avenue
South Plainfield, New Jersey 07080
USA

Ragonot
15 Bld Gabriel Peri
Malakoff 92240
FRANCE

Randtronics, Inc.
150 Constitution Drive
Menlo Park, California 94025
USA

Renault
Division Autocars-Autobus
8 quai Leon Blum
92156 Suresnes Cedex
FRANCE

Gianni Rogliatti
Cas Post 116
Turin
ITALY

S A E M
via Mentana 16
Monza (Milano)
ITALY

SGL Batteries Manufacturing Co.
14650 Dequindre
Detroit, Michigan 48212
USA

Salisbury Transmission Ltd.
P.O. Box 281B
Birmingham B8 2RQ
ENGLAND

Sevcon
Division of Technical Operations, Inc.
40 North Avenue
Burlington, Massachusetts 01803
USA

Siemens AG
Dep E 41
Werner-von-Siemens-Strabe 50
Erlangen D 8520, Bayern
WEST GERMANY

Smith's Electric Vehicles Limited
Marquisway, Team Valley Trading Estate
Gateshead, Tyne & Wear NE8 1YT
ENGLAND

South Coast Technology, Inc.
15001 Commerce Drive, Ste. 406
Dearborn, Michigan 48120
USA

SOVEL S.A.
164 Rue Leon Blum
69608 Villeurbanne
FRANCE

Stewart Warner Corporation
South Wind Division
1514 Drover Street
Indianapolis, Indiana 46221
USA

Surrette Storage Battery Co., Inc.
Jefferson Avenue
Salem, Massachusetts 01970
USA

Team Scarab, Inc.
P.O. Box 9334
Marina del Rey, California 90291
USA

Teilhol Electrique
Societe des Establissements Teilhol
63120 Courpiere
FRANCE

Towmotor Corporation
Sub. of Caterpillar Tractor Company
7111 Tyler Boulevard
Mentor, Ohio 44060
USA

Toyo Kogyo Company, Ltd.
3-1, Shinchi, Fuchu-cho
Aki-gun, Hiroshima 730-91
JAPAN

Toyota Motor Sales Company, Inc.
No. 3, 2-Chome Kudan, Chiyoda-Ku
Tokyo
JAPAN

Trojan Battery Company
9440 Ann Street
Santa Fe Springs, California 96070
USA

Twenty-First Century Electric Vehicles
8136 G Byron Road
Whittier, California 90606
USA

Twildo AB
Box 1286
171 25 Solna
SWEDEN

U.S. Electricar Corporation
250 South Main Street
Athol, Massachusetts 01331
USA

Unique Mobility, Inc.
3700 South Jason Street
Englewood, Colorado 80110
USA

Vantage Boats
R-1, Box 309
Mount Dora, Florida 32757
USA

VARTA Batterie AG
Am Leineufer 51, Postfach 210540
D3000 Hannover 21
WEST GERMANY

VARTA Batteries Inc.
85 Executive Boulevard
Elmsford, New York 10523
USA

Volkswagen Werk A G
Abteilungsleiter Forschung 6
D-3180 Wolfsburg
WEST GERMANY

Volvo, Car Division
Advanced Engineering Projects
Dept. 56500
S-405 08 Goteborg
SWEDEN

W. & E. Vehicles
Harlescott
Shrewsbury SY1 3AE
ENGLAND

Western Research Industries, Inc.
3100 Sirius Avenue, Bldg. C
Las Vegas, Nevada 89102
USA

Westinghouse Electric Corporation
Westinghouse Building, Gateway Center
Pittsburgh, Pennsylvania 15222
USA

White Materials Handling
130 Ninth Avenue South
Hopkins, Minnesota 55343
USA

Yardney Electric Corporation
82 Mechanic Street
Pawcatuck, Connecticut 02891
USA

Yuasa Battery Company, Ltd.
6-6 Josai-cho, Takatsuki
Osaka 569
JAPAN

Zagato International S.A.
Viale Stefano Franscini 22
6901 Lugano
SWITZERLAND

BIBLIOGRAPHY

BOOKS

CYCLOPEDIA OF AUTOMOBILE ENGINEERING
Chicago, American Technical Society, 1915.

Anderson, Edwin P.
ELECTRIC MOTORS
Theodore Audel & Co., 1968.

Bergere, Thea
AUTOMOBILES OF YESTERYEAR
New York, Dodd, Mead & Co., 1962.

Bishop, Calvin C.
FUNDAMENTALS OF ELECTRICITY
New York, N.Y. Chiton Company Books, 1960.

Bishop, Denis and Marshall, Prince
TRUCKS AND VANS 1897-1927
New York, The MacMillan Co. 1972.

Prepared by the Bureau of Naval Personnel
BASIC ELECTRICITY
New York, Dover Publications

Butterworth, W. E.
WHEELS AND PISTONS: THE STORY OF THE
AUTOMOBILE
New York, Four Winds Press, 1971.

Christian, J. M.
WORLD GUIDE TO BATTERY-POWERED ROAD
TRANSPORTATION
New York, N.Y., McGraw-Hill Publishing Co., 1980.

DiCerto, Joseph J.
THE ELECTRIC WISHING WELL: THE SOLUTION TO
THE ENERGY CRISIS
New York, Collier Books, 1976.

Donovan, Frank
WHEELS FOR A NATION
Thomas Y. Crowell Company, 1965.

Ewers, William I.
SOLAR ENERGY: A BIASED GUIDE
Northbrook, Ill., DOMUS BOOKS, 1977.

Flink, James J.
AMERICA ADOPTS THE AUTOMOBILE 1895-1910.
London, England, Cambridge, Mass., The MIT Press,
1970.

Georgano, G. N.
THE COMPLETE ENCYCLOPEDIA OF MOTORCARS
1885 TO THE PRESENT
New York, E. P. Dutton & Co., Inc., 1968, 1972.

Jamison, Andrew
THE STEAM-POWERED AUTOMOBILE
Bloomington, London, Indiana University Press, 1975.

Karolevitz, Robert F.
THIS WAS PIONEER MOTORING
Seattle, Wash., Superior Publishing Co., 1968.

Lewis, Albert L. and Musciano, Walter A.
AUTOMOBILES OF THE WORLD
New York, Simon and Schuster, 1977.

Mantell, Charles L.
BATTERIES AND ENERGY SYSTEMS
New York, McGraw-Hill, 1970.

Nicholson, T. R.
PASSENGER CARS 1863-1904
855 Third Ave., New York, The MacMillan Co., 1970.

Ruchlis, Hyman
THE WONDER OF ELECTRICITY
49 E. 33rd St., New York, N.Y., Harper & Row, 1965.

Scheel, J. D.
CARS OF THE WORLD IN COLOR
New York, E. P. Dutton & Co., Inc., 1963.

Edited By: Schroeder, Jr., Joseph J.
THE WONDERFUL WORLD OF AUTOMOBILES
1885-1930
Northfield, Ill., DBI Books, Inc., 1971.

Waard, John De and Klein, Aaron E.
ELECTRIC CARS
New York, Doubleday & Co., Inc., 1977.

Wellman, William R.
ELEMENTARY ELECTRICITY
450 W. 33rd St., New York, N.Y., 10001, Van Nostrand
Reinhold Co., 1971.

Edited by L'EDITRICE DELL'AUTOMOBILE LEA
WORLD CARS 1980
Pelham, New York, Herald Books, 1980.

MAGAZINE ARTICLES

Electric Vehicle News
February through November, 1974 to 1981.

"ENGINEERS IN, STYLISTS OUT"
Machine Design (Oct. 17, 1974) p. 120.

"HOW MANY SPEEDS?"
Machine Design (Oct. 17, 1974) p. 139.

"A NEW SPARK REVIVES ELECTRIC CAR MAKERS."
Business Week (Jan. 17, 1977) p. 86.

"A PIONEER STRUGGLES TO KEEP HIS PRODUCT
PLUGGED IN"
Industry Week (April 25, 1977) p. 76.

"REDDY-KILOWATT WAS MY CO-PILOT"
Car and Driver (Jan. 1978) p. 12.

"ROAD TESTING THE ELECTRICS"
Machine Design (Oct. 17, 1974) p. 19.

"SEMICONDUCTORS MEAN EXTRA RANGE"
Machine Design (Oct. 17, 1974) p. 19.

"THE WAR AGAINST THE AUTOMOBILE"
Car and Driver (Jan. 1978) p. 31.

"MAGNETIC 'WANKEL' FOR ELECTRIC CARS"
Popular Science (June 1979) p. 80 and 81.

"A BATTERY ELECTRIC DELIVERY VAN—THE I.M.P.
PROJECT"
Electric Vehicle Developments (March 1980) p. 23.

"AMAZING MAGNET-POWERED MOTOR"
Science & Mechanics Magazine (Spring 1980) p. 45.

"HIGH-ENERGY TUBULAR BATTERY DEVELOPED IN
U.K."
Automotive Engineering (April 1979) p. 34.

"BATTERYMAKERS' VIEWS ON GM ADVANCE"
American Metal Market (Sept. 28, 1979).

"THE ALUMINUM-AIR BATTERY FOR ELECTRIC
VEHICLES"
Energy and Technology Review (November 1978)
Reprint.

"VOLTS WAGON DOES IT, AGAIN—ELECTRIC CARS
LOOK SHARP, RUN CHEAP, BUT WILL THEY
SELL?"
Time (June 16, 1980) p. 52.

"SUPERBATTERIES: A PROGRESS REPORT"
IEEE Spectrum (March 1979) p. 49.

"HARNESSING THE POWER OF THE LASER"
Mechanix Illustrated (August 1980) p. 58.

"ARGONNE IS A STEP CLOSER TO ION-BEAM
FUSION—FIRST ION BEAM ACCELERATED"
Argonne News (June 1979) p. 3.

"THE E/HV COMPONENTS AND SUBSYSTEMS
TECHNOLOGY DEVELOPMENT PROGRAM"
Electric Vehicle News (August 1979) p. 14–21.

"HYBRIDS GET CLOSE SCRUTINY BY DOE"
Electric Vehicle News (May 1980).

"SCIENCE NEWSFRONT"
Popular Science (June 1980).

"HARNESSING THE POWER OF THE LASER" by
Victor D. Chase
Mechanix Illustrated (August 1980).

"CHURNING & BURNING—GARBAGE FOR POWER"
Mechanix Illustrated (August 1980).

"AMERICA ON THE THRESHOLD"
Mechanix Illustrated (August 1980).

"SHOULD YOU GO SOLAR THIS YEAR?"
Mechanix Illustrated (August 1980).

"HAULING IN THE WIND"
Mechanix Illustrated (August 1980).

"TURNING SAND INTO OIL"
Mechanix Illustrated (August 1980).

"ALTERNATIVE SOURCES OF ENERGY"
Independent Banker (July 1980).

"COAL FOR YOUR CAR"
Popular Mechanics (December 1979).

"FUEL FOR THE 'FÜHRER'"
Popular Mechanics (November 1979).

"ALCOHOL FUELS—CAN THEY REPLACE
GASOLINE?"
Popular Science (March 1980).

MISCELLANEOUS

U.S. Department of Energy Report
"ELECTRIC & HYBRID VEHICLE PROGRAM"
EHV/Quarterly Report Vol. 2 No. 1, January, 1978.

U.S. Department of Energy Report—Public Law 94-413
The Electric & Hybrid Vehicle Research, Development &
Demonstration Act of 1976.
ELECTRIC & HYBRID VEHICLE PROGRAM,
December 1977.

EVC No. 8013 Report
A BRUSHLESS DC MOTOR-POWER CONDITIONER
UNIT DESIGNED AND BUILT FOR PROPULSION OF
ELECTRIC PASSENGER VEHICLES—PHASE I
Dermerdash, N.A., Lee, F.C., Nehl, T.W., Overton, B.P.

ENERGY RESEARCH CORPORATION News Release.

EVC No. 8031
Hudson, Ray, DEVELOPMENT OF THE NICKEL-IRON
BATTERY SYSTEM FOR ELECTRIC VEHICLE
PROPULSION.

Eagle Picher Product Description/Pamphlet
"NIFE: THE NEAR-TERM BATTERY."

Cooper, John F., LAWRENCE LIVERMORE
LABORATORY, and Littauer, Ernest L., LOCKHEED
MISSILES AND SPACE COMPANY.
"MECHANICALLY RECHARGEABLE, METAL-AIR
BATTERIES FOR AUTOMOTIVE PROPULSION."

EVC No. 8048.
Bellows, R.J., Grimes, P., Shropshire, J.A., Zahn, M.
"ADVANCES IN ZINC BROMINE BATTERIES FOR
MOTIVE POWER."

Society of Automotive Engineers International Congress and Automotive Engineering Exposition, Detroit, 1977 Paper.
Unnewehr, L.E., Minck, R.W., Owens, C.
"APPLICATION OF THE FORD SODIUM-SULFUR BATTERY IN ELECTRIC VEHICLES."

Yao, N.P., Ludwig, E.A., Hornstra, F.
"OVERVIEW OF NEAR-TERM BATTERY DEVELOPMENTS," presented at The Fifth International Electric Vehicle Symposium.

Energy Development Associates Product Description Pamphlet
"EDA CREATIVE ENERGY STORAGE SYSTEMS."

GEL Product Description Pamphlet
"GEL ENERGY CONVERTER."

Selected Articles on Magnetic Fusion Energy from ENERGY AND TECHNOLOGY REVIEW, Prepared for DOE, Contract No. W-7405-ENG-45.
"LLL MAGNETIC FUSION RESEARCH: THE FIRST 25 YEARS."

Department of Energy Press Conference Paper
Halsall, Vincent M., Vice-President Battery Engineering, Globe-Union, Inc.,
"THE ELECTRIC VEHICLE BATTERY SYSTEM."

Japan Storage Battery Co., Ltd., Product Descruotuib
Kamada, K., Okazaki, I., Takagaki, T.
"NEW LEAD-ACID BATTERIES FOR ELECTRIC VEHICLES."

ESB RAY-O-VAC News Release
"TODAY'S BATTERIES COULD PROVIDE THE ENERGY FOR MOST COMMUTERS TO USE ELECTRIC CAR."

International Automotive Engineering Congress Exposition Paper
Von Krusenstierna, Otto, Reger, Mats
"A HIGH ENERGY NICKEL-ZINC BATTERY FOR ELECTRIC VEHICLES."

EVC No. 8032
Pearlman, Eugene, Program Manager, VIBROCEL™
"NICKEL/ZINC VIBROCEL BATTERY FOR EV APPLICATIONS."

Energy Research Corporation Pamphlet
"NIVOLT™ NICKEL-ZINC RECHARGEABLE BATTERY."

The 29th Power Sources Conference Paper
Yao, N.P., Christianson, C.C., Lee, T.S., Argonne National Laboratory, CHEMICAL ENGINEERING DIVISION, "IMPROVED LEAD-ACID BATTERIES—THE PROMISING CANDIDATE FOR NEAR-TERM ELECTRIC VEHICLES."

EVC No. 8029
Yao, N.P., Christianson, C.C., Elliott, R.C., Lee, T.S., Miller, J.F.
"DOE'S NEAR-TERM ELECTRIC VEHICLE BATTERY PROGRAM—STATUS OF IMPROVED LEAD-ACID, NICKEL/IRON, AND NICKEL/ZINC BATTERY DEVELOPMENTS."

Los Alamos Scientific Laboratory Publication LASL 78-1
"LASER FUSION."

Paper Presented at 9th Energy Technology Conference and Exposition, Washington, D.C., March 25, 1980.
"A VIEW OF THE FUTURE POTENTIAL OF ELECTRIC AND HYBRID VEHICLES," by Kirk, Robert S., and Davis, Philip W.

U.S. DEPARTMENT OF ENERGY
Information Bulletin No. 404, June 1979, October 1979.
"THE GENERAL ELECTRIC/CHRYSLER NEAR-TERM ELECTRIC TEST VEHICLE (ETV-1)."

"Electric Vehicle/Battery Technology"
Newsletter April, 1980, vol. 4, no. 1.

U.S. Department of Energy
Information Bulletin Nos. 101, 102, 103, 105, 107, 108, 201, 301, 304, 306, 402, 405, 406, 501–504, 506.

U.S. Department of Energy
Information Bulletin No. 403-1 December 1979
"THE GARRETT NEAR-TERM ELECTRIC TEST VEHICLE (ETV-2)."

U.S. Department of Energy Environment Assessment
May, 1980
"INCLUSION OF ELECTRIC AND HYBRID VEHICLES IN CORPORATE AVERAGE FUEL ECONOMY STANDARDS."

Los Alamos Scientific Laboratory, Mini-Review
September 1978.
"DIRECT CURRENT SUPER-CONDUCTING POWER TRANSMISSION."

Chicago Tribune, Wednesday February 20, 1980.
"EXPERT ADDS FUEL TO THE FISSION VS. FUSION DEBATE."

Report to the Congress by the Comptroller General, April 9, 1979.
"THE CONGRESS NEEDS TO REDIRECT THE FEDERAL ELECTRIC VEHICLE PROGRAM."

2ND ANNUAL REPORT TO CONGRESS FOR FISCAL YEAR 1978
"ELECTRIC AND HYBRID VEHICLE PROGRAM"
January 1979
U.S. Department of Energy.

INDEX